• • •

Nicos Rossides

THE **FUTURE** OF **WORK**

•

Managing in the Age of AI

Published by Stoic Owl Press

First Edition

ISBN (Print Edition): 979-8-35094-598-0
ISBN (eBook Edition): 979-8-35094-599-7

AUTHOR BIOGRAPHY

Dr. Nicos Rossides is a seasoned CEO, respected management consultant, and startup coach. His career spans academia as well as industry, where he has held leadership roles in global corporations, marketing insights agencies, and academic incubators.

He is recognized for his expertise in combining academic rigor with managerial relevance and for setting up successful entrepreneurial ventures. Dr. Rossides co-owns MASMI Research Group, a marketing insights agency with a network of offices across Central and Eastern Europe, as well as the Middle East. He also co-founded DMR, a digital marketing insights agency based in London, and currently serves as the Chairman of its Advisory Board.

As the CEO of CREF Business Ventures, an incubator associated with The Cyprus Institute, Dr. Rossides mentors and guides founders of academic spinoffs, assisting them in crafting and implementing effective go-to-market strategies.

Dr. Rossides has a long history in senior management roles. He honed his leadership skills at several global organizations, including Medochemie, a global pharmaceutical company, and Synovate, a top-four global marketing insights firm, where he served as CEO for EMEA & Global Solutions. Earlier, his extended tenure as MEMRB International's CEO spanned nearly two decades before it was acquired by Synovate.

He started his academic journey in the United States as a Fulbright scholar, earning both his Bachelor's and Master's degrees. He then attended Japan's prestigious Kyoto University, where he received his Doctor of Engineering degree and continued in postdoctoral and teaching capacities. After transitioning to his professional career, he engaged deeply in marketing insights, a career that spanned over 25 years. Before assuming his first international CEO role, he received his senior management training at MIT's Sloan School.

Dr. Rossides' most recent book, "Engaging the Workforce: The Grand Management Challenge of the 21st Century," was published by Routledge/Taylor & Francis in 2023. This work offers a unique perspective on the modern challenges of management, especially focused on effective engagement strategies. His other publications include "Exploring Japanese Culture: Not Inscrutable After All" (Matador, 2020), and "Eureka! to Market: A Guide for Academic Startups" (Stoic Owl Press, 2023). He has also written numerous articles and white papers on management and innovation.

Dr. Rossides often speaks at international conferences and symposia and serves on the boards of a diverse range of companies, including academic startups.

BACK COVER - FIRST ENDORSEMENT:

"A forward-thinking examination of how digital technologies, particularly AI, are transforming work. Nicos Rossides draws on an impressive grasp of historical context, contemporary challenges, and the latest research to provide leaders and managers with prescient insights and sage advice on navigating this new world. He skillfully explores opportunities and risks, providing actionable strategies rooted in ethics and social responsibility. Technology is not neutral; it co-shapes human systems."

— Norberto Patrignani, Politecnico di Torino;
Expert on AI Ethics for the European Commission;
Author of "The Ethics of Clinical Risk in Innovative Medical Technologies"
and "The Robotics Divide: A New Frontier in the 21st Century?"

BACK COVER - SECOND ENDORSEMENT:

"In an era where the future of work is shaped by rapid technological progress and other megatrends, this book emerges as a crucial resource. It navigates us through emerging opportunities and challenges with insight and foresight. Nicos Rossides addresses the key forces at play, and how they impact organizational management. Essential reading for leaders, policymakers, and anyone invested in the future of work and our world."

— Bud Taylor, Management Consultant and Author of "Customer Driven Change."

BACK COVER BLURB

In "The Future of Work: Managing in the Age of AI," Nicos Rossides embarks on a thought-provoking exploration of the evolving world of work, where the convergence of human ingenuity and AI is fundamentally reshaping not only work but also the very fabric of society.

Rossides traces work's fluid evolution from our early hunter-gatherer origins to the current era of exponential technological change, where traditional job structures are giving way to a dynamic blend of adaptive skills and fluid workflows. As AI assumes a dominant role in key economic functions, he confronts the reality that work's meaning and purpose may need to be fundamentally redefined.

In light of these transformative shifts, Rossides provides invaluable guidance for managers and leaders, emphasizing the systematic integration of AI capabilities while upholding sustainability and ethical practices. He encourages us to rebalance our priorities and seek fulfillment beyond traditional career metrics, paving the way for a human-centric future of work.

This well-researched and insightful guide offers pragmatic management strategies for staying competitive while remaining rooted in enduring values that uplift our organizations and our shared humanity.

CHAPTERS:

FIGURES:

CHAPTER 1:
INTRODUCTION

From its humble origins as a means of survival in hunter-gatherer societies to its current role as a symbol of status and power in advanced economies, work has undergone a remarkable transformation. Today, work is not just a means to an end or a way to earn a livelihood; it is deeply woven into the fabric of our identity. When we answer the age-old question, "What do you do?", we are not merely stating our occupation; we are defining our sense of self-worth, social identity, and even our perceived relevance to others. It's a testament to our status, power, and place in the world.

For businesses, the link between work and identity is equally significant. Understanding the intricate dynamics of work is crucial for shaping organizational hierarchies, defining roles, and ensuring efficient functioning. This understanding is evident in the metaphors we use to describe work, such as likening it to a machine, warfare, an organism, or a brain. These metaphors not only illustrate different aspects of work and working environments but also influence our discourse on this existentially fundamental topic. The 'machine' metaphor, for instance, emphasizes efficiency and precision, while 'warfare' suggests strategy and competition. Viewing organizations as 'organisms' highlights interdependence and growth, and the 'brain' metaphor underscores intelligence and problem-solving. Each of these perspectives offers unique insights into the nature of work and its role in both individual lives and organizational structures.

In the modern era, the nature of work and its relationship with capital have taken center stage. As Warren Buffett once remarked, the allure of products that cost mere cents to produce but yield immense profits highlights a shift in how we perceive value, especially economic value. Such products, requiring minimal labor or raw material input, represent a form of work that, while profitable, may not always align with societal benefits. This raises questions about the true essence of 'value' in our capitalist structures.

Today, significant advances in artificial intelligence are fundamentally altering our understanding of "work" and its execution. This change is more than a fleeting trend; it represents a profound shift. It's transforming the way businesses interact with their employees and how roles within these evolving environments are defined.

As AI continues to blur the lines between tasks deemed 'routine' and 'non-routine', we're confronted with deeper questions about our identity. If machines can now handle tasks that were once the exclusive domain of humans, where does that leave us? The intertwining of our identity with our work is being tested, pushing us to redefine our understanding of purpose, value, and self-worth in an increasingly technologically driven world.

Historically, the perception of work and its association with status and power has varied. In fact, the upper classes or elites (tied to the notion of *aristokratia* in ancient Greece) shunned manual labor as drudgery, subservient to the more noble pursuits of leisure and learning. This perspective spanned from the ancient Athens of Pericles to the aristocracies of the Renaissance and Enlightenment; work was best left to those outside the circles of privilege.

Now coming to our current era and the advent of AI, we are attempting to predict what aspects of our jobs may or may not be automated, partially or fully, in the foreseeable future. The ones classified as routine are those with clearly defined steps and where a logical sequence can be programmed, while non-routine tasks are those classified as complex, requiring nuanced articulation or human judgment.

Recent advances in computing power, data storage, and deep learning-enabled algorithms have started to blur the lines between routine and non-routine tasks. Machines are increasingly capable of handling jobs previously thought to be non-routine. Their ability to access and process vast amounts of information allows them to recognize patterns with unprecedented scale and speed. More impressively, they can potentially explain their reasoning and adapt to different contexts.

This evolution is redefining the traditional boundaries of cognitive labor that AI can undertake, with AI-driven processes increasingly venturing into areas once thought exclusive to human cognition. We are witnessing AI systems develop forms of self-improvement and operational autonomy, though they still rely on foundational design and oversight by human experts. The progression towards self-design and enhanced operational autonomy in AI systems is significant, marking a major shift in the field. This development is simultaneously exciting and daunting, reflecting the dual nature of advanced technology. While full autonomy and complete self-design without human intervention are not yet realities, the direction of current research and development points towards this as a future certainty. As AI technology continues to evolve, the likelihood of AI systems operating independently becomes a matter of when, not if.

The rapid advancement of automation and augmentation technology is reshaping our understanding of identity and purpose. We are faced with profound questions about the role of work in our lives, our societal contributions, and the sources of our livelihood and meaning. As we contemplate a future where traditional work may become obsolete – a future where humans might not be needed for most or all economic tasks – we are challenged to reconsider what gives our lives meaning beyond conventional employment. This scenario invites a return, perhaps, to a eudaimonic conception of human endeavors, with AI potentially freeing humans for more fulfilling pursuits, akin to the philosophical ideals of flourishing and well-being in Aristotle's Athens.

This is a deeply personal question with no straightforward answers. Our perception of a future without work as either utopian or dystopian depends on a multitude of factors, including our individual values, beliefs, and perspectives on the human experience. For some, the prospect of a world unburdened by the necessity of work evokes excitement, offering the freedom to pursue personal passions and live more fulfilling lives. Others find the idea of a work-free world unsettling, fearing the loss of identity, purpose, and community that work often provides.

Setting aside work's personal significance, we have also been debating the promise as well as peril of AI. Some thought leaders, such as Ray Kurzweil, hold a largely optimistic perspective on AI's potential to solve humanity's greatest challenges like climate change and disease while dramatically prolonging life expectancy.

In his 2005 book "The Singularity is Near", Kurzweil envisions that by 2045, AI will help create a technological singularity—the moment when AI surpasses human intelligence in all domains. This will mark a critical juncture beyond which events cannot be predicted because the world will have become so fundamentally altered by technology that the human mind will be incapable of understanding let alone controlling it.

Other experts, such as Geoffrey Hinton and Nick Bostrom, while agreeing with AI's huge potential for good, have warned of its dangers, such as the possibility of AI systems evolving in ways that elude human control and become misaligned with our values. Industry voices have also chimed in—Elon Musk and Bill Gates advocating a slowing of the pace of AI development to allow time for properly integrating ethical and other safeguards.

While ongoing concerns about the potential dangers of AI persist, the prevailing view is that its substantial potential benefits outweigh these risks. Moreover, the mistrust among key stakeholders adds another layer of complication to this issue, underscoring the need for a pragmatic, yet not overly restrictive, approach to AI development.

This approach should aim to balance progress with responsible innovation, avoiding the drawbacks (and perhaps impracticality) of pressing the 'pause' button on advancement. As AI increasingly becomes a focal point in our future, comprehending its capabilities and limits, along with finding practical governance strategies, becomes vital to ensure its beneficial impact on society.

A central debate in AI's evolution concerns how it's redefining the boundary between routine and non-routine tasks, challenging conventional views of 'expertise.' AI systems, such as ChatGPT and Bard, are increasingly adept at tasks traditionally considered creative and reliant on judgment, blurring the lines between these cognitive categories. This trend was presciently anticipated by Richard and Daniel Susskind in their 2015 work, 'The Future of the Professions.' They foresaw automation's transformative effect on knowledge-intensive occupations, even those demanding nuanced expertise and judgment.

Consider pathologists in the medical field. These professionals, tasked with diagnosing diseases by examining cells and tissues, can significantly benefit from AI's image recognition capabilities. AI's ability to detect patterns or anomalies that might escape the human eye can lead to life-altering diagnoses. However, AI still lacks the capacity to fully understand the complexities of a patient's overall health context, which is vital for accurate diagnosis.

Pathologists integrating AI tools into their practice can enhance diagnostic accuracy, while those who resist may find themselves disadvantaged.

In the finance sector, investment strategists can leverage AI to analyze extensive market data, identifying trends and potential investment opportunities. Human expertise remains essential, as final investment decisions often require a deep understanding of global economic dynamics, geopolitical risks, and company-specific factors. This expertise serves to complement, not replace, AI-driven analysis.

The implications are therefore clear. Professionals who seamlessly integrate AI capabilities into their expertise will be well-equipped to navigate future challenges effectively. It is not entire professions, such as pathologists or financial analysts, that face the looming threat of obsolescence. Rather, it is individuals who fail or refuse to embrace AI who are almost certain to be left behind.

At its core, this book examines the multifaceted realm of work, dissecting its past, scrutinizing its present, and envisioning its future through three comprehensive lenses. It embarks on a journey through the historical evolution of work, unraveling the intricate tapestry of economic and social forces that have shaped its significance. The narrative then transitions into an in-depth analysis of today's landscape, where megatrends such as technological innovation, demographic transformations, and the imperative for sustainability are driving unprecedented shifts.

Concluding with a forward-looking perspective, the book offers a strategic roadmap, spotlighting actionable strategies for individuals, leaders, and organizations. These strategies are designed to harness emerging opportunities within a framework that upholds ethical values, ensuring a balanced approach to the future of work.

This multifaceted exploration of work, spanning its origins, current transformations, and future prospects, converges into a singular, pivotal message:

we are not mere spectators but active participants in shaping the narrative of work. As sentient beings, we bear a collective responsibility to steer this evolution in a direction that aligns work with human welfare and dignity.

The future of work is a journey through a dynamic interplay of multifaceted forces of change, touching upon three core dimensions (see Figure 1):

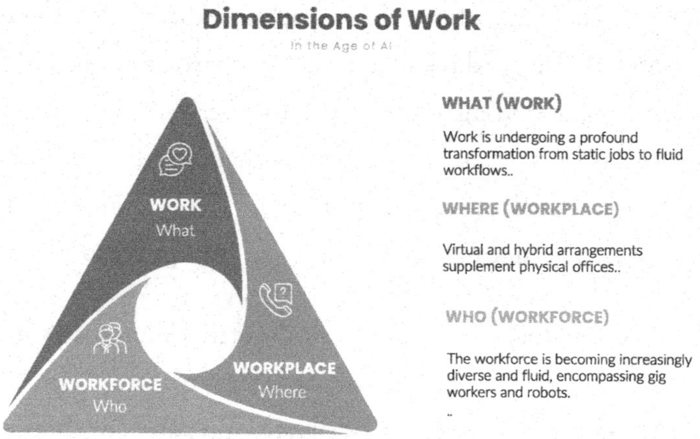

Dimensions of Work
In the Age of AI

WHAT (WORK)

Work is undergoing a profound transformation from static jobs to fluid workflows..

WHERE (WORKPLACE)

Virtual and hybrid arrangements supplement physical offices..

WHO (WORKFORCE)

The workforce is becoming increasingly diverse and fluid, encompassing gig workers and robots.
..

FIGURE 1: THE DIMENSIONS OF WORK

Work: We'll explore the transformative power of technology, especially AI, in redefining our tasks and responsibilities. By understanding historical contexts, we can gain insights into the evolution of work and its potential trajectories.

Workforce: The boundaries that once defined the workforce are becoming increasingly porous. The impact of AI on more fluid workflows, the rise of the gig economy, and global collaborative platforms mark a departure from the rigid employment structures of the past.

Workplace: The very concept of a 'workplace' is undergoing a metamorphosis. From remote offices to co-working spaces and virtual collaborations, we're witnessing a reinvention of work spaces (physical and virtual).

Change has been afoot for some time now, but the COVID-19 pandemic acted as a catalyst that greatly accelerated it. It forced companies to act with urgency. It demonstrated the feasibility and efficiency of remote work, accelerating the already ongoing digitalization of the workplace. This trend is not only poised to continue but will do so at accelerated pace.

A McKinsey Global Institute report projects significant workforce changes by 2030, driven by automation and AI, which are expected to both create and displace jobs. The demand for skilled workers, particularly in STEM fields such as mathematics and engineering, is on the rise. This increase is attributed to their specialized expertise and ability to manage complex, technical tasks. Conversely, traditional roles, especially those involving routine, manual tasks, may experience a decline as they become more susceptible to automation.

The McKinsey Global Survey on AI 2023 further illuminates this transformation. It reveals that 93% of business leaders recognize AI's disruptive potential. However, only 15% feel adequately prepared for its integration, pointing to significant challenges in securing resources, developing expertise, and implementing AI strategies effectively.

In response to these changes, there's a growing need to shift management paradigms from traditional, hierarchical models to more agile, systems-oriented approaches. Traditional management often involves top-down decision-making and rigid structures, whereas agile management emphasizes flexibility, cross-functional teams, and rapid response to change. Systems-oriented management focuses on understanding and managing complex systems, recognizing the interdependence of various components within an organization.

This transition in management styles involves a greater emphasis on enabling, coaching, and facilitating, rather than merely directing or controlling. Enabling involves providing teams with the tools and autonomy they need to solve problems creatively. Coaching refers to offering guidance and support to help employees develop their skills and capabilities. Facilitating involves creating an environment that encourages collaboration and innovation.

By adopting these new management approaches, organizations can help their employees contribute more effectively while balancing the increasing demands of work and personal life. For example, a manager in an agile setup might facilitate a team brainstorming session to solve a technical challenge, coach team members through a complex project, and enable them by providing access to advanced AI tools and training. This shift is crucial for businesses to remain competitive and for employees to stay relevant and fulfilled in the evolving job market.

Additionally, AI systems have the potential to transcend the limitations of human decision-making, often characterized by 'bounded rationality.' This term, coined by Nobel laureate Herbert Simon, describes how our decision-making is constrained by cognitive limitations and the information we have access to, leading us to opt for 'satisficing' or sufficiently good solutions; not ones that are necessarily perfect or optimal. AI, with its ability to process vast amounts of data and learn from complex patterns, offers a means to surpass these constraints, enabling more optimized and informed decision-making.

Emerging innovations like the metaverse and Web3 are prime examples of shifts in the digital and work landscape, despite facing resistance and skepticism from users and consumers. Concerns about disruption and the perceived benefits of these technologies are prevalent, especially given the negative associations with the volatile cryptocurrency market and the prevalence of scams in the virtual space.

The metaverse, which encompasses shared virtual environments accessible through augmented and virtual reality, merges digital and physical experiences. It opens up new possibilities for work, collaboration, and customer engagement, redefining traditional concepts of the workplace. For instance, virtual reality could enable more immersive remote meetings, creating a sense of presence that traditional video conferencing lacks.

Web3, based on blockchain technology, represents a shift towards a more decentralized internet phase. It promises users greater control over their data and digital interactions, though its adoption faces hurdles due to its association with the unstable cryptocurrency market and concerns about the legitimacy and security of blockchain-based applications. Despite these challenges, Web3's potential for creating more secure, user-controlled digital experiences could significantly impact how businesses interact with customers and manage data.

Both the metaverse and Web3 are setting the stage for significant changes in digital interaction, potentially transforming how we understand and engage in work. These technologies are reshaping traditional notions of the 'workplace' and 'workforce,' prompting organizations to adopt more flexible, global strategies and leverage talent pools beyond geographical boundaries. For example, a company might use blockchain technology for secure, transparent supply chain management or create a virtual workspace in the metaverse for its globally dispersed team.

In parallel with these technological shifts, there is another important dimension evolving in the workforce: diversity. The increasing diversity in terms of culture, gender, and ethnicity is becoming more recognized as an asset rather than a burden. This shift is crucial in the context of technological innovation and AI, as diverse teams can provide varied perspectives and insights, which are essential for developing inclusive and effective AI systems. A diverse workforce can help mitigate biases in AI algorithms and ensure that these technologies are beneficial and accessible to a broader range of people.

Adaptable management approaches are necessary to embrace this diversity, viewing it as integral to a healthy and dynamic work environment. This perspective goes beyond seeing diversity as a mere compliance or 'woke' requirement; it's about recognizing the value diversity brings in fostering resilience and effectiveness in organizational cultures. For instance, a diverse team might bring a range of perspectives to the development of an AI-driven product, ensuring it caters to a wider audience and addresses varied needs.

In summary, as we witness the convergence of technological advancements like AI, the metaverse, and Web3, alongside a growing emphasis on workforce diversity, the landscape of work is undergoing a profound transformation. This evolution requires organizations to rethink traditional workplace structures and embrace more flexible, and innovative approaches to remain competitive in a rapidly changing world.

CHAPTER 2:
THE EVOLUTION OF WORK

The concept of work is as ancient as humanity itself, rooted in our very survival. Our hunter-gatherer ancestors embarked on the first form of work, foraging the wild for sustenance. They learned to work together, understanding that collective effort enhanced their chances of survival. Work, at this stage, was directly linked to human existence. It was tactile, immediate, and had life or death implications.

Gradually, humans transitioned from being nature's guests to its masters. The advent of agriculture signaled a shift from the transient, nomadic lifestyle of hunter-gatherers to a settled, organized society. This change had profound implications on work. Labor became centered on planting, harvesting, and tending to animals. Societies became more sedentary, leading to the formation of communities structured around agricultural cycles. The shift from hunter-gathering to agricultural societies is very significant. Agriculture allows specialization, giving rise to professions and for work to form a part of a person's identity. Specialization decouples work from the immediate survival of the community, as the new surplus of food means that not every member of society need perform substistence labor. While this shift generates greater wealth for the community, the effect on the individual worker is a more complex matter, with some seriously negative consequences arising alongside the higher standard of living.

Consider the hours worked where the debate among anthropologists is rather inconclusive. Some studies indicate that hunter-gatherers dedicated fewer hours to sustenance, while other research suggests the opposite, with early farmers potentially working fewer hours. Beyond the mere number of hours worked, it's essential to consider the nature of the labor and its impact on the workers' lifestyle. Jared Diamond, in his 1987 work, argued that the adoption of agriculture brought significant negative consequences for the first farmers. The labor involved in early farming was intensive and physically taxing, often leading to discernible damage in the farmers' skeletons, unlike their hunter-gatherer counterparts. Additionally, hunter-gatherers enjoyed a more diverse diet, which likely contributed to better overall health compared to the more monotonous diet of early farmers.

While agriculture is capable of generating a greater surplus of food than was possible before, this surplus is rapidly consumed by a corresponding increase in population. Local natural resources become strained, and the now sedentary community cannot move to new foraging grounds. Hierarchies emerge that demand greater standards of living, putting pressure in those professions further down the chain. These all increase the demands on human labor. The issue is complex, and it is difficult to make a definitive claim about the amount of leisure time enjoyed by hunter-gatherers versus early farmers.

One change that is clear, however, is the shift in human attitudes towards their work. Hunter-gatherer socieites often have little concept of wealth, the amassing of which only really becomes possible with agriculture and the settled hierarchies it creates. As a result, hunter-gatherers' identities are not bound up in their work, and they tend to view it as a mere means for survival. Their leisure time is thus concentrated on deepening their relationships, engaging in ritual practice and strengthening their communities. Outside of the necessary labor for survival, the focus is thus on the pursuit of human flourishing, a view made possible by the disconnect present in their attitude between wealth and work. This is an idea which we will return to later in discussions about the state of work post-AI.

The Agricultural Revolution represents arguably the single greatest shift in our relationship to work in history, and is where "work" in the modern sense of the word arises. The consequences of such a change can offer insight into the potential and pitfalls of future paradigm shifts, and help humanity steer this present period of transformation in a positive direction.

As societies grew more sophisticated and organized, so did the nature of work. The pyramids of Egypt, the Great Wall of China, the Parthenon of ancient Greece, or Rome's Colosseum – these monumental feats of engineering marked the dawn of project-based work, requiring meticulous planning, intricate logistics, and a coordinated workforce.

Slave labor played a prominent role in these societies, where the distinction between manual labor and intellectual pursuits was starkly drawn. While slaves were bound to manual toil, free citizens enjoyed the privilege of engaging in philosophical discourse, artistic endeavors, and the pursuit of knowledge. This stark division between mental and physical labor persisted for centuries, shaping social hierarchies and societal norms.

Work continued to evolve in the Middle Ages with the rise of craftsmanship, a form of work that involves skill acquisition through rigorous apprenticeships and the mastery of specialized techniques. While craftsmanship itself was not a new phenomenon, having been a fundamental aspect of human activity for centuries, it became more structured and formalized during this era.

In Western societies, the establishment of trade guilds played a pivotal role in this formalization. These guilds regulated practices, oversaw apprenticeships, and exerted economic control over specific trades. They were instrumental in preserving artisanal knowledge, ensuring the high quality of goods, and safeguarding the interests of skilled craftsmen. By standardizing methods and setting benchmarks for quality, these guilds helped elevate craftsmanship to a recognized and respected profession, distinct in its emphasis on skill and expertise.

Meanwhile, in the East, craftsmanship traditions thrived, with Japan developing traditions that are still alive today. Indeed, the rich Japanese craftsmanship tradition, *shokunin kishitsu,* still lives on today in many domains where mastery of a craft or art is prized: pottery, carpentry, sushi-making even flower arrangement. Disciples may spend their entire lives perfecting their art, making a living out of it and ensuring it passes to the next generation.

This master-apprentice tradition is echoed across various Eastern cultures. In China, it's referred to as *taizidao,* translating to "the way of the master" while in Korea it has an almost identical connotation, "the way of the teacher" (*cheonjaedo*). Finally, in India, it is known as *guru-shishya parampara,* translated as "the tradition of the guru and the disciple."

At its core, the master-apprentice tradition is a learning system wherein a novice, or apprentice, acquires skills and knowledge under the tutelage of a seasoned expert, the master. The apprentice works closely with the master, absorbing the intricacies of the trade. In turn, the master guides, mentors, shares his experience and assesses the apprentice's development.

This means of gaining expertise offers a holistic approach to skill acquisition and experiential learning. Apprentices benefit from hands-on experience, learning directly from someone who is recognized as a master. The immersive process, unfolding over years, equips them with practical skills and deep expertise while preparing them to become masters themselves. Indeed, craftsmanship demands both physical exertion and intellectual engagement, requiring the craftsman to manipulate materials while also grappling with the complexities of design, planning, and problem-solving.

This fusion of physical and intellectual effort, coupled with an emotional investment in the craft, elevates craftsmanship beyond the labor involved to a deeply meaningful and fulfilling form of creation. It is a way of life that fosters a sense of mastery, purpose, and connection to one's work and the broader world. Through the embodied experience of creating, we find meaning, fulfillment, and a sense of belonging to something larger than ourselves.

In his seminal book "The Craftsman," Richard Sennett identifies three key elements of craftsmanship: skill, judgment, and responsibility. Skill involves mastering techniques and executing tasks with precision. Judgment entails making informed decisions based on experience and understanding of materials and techniques. Responsibility includes a commitment to quality and pride in the finished product. Each creation, bearing the unique touch of its creator, is an embodiment of human creativity, ingenuity, and perseverance.

The master-apprentice paradigm has endured through history, representing an intergenerational transfer of knowledge, skills, and values. It symbolizes a symbiotic relationship where the master shapes the future of the craft through the apprentice, who, in turn, revitalizes traditional practices.

Leonardo da Vinci exemplifies this tradition's potential for sublime mastery. Apprenticed at 14 to Andrea del Verrocchio, a master of painting, sculpture, and engineering, Leonardo acquired a diverse skill set. Within six years, he was ready to embark on his own, eventually becoming one of history's most celebrated artists.

The era of craftsmanship, marked by skilled artisans, precise methods, and a personal touch, waned with the Industrial Revolution's onset. Work underwent a transformation, becoming more standardized, regimented, and impersonal, with a focus on efficiency, output, and profit rather than creativity. Although specialized expertise was essential for operating machinery, most labor tended to be monotonous. The unique, handcrafted items of the past gave way to uniform, machine-made products, as factory floors replaced local workshops.

Significantly, China's early industrial shift during the 11th century Song Dynasty foreshadowed these changes. Advanced smelting and minting techniques led to specialization in various trades and commerce, attracting rural farmers to growing urban centers. This local innovation in production and trade, along with silk exports, integrated China's economy into the global market.

However, the master-apprentice tradition, once central to craftsmanship, wasn't completely lost. It adapted to the evolving societal context, maintaining relevance in areas like high fashion and specialized crafts. Thus, elements of this model persisted, preserving a degree of creativity and personal involvement in producing luxury goods. This tradition transformed into a specialized niche, distinct and somewhat removed from the mainstream, continuing to thrive in sectors where bespoke quality and artisanal skills are highly valued.

Consequently, factories, driven by mechanization, became the industrial economy's backbone. Labor, previously creative and self-directed, turned largely regimented, reduced to repetitive, uniform tasks. Work, once tied to the craftsman's identity, evolved into an impersonal series of actions, detached from the final product.

The relentless pace of the time clock and the monotonous drone of machinery began to define the workplace as the revolution took hold. A significant portion of the workforce, once engaged in creative tasks, was relegated to mere components in a vast machine, valued more for physical than intellectual labor.

Yet, no economic era is static. By the late 20th century, a shift towards services, information, and knowledge work emerged. Intellectual capital became the primary differentiator for businesses and nations, signifying a move from tangible to intangible assets. In this new era, coding and innovation surpassed traditional manufacturing, as technology redefined work's possibilities.

Today, we find ourselves at the heart of a digital economic revolution, a pivotal moment that re-emphasizes the value of expertise and creativity over the rigidity of fixed production lines. Once again, the essence of work is being reshaped, with algorithms and artificial intelligence not just supplementing, but significantly enhancing human capabilities. This technological advancement is reintroducing a sense of purpose and autonomy into the workplace, reminiscent of a time when individual skill and creativity were paramount.

In many respects, today's economy, with its focus on skill and creativity, echoes the artisanal era of old. Yet, it transcends it through digital connectivity, sophisticated tools, and a global reach. This fusion of the old and the new marks a remarkable evolution in the way we work, a progression that unfolds in cycles rather than straight lines, seamlessly blending timeless traditions with the transformative power of cutting-edge technology. As civilization progresses, the nature of work will continue to evolve, relentlessly pursuing enhanced productivity while simultaneously unlocking humanity's innate talents, abilities, and aspirations.

The Rise of the Knowledge Economy

The emphasis on physical labor and mass production gradually gave way to the Knowledge Economy, particularly in the latter half of the 20th century. This transformation marked a significant paradigm shift, valuing intellectual capital, creativity, and knowledge management above all. Workers were increasingly appreciated for their ability to generate, process, and apply knowledge, reflecting the growing importance of information in driving innovation and economic growth.

The emergence of the Knowledge Economy didn't completely displace the Industrial Revolution's legacy of mass production and mechanization but represented a dramatic shift in the dynamics of value creation and capture. The focus moved from producing goods to creating and disseminating knowledge, with intangible assets like knowledge, innovation, and intellectual property becoming paramount.

In this new economy, skills and expertise became the primary value drivers. Individuals with specialized knowledge and creative abilities commanded higher wages and wielded greater influence. Even knowledge-based jobs, such as accounting and paralegal work, which may not inherently stimulate creativity, demand high levels of precision, attention to detail, and analytical skills. These abilities are crucial for the smooth operation of modern organizations and the creation of valuable intellectual assets.

Indeed, the changing nature of work in the Knowledge Economy prompted a reevaluation of corporate value. Companies like Ford and GE, once giants of the manufacturing era, were gradually overtaken by firms like Microsoft, whose primary assets were intangible, such as software and data. By the early 21st century, intangible assets accounted for 84% of the total value of S&P 500 companies, a stark contrast to the tangible asset-dominated balance sheets of the previous century.

Yet, amidst these shifts, one constant remains: change itself, ever-accelerating. Today, we are in the midst of another transformation. The 'knowledge' fulcrum that ushered us into the 21st century continues to evolve, from the widespread adoption of the internet to the digitalization of nearly every life aspect, and now to the rapid application of artificial intelligence. This ongoing evolution further distills the essence of work from machinery and raw materials to ideas, information, creativity, and unprecedented leaps in 'intelligence'.

Work has become more intellectual, workplaces more virtual, and time more flexible. Transformative innovations like the internet, artificial intelligence, and digital technologies have seamlessly integrated work into our daily lives, leading to a blurring of traditional boundaries and creating a continuum of work-life integration (or, for some, confusion). These developments have unlocked vast potential but also brought new challenges, as the balance between our physical and mental well-being is often disrupted.

Ironically, in this rapidly evolving environment, we witness a subtle renaissance of the craftsmanship ethos. Today's workers increasingly seek purpose, autonomy, and mastery in their work, echoing the values of craftsmen. They aspire not only to work but to create, innovate, and leave a unique imprint on their work, taking pride in it. In this sense, the trajectory of work seems to have come full circle, albeit in a highly digitized, globalized, and complex world where our efforts are augmented by artificial intelligence.

Seminal Thinkers on Work

As we trace the journey of work from ancient times to the present, let's review the philosophers and thinkers who have shaped our understanding of work and its role in society. While their ideas certainly reflect the spirit of their times, they also provide a compass for navigating the complexities of our contemporary environment. From the ancient wisdom of Aristotle to the modern philosophies of Karl Marx and Zygmunt Bauman, these thinkers offer insights that challenge and enlighten us. They remind us that our relationship with work is not just economic but deeply human and, perhaps, existential.

Aristotle's *Eudaimonia*: Human Flourishing

Aristotle, a towering figure in philosophical thought, championed the concept of *eudaimonia*, often translated as "human flourishing" or "well-being." Distinguished from fleeting happiness or pleasure, Aristotle viewed *eudaimonia* as a sustained state of virtuous living, an "activity of the soul in accordance with moral excellence."

His most immediate influences were his predecessors, Socrates and Plato. Socrates, widely regarded as the 'philosopher of philosophers,' placed particular emphasis on self-knowledge, virtue cultivation, and his signature Socratic method of inquiry, a process that challenged assumptions and engaged in rigorous critical thinking to seek the truth.

Plato, Socrates' student and another great philosopher, was known for his exploration of ideas like the theory of forms, proposing a realm of ideal forms or concepts beyond the material world, and the concept of philosopher-kings, as outlined in "The Republic." He advocated for a life dedicated to wisdom, examining the connection between the ideal and the real and the significance of knowledge in achieving a just and virtuous society.

Aristotle, Plato's student, built upon these philosophical foundations, developing a comprehensive theory of human flourishing. He viewed its pursuit as the cornerstone of a well-lived life, intricately woven into the societal structure of ancient Athens. In this society, where manual labor was primarily performed by slaves, citizens had the opportunity to engage in scholarly and political pursuits. This structure enabled citizens to dedicate themselves to learning, philosophical contemplation, and civic engagement, mirroring the ideals of *eudaimonia*.

Within Aristotle's framework, intellectual virtues pertain to the mind's capabilities, emphasizing the importance of sound reasoning and wisdom. Moral virtues, in contrast, focus on character and the consistent choice and action of what is morally right. Indeed, he argued that the pursuit of knowledge was essential for comprehending the world and our position within it. Similarly, moral virtues were crucial for leading a good and meaningful life.

Today, the concept of eudaimonia remains relevant, offering a comprehensive vision of the good life that extends beyond mere happiness or pleasure, advocating for a life lived in virtue and excellence.

Fast forward to our current era, where automation and robotics are poised to take over numerous labor-intensive tasks, and we find ourselves on the cusp of a societal shift reminiscent of ancient Athens, minus the pesky slavery bit. This technological advancement could potentially redefine our labor structure, freeing us to pursue more intellectually fulfilling lives.

The Protestant Work Ethic

Thomas Aquinas and John Calvin, two Christian scholars, had a profound influence on our understanding of work, seeing it as a sacred obligation - a "divine duty."

Aquinas argued that work was necessary for our physical and moral well-being. He wrote, "Man is bound to work, not only for his own preservation but also for the good of others, that he may help them in their needs."

Calvin also emphasized the importance of work and believed it is a way to achieve virtue and to live a meaningful life. He wrote, "We ought to consider it a sacred duty to labor in our callings, and to do all we can to help others."

The ideas of Aquinas and Calvin were further developed by Protestant reformers such as Martin Luther and John Wesley, who emphasized the importance of hard work, diligence, and frugality. This set of beliefs and values, known as the Protestant work ethic, has had a major impact on Western culture, and it continues to influence our attitudes towards work today.

In fact, the Protestant work ethic manifests itself in the way that many people work long hours at the expense of their personal lives. They may also be stigmatized for not being "hardworking" enough.

Émile Durkheim: Social Solidarity and Work

Émile Durkheim, a pioneering sociologist of the late 19th and early 20th centuries, explored the social dimensions of work and its role in fostering social cohesion. He introduced the concepts of mechanical and organic solidarity to describe the evolution of societies. He argued that in societies that he characterized as rather simple, mechanical solidarity prevails, where individuals perform similar tasks and share a collective consciousness.

Nevertheless, as societies become more complex, organic solidarity emerges, characterized by interdependence as a result of the specialized roles each individual performs. For Durkheim, work was not just an economic activity but a crucial factor in maintaining social order and cohesion. In the context of modern work, these insights remind us of the importance of social connections and the role of work in fostering a sense of belonging and purpose.

Karl Marx: The Alienation of Work

The 19th-century philosopher Karl Marx was one of the first to address the profound impact of the economic structure on the nature and experience of work. He argued that under capitalism, workers were alienated from the products of their labor, the labor process, their fellow workers, and their own human potential. This, he believed, led to a sense of estrangement, turning work from a fulfilling human activity into a mere means of survival.

Marx's analysis of the alienation of work was deeply influenced by the historical context of his time. The Industrial Revolution was transforming Europe with new technologies leading to the rise of mass production and the factory system. While this created employment opportunities, it also gave rise to novel forms of exploitation and oppression.

Marx was particularly concerned about the plight of the factory worker. He saw that capitalism was creating a system in which workers were stripped of their autonomy and creativity as they were forced to perform repetitive tasks in dangerous and unhealthy conditions. They had no control over the products of their labor, which were owned by the capitalists.

Marx's analysis of the alienation of work remains relevant today. While the nature of work has changed in many ways since then, some of the fundamental dynamics of capitalism remain in place. Many workers are still alienated from the products of their labor, the labor process, their fellow workers, and their own human potential.

Neo-Marxist perspectives have further developed Marx's ideas, emphasizing how the structures of capitalism have evolved but continue to produce forms of alienation, especially in the context of globalized economies and technological advances. For example, neo-Marxist thinkers have argued that the rise of precarious work, the decline of unions, and the increasing use of surveillance technologies have all contributed to new forms of alienation.

Marx's work is a reminder that the way we organize work has a profound impact on our lives and the need to be mindful of the potential negative consequences of rampant capitalism – at the expense of human dignity and well-being.

Thomas Piketty: Capital in the Modern Age

Thomas Piketty's seminal work "Capital in the Twenty-First Century" provides a comprehensive analysis of the dynamics of capital and its relationship to inequality. Piketty argues that the rate of return on capital frequently exceeds the rate of economic growth, leading to a systematic increase in wealth concentration and income inequality. This dynamic, which Piketty terms the "r>g inequality," is particularly concerning in light of the fact that capital is able to reproduce itself and grow at a faster rate than the economy as a whole.

Piketty's work is particularly relevant in the context of the future of work, which is likely to be characterized by increasing automation and technological advancements, further tilting the balance towards capital at the expense of labor. So, while these advancements have the potential to create new jobs and improve our quality of life, they also pose a risk of exacerbating inequality and poor labor conditions.

For example, automation is already displacing workers in some industries, and this trend is likely to continue in the future. As a result, some workers may find it difficult to find new jobs, and others may be forced to take jobs that pay lower wages and offer fewer benefits. Additionally, technological advancements can lead to the creation of new monopolies, which can further concentrate wealth and power in the hands of a few.

Piketty's work suggests that we need to be mindful of the potential negative consequences of technological change and take steps to mitigate them. One way to do this is to focus on creating jobs that require human ingenuity and creativity. These jobs are less likely to be automated and are more likely to provide meaningful work and value to society, at least in the foreseeable future.

Another way to mitigate the negative consequences of technological change is to implement policies that redistribute wealth and reduce inequality. For example, governments could raise taxes on the wealthy and use the revenue to fund programs that support low- and middle-income families, such as affordable housing, quality education, and healthcare. They could also invest in education and training programs to help workers develop the skills they need to succeed in the new economy.

Ultimately, Piketty's work is a powerful reminder that we need to rethink the way our economy works, making it more equitable and valuing human ingenuity and creativity over mere profitability.

Warren Buffett's investment strategy provides a cautionary tale about the potential misalignment between profit and social value. The legendary investor is known for investing in highly profitable companies, including some that sell addictive and harmful products, such as tobacco and sugary drinks. These products are highly profitable, even though they provide little or no value to society.

In a world where capital is able to reproduce itself and grow at a faster rate than the economy as a whole, those who already own capital like Buffett are able to accumulate additional wealth, even if they are doing so by investing in products that harm society. This is indeed one of the challenges of the capitalist system as it is currently structured.

Piketty's work is a powerful reminder that we need to create an economic system that is more equitable and that values human ingenuity, creativity and well-being over mere profitability. This means creating a system where businesses are rewarded for creating true value for society, not just for generating profits.

Max Weber: Bureaucratization and the 'Iron Cage'

Max Weber, a German sociologist and political economist in the early 20th century, probed deeply into the nature and evolution of organizations, particularly focusing on the rise of bureaucracy.

He observed that as societies grew more complex, there was an increasing need for structured and predictable systems to manage this complexity. So he saw bureaucracy as the solution to the need for structured and predictable systems, with its emphasis on rationality, hierarchy, and impersonal relationships. He believed that this form of organization was not just a byproduct of modernity but its very essence, capable of delivering efficiency, predictability, and control.

However, Weber was not without his reservations. He introduced the concept of the "iron cage" of rationalization, a metaphor describing the potential pitfalls of an overly bureaucratic system. In this cage, individuals become ensnared in a web of rules and procedures, often at the expense of creativity, autonomy, and personal fulfillment. The very systems designed for efficiency could, paradoxically, stifle the human spirit, leading to feelings of disenchantment and alienation.

In the context of today's organizations, Weber's insights remain profoundly relevant. Many contemporary workplaces, from multinational corporations to governmental bodies, clearly exhibit the characteristics of a bureaucratic system as he described it. While it can ensure consistency and fairness, it can also be inflexible, resistant to change, and dehumanizing.

Moreover, in the age of AI and remote work, Weber's concerns about the "iron cage" take on new dimensions. As organizations increasingly rely on algorithms and data-driven decision-making, there's a risk of over-rationalizing processes, sidelining human judgment and intuition. So, the challenge lies in harnessing the benefits of technology without falling into a digital "iron cage" where human values and connections are eclipsed by cold efficiency.

Comparatively, while Marx focused on the economic structures and the alienation of workers from their labor, Weber concentrated on the organizational structures and the potential alienation from overly rationalized systems. Both offer critical perspectives on the challenges of modern work but from slightly different angles. Meanwhile, thinkers like Terkel provide a more bottom-up view, focusing on the lived experiences of workers.

Studs Terkel: The Human Work Experience

Studs Terkel, a 20th-century American author, broadcaster, and historian, is best known for his oral histories that chronicled the lives and experiences of everyday Americans. His book, "Working," is a seminal piece that delves into the human experience of work, capturing the voices of people from diverse professions and backgrounds.

In "Working," Terkel presents a series of narratives, from the waitress to the steelworker, the stonemason to the cab driver. Through these intimate accounts, he paints a vivid picture of the joys, frustrations, successes, and challenges that define the world of work. Terkel's genius lay in his ability to make the ordinary seem extraordinary, revealing the depth of human experience in even the most mundane tasks.

One of the recurring themes in "Working" is the search for meaning. Many of Terkel's interviewees expressed a desire to find purpose in their work, to feel that they are contributing to something larger than themselves. But this quest for meaning is often juxtaposed with the harsh realities of the workplace: the monotony, the exploitation, the lack of recognition.

Another significant aspect of Terkel's exploration is the sense of identity that work provides. For many, their profession becomes an integral part of who they are. It shapes their self-perception, their relationships, and their place in society. Yet, this intertwining of work and identity also brings with it challenges, especially when one's job is underappreciated or undervalued.

So, "Working" serves as a poignant reminder that behind every job title, there's a human story. It underscores the importance of recognizing the dignity of all forms of work and understanding the profound impact that our professional lives have on our personal identities.

As we reflect on Terkel's insights, it becomes evident that while work is a universal experience, it is also deeply personal and varied. This variation becomes even more pronounced when we consider the gendered dimensions of work. Historically, societal norms and expectations have shaped and often limited the roles and opportunities available to women, potentially creating gender inequalities that could have a negative impact on society as a whole. This brings us to the writings of thinkers like Simone de Beauvoir, who explored the gendered experience of work and its implications for personal and societal growth.

Simone de Beauvoir: The Gendered Perspective

In the realm of understanding work's human dimension, it's essential to consider the gendered nuances that have historically shaped our experiences and perceptions. Simone de Beauvoir, in her groundbreaking work "The Second Sex," delved deep into the ways women have been historically considered the 'Other' in a male-centric world. In that sense, gender is a fruitful lens to examine attitudes to work throughout history and demonstrating how fluid its nature can be.

Indeed, the way 'women's work' is defined is a great example of the ways our cultural perceptions of work create its structure and define its boundaries. Domestic labour and childcare are both essential for the running of society on a fundamental level, but the way patriarchal societies manage this labour is radically different to regular employment. Perceived as of a different class of work than salaried employment, it is motivated by the expectations put upon women, whose contributions are thus erased.

Beauvoir's writings help illuminate how our cultural perceptions of work are neither static nor neutral; by defining some labour as implicitly inferior, the workers' contributions are left invisible and any costly demands for recognition can be safely ignored. Indeed, women's roles in the workforce and society have been defined by men, limiting opportunities and potential. Work goes beyond just earning a living; its also a path to freedom and self-realization and societal constraints and expectations can hinder this journey.

Of course, the issue of women's economic empowerment was not limited to their lack of adequate access to salaried jobs. It also involved questioning why the work that women were expected to perform was not a reliable path to independence and fair compensation. What counts as 'women's work' has shifted historically and is another example of the way changing circumstances radically re-shape our perception of work. For example, early in the development of computing technology, the practice of writing code for the machines was heavily female gendered; this was drudgery the engineers would delegate to their secretaries, or teams of low status female number crunchers (their 'computers').

As information technology began to take off and it became clear that real money could be made off the intangible assets created by coders, programming rose in status. Concurrently it increasingly became regarded as 'man's work' and women's prominence in the field rapidly decreased. Today, 'getting women into STEM' is a well known feminist goal, demonstrating the scale of the shift in perceptions.

There's another parallel here with the way work is often divided into routine and creative tasks – this is discussed elsewhere in the context of new developments in AI allowing the routine tasks to be automated. In intellectual work a similar division used to exist, with the routine tasks performed by 'human computers' – teams of typically women whose job it was to perform repetitive calculations in support of the man carrying out the creative side of the work.

Automation has historically thus been an inherently gendered process and there is a record of framing the routine tasks as worthy of being performed by depersonalised or dehumanised laborers. Before the widespread use of mechanical computers, this meant those lower down social hierarchies – particularly women.

While we have made significant strides in addressing gender inequalities, remnants of traditional gender roles persist in the workforce, reflecting a reluctance to fully embrace the realignment of societal priorities. Simone de Beauvoir's insights into the gendered division of labor offer a stark reminder that we must continue to recognize and challenge these deeply ingrained social norms and structures to create workplaces that are inclusive and equitable.

Richard Sennett: The Enduring Value of Craftsmanship

Transitioning from Simone de Beauvoir's exploration of gender's profound impact on societal roles and labor, we now turn to the insights of Richard Sennett and his seminal work on craftsmanship that I've already referenced. While de Beauvoir's analysis provides a critical understanding of how gender shapes our experience and expectations of work, Sennett's perspective offers a complementary lens, focusing on the intrinsic value and identity aspects of work in modern society.

Richard Sennett, in his influential book "The Craftsman," explores the philosophical and sociological dimensions of craftsmanship. He argues that work should be viewed not merely as a means to material outcomes but as a craft – a pursuit of excellence for its own sake and a deep, meaningful connection to labor itself. This craftsmanship ethos centers on dedication to quality, skill mastery through practice, and intrinsic rewards through the process of creation.

In this light, the craftsman's focus lies not solely on the destination but on the ongoing journey of learning, refining techniques, and solving problems. This fusion of intellectual and physical pursuits elevates craftsmanship, fostering purpose, identity, and a profound connection to one's work.

While Marx's critique of alienation focused primarily on industrial labor and the commodification of labor, it also applies to craftsmanship in certain contexts. Skilled artisans, once esteemed for their expertise and autonomy, saw their value diminished with the rise of capitalism and its emphasis on efficiency and productivity. Mass production techniques standardized skills, making artisans' contributions more replaceable and eroding their sense of ownership and control over their work.

Nevertheless, Sennett took a more optimistic view, recognizing the enduring value of craftsmanship in fostering personal fulfillment. Through his analytical lens, craftsmanship offers individuals a chance to reconnect with their work and find a sense of purpose and identity. Creating something meaningful helps the craftsman find fulfillment. Indeed, craftsmanship is timeless in its ability to impart personal meaning and societal value.

As work continues to evolve, the craftsman's ethos endures, upholding the values of skilled mastery, purposeful labor, and the inherent human drive to create. This enduring legacy helps bridge the chasm between past and present and serves as a timeless reminder of the profound satisfaction that arises from dedicated work.

Zygmunt Bauman: Liquid Modernity

While Sennett contends that craftsmanship's essence of creation holds enduring relevance even as work evolves and transforms, sociologist Zygmunt Bauman presents a counterpoint through his concept of "liquid modernity." He asserts that today's world is defined by flux and uncertainty, challenging the stability and continuity that craftsmanship traditionally embodies. So, while Sennett sees craftsmanship as an enduring ethos, Bauman would likely argue that liquid modernity's turbulent change makes it challenging for any single skill or occupation to remain relevant.

As technology, globalization, and automation transform the nature of work, traditional craftsmanship faces major disruptions. Mastering a single craft no longer guarantees a stable livelihood; instead, lifelong learning is essential to adapt to shifting skills and technologies. Precarious careers, rather than stable occupations, are increasingly common as the job market becomes more fluid and unpredictable.

In liquid modernity, change is the only constant. Traditional assumptions about work, skills development, and career progression face major challenges. Sennett celebrates craftsmanship's ability to impart lasting meaning amidst change, but Bauman questions whether craftsmanship can survive in such a turbulent era.

Bauman characterizes liquid modernity by several key features, including the rise of precarious work, the pervasiveness of lifelong learning, and the blurring of boundaries between work and personal life.

One of the most significant changes in the world of work is the proliferation of precarious work arrangements, such as temporary contracts, freelance work, and zero-hours contracts. These jobs offer little security and predictability, hindering workers' ability to plan for the future or build a stable career path.

In liquid modernity, workers must continuously invest in their education and training to stay abreast of ever-changing technologies and skills demands. This constant learning curve places additional pressure on workers and fuels a sense of lifelong insecurity as they grapple with the fear of their skills becoming obsolete.

Another key challenge of liquid modernity is the erosion of clear distinctions between work and personal life. Workers are increasingly expected to be available beyond traditional working hours, responding to work demands at all times of the day and night. This blurring of boundaries can lead to stress, burnout, and a struggle to maintain a healthy work-life balance.

Frithjof Bergmann: The Crisis of Work

In agreement with Bauman, Philosopher Frithjof Bergmann sees prevailing work arrangements as no longer meeting the needs of workers or society. He envisions a future where work is more meaningful, fulfilling, and sustainable, and advocated for a new way of working that he dubbed "New Work."

Bergmann argues that the crisis of work is a complex phenomenon with a number of contributing factors, including automation, globalization, and the rigid division of labor in the traditional job system. He envisions a future where people are free to do work that they are passionate about and that contributes to the common good. He also argues for a more democratic and participative approach to management, where workers have a greater say in decision-making and how their work is organized.

Bergmann's vision of New Work may seem aspirational, but it is also realistic. There are already a number of such organizations emerging around the world, characterized by a focus on meaningful work, a democratic and participative approach to management, and a commitment to social and environmental responsibility.

The shift to New Work will require changes in both the public and private sectors. Governments can support it by creating policies that promote entrepreneurship and innovation, and by providing support for workers who are transitioning to new jobs. Businesses can support it by adopting more democratic and participative management models, and by investing more in the development of their employees.

Where is Work Heading? A Collective Quest

Our exploration of work's evolution reveals a fascinating interplay between human ingenuity and the ever-changing nature of labor. Today, as we stand at the threshold of an AI-driven future, we are presented with a unique opportunity to reshape the narrative of our existence. The metamorphosis of work, from mundane tasks through to highly complex knowledge processes, holds immense potential to enhance productivity, liberate us from drudgery, and open up new avenues for creativity and innovation. It can also help address societal challenges such as climate change, inequality, and resource depletion.

The automation of many routine tasks raises concerns about job displacement and the need to redefine our relationship with work. In a world where AI and advanced technology become increasingly capable, we must explore alternative societal structures and reimagine the concept of "work" for as long as the notion is still relevant.

In a nascent "post-work" society, traditional concepts of employment and economic productivity may require a fundamental reimagining. The gig economy, with its focus on flexibility, personal fulfillment, and skills development, may offer glimpses into potential future models of economic organization, albeit as a temporary phase on the way to a fully realized "post-work" future. We may also witness an emergence of cooperative and community-driven enterprises, where individuals collaborate to pursue shared goals and contribute to their communities as more and more economic work is undertaken by AI driven systems.

Untethered from the traditional framework of work, we must seek new avenues for self-definition and fulfillment. Lifelong learning, creative expression, and community contributions may emerge as central pillars of our identities. Activities such as mentorship, volunteerism, and artistic pursuits, while not necessarily falling under the conventional definition of "work," can provide immense satisfaction and a sense of purpose.

In a post-work world, the role of organizations is poised for a profound transformation. Traditional hierarchical structures may be the first to come under strain, often replaced by more fluid and collaborative networks. This is already underway, as we shall examine in later chapters, even though there may be counter-currents that have to do with our innate need for structure and hierarchy (and yes, power). So the question remains: what will be the role of organizations in a world where labor is driven largely or wholly by AI?

As we grapple with these profound questions, the diverse philosophical perspectives we've explored in this chapter serve as a gentle reminder that the meaning we derive from our labors remains deeply intertwined with our sense of purpose and identity. While the nature of work undergoes constant evolution, we must also continuously evolve our understanding of these fundamental humanistic concepts.

From Aristotle's concept of *eudaimonia*, which emphasizes the pursuit of happiness through meaningful activity, to Marx's theory of alienation, which highlights the detrimental effects of unfulfilling labor on the human spirit, the thinkers we've encountered underscore the complex relationship between work and self-realization. As AI redefines the future of employment, potentially ushering in a "post-work" society, we have an unprecedented opportunity to reimagine our relationship with work and embrace values that transcend traditional notions of productivity and economic value. By cultivating community, dignity, and human flourishing, we can create a framework that supports our well-being, with or without work.

In a curious revival, such a post-work society might resemble that of our earliest hunter-gatherer ancestors, where work and wealth were also decoupled. This allowed them to focus their free time on community wellbeing and the pursuit of *eudaimonia*, a state that became less prominent with the rise of more standardized, systematic and hierarchical forms of work. In our era, however, this decoupling would stem from economic abundance rather than scarcity, with work continuing to play a key role in our pursuit of a meaningful life.

To conclude this chapter on the evolution of work, informed by the insights of seminal thinkers, we turn to two case studies that signify monumental shifts: the Agricultural Revolution and the implementation of Ford's assembly line workflows. Despite being separated by centuries, these events are not disparate phenomena but rather interconnected landmarks in the continuous evolution of work.

Each milestone built upon its predecessors, setting the stage for the knowledge and digital eras that define our current era. These developments have significantly shaped our understanding of work and its role in society. As we move forward, by adopting values that go beyond conventional measures of productivity and economic gain, we can establish a framework that nurtures well-being, whether in the context of work or beyond it.

CASE STUDY 1:
THE AGRICULTURAL REVOLUTION

The Agricultural Revolution, a pivotal chapter in human history, unfolded around 10,000 years ago, marking a profound shift from nomadic hunter-gatherer lifestyles to settled agricultural societies. This era of transformation began when our ancestors started to domesticate plants and animals, leading to a dramatic increase in food production. This abundance allowed us to establish more permanent communities and gave rise to complex societal structures.

In the fertile crescent of Mesopotamia, the cradle of this revolution, early humans began cultivating wheat, barley, peas, lentils, and chickpeas, and domesticating animals like sheep, goats, pigs, and cattle. This groundbreaking shift from foraging to farming was not just a change in food procurement methods; it was the cornerstone of modern civilization.

As agriculture spread from the Middle East to Europe and eventually to North America over thousands of years, it catalyzed a series of innovations and societal changes. The development of tools such as hoes,

sickles, plows, and irrigation systems revolutionized food production. The construction of grana-
ries and other storage techniques ensured a steady
food supply, mitigating the unpredictability of sea-
sonal harvests.

This newfound stability in food supply led to a population boom and the expansion of human settle-
ments, giving rise to towns and cities. With this, the
societal fabric transformed. A more stable food supply meant not everyone needed to be involved in food
production, leading to the emergence of specialized
roles like craftsmen, merchants, and farmers. This
specialization marked a departure from the egalitarian tribal structure to a more complex, hierarchical
societal system.

The rise of these new classes and the growth of set-
tlements spurred the development of trade networks.
Merchants became the linchpins in these networks,
facilitating the exchange of goods and services, and
connecting communities far and wide. This not only
enhanced the flow of resources but also fostered
cultural exchanges and economic development.

Craftsmanship and specialized production led to the
creation of tools and utensils, further enhancing agricultural efficiency and daily life. Nevertheless, this
revolution was not without costs, not least of which
were environmental: deforestation, soil erosion, and
species extinction, consequences we are still grappling with today. Added to that were the human costs:

the replacement of hunter-gatherer culture and ways of living with a system that in many ways harmed human wellbeing, despite offering greater wealth.

Jared Diamond in his article "The Worst Mistake in the History of the Human Race" (Diamond, 1987) makes the point that the agricultural revolution brought about gross social and sexual inequality, disease, and despotism, which continue to plague our existence.

Highlight: The agricultural revolution was a significant milestone in human history, with far-reaching effects on the way people lived and worked. It laid the foundation for the development of modern societies, with both positive and negative consequences. In several ways, it still forms the basis of our modern food system, shaping the way we live and work today.

CASE STUDY 2:
FORD MOTOR COMPANY

Henry Ford's introduction of the assembly line in 1913 marked a pivotal moment in manufacturing history, revolutionizing the production of cars and profoundly impacting society as a whole. The assembly line's innovative approach, characterized by compartmentalizing the production process into small, repetitive tasks, transformed the automotive industry and opened up a new era of mass production.

From an economic standpoint, Ford's assembly line innovation was a great success. The Model T, the first mass-produced car, became an affordable and accessible mode of transportation for the middle class, slashing the production cost by an astounding 95%. This affordability fueled the creation of a burgeoning automotive market, fundamentally altering urban landscapes and shaping the modern world.

The assembly line's impact extended far beyond the factory floor. It triggered economic growth by fueling the demand for automobiles, generating millions of new jobs, and transforming the way cities were designed and functioned. The rise of the automobile spurred suburbanization, as families sought the spaciousness and relative tranquility of suburban life beyond the confines of densely populated cities.

While the assembly line's impact on labor was undeniably significant, it also brought about mixed consequences. On the one hand, it created employment opportunities for millions, raising the standard of living of many ordinary Americans. On the other hand, it resulted in the deskilling of workers, as repetitive tasks minimized the need for specialized skills. A new class of factory workers emerged: often unskilled and with limited education and with minimal autonomy and fairly limited prospects for upward mobility.

Highlight: Ford's assembly line stands as an important milestone in manufacturing history, forever changing the way we produce goods and the way we live. Its impact extended far beyond the factory floor, shaping the modern world in profound ways. From democratizing personal transportation to transforming urban landscapes, the assembly line remains an enduring testament to the transformative power of technological innovation, even as it led to some unintended consequences, such as the deskilling of labor, the decline of inner cities and the rise of long-distance commuting.

CHAPTER 3:
THE METAPHORS WE WORK BY

You walk into a busy office and hear two people talking.

"We need to think outside the box on this project. We absolutely must win this battle!"

"We're just cogs in the machine. We'll need to sell the idea to the CEO."

What do these two conversations reveal about our relationship with work?

The metaphors we use to describe our work reveal our culture, values, and experiences, shaping how we perceive its essence and dynamics - and as I argued in the previous chapter, the narrative has evolved through the ages.

In this chapter, we will explore the role of metaphors in shaping our work lives. We will examine how they reflect and reinforce cultural values, influence decision-making, and shape our sense of identity and purpose. We will also discuss how metaphors can be used to challenge the status quo as we envision a more equitable and sustainable future.

So, the words and phrases regarding work reflect our experiences and values, and, ultimately, our culture. Edgar Schein's deepest layer of organizational culture (Schein, 1985) reflects the basic underlying assumptions or deeply ingrained beliefs and values that are taken for granted and often go unspoken.

Yet, these fundamental assumptions even if not overtly articulated profoundly influence our behavior at work.

In the realm of management, metaphors extend beyond mere linguistic flourishes. They mold our thinking and steer our comprehension. For instance, when we describe an organization as a 'well-oiled machine,' we underscore its efficiency and predictability. On the other hand, likening it to a 'living organism' conjures up ideas of adaptability, growth, and interconnectedness - a significant shift in both our approach and desired outcomes.

Our language is replete with metaphors that underscore work's competitive nature. Phrases like 'war for talent,' 'conquer the market,' or 'going head-to-head with competitors' shed light on our views of success and its inherent challenges. Conversely, expressions such as 'racking our brains' or 'brain teaser' hint at the complexities of work and the necessity for creativity and innovation, thereby illuminating a different facet of our efforts - one that values mental agility and problem-solving.

Indeed, these metaphors reveal work as more than a mere competition; they portray it as a puzzle requiring our creativity and intelligence to devise new and innovative solutions. In essence, metaphors serve as vivid frameworks in our discourse about work, enabling us to grasp various perspectives along with their associated nuances.

George Lakoff and Mark Johnson, in their seminal work (1980), posited that metaphors are foundational to our cognition. They argued that metaphors do more than merely decorate speech; they are central to our understanding and interaction with the world, profoundly influencing our perception and actions. Expanding on this, Steven Pinker suggested that metaphors serve as cognitive shortcuts, aiding us in navigating complex ideas. He saw them as linguistic tools that help streamline our brain's processing of intricate concepts - simplifying our interaction with them. In this sense, they are a key mechanism to synthesize and interprete the vast array of information we encounter daily.

So as we explore the concept of work and its management, metaphors stand out as powerful narratives that reflect cultural dynamics but also guide decision-making and shape our sense of identity and purpose. They hold the potential to both inspire and constrain, to empower and hinder.

As the nature of work undergoes transformative shifts, grasping the metaphors that mold our perceptions is a pivotal step in redefining work's fundamental aspects. This isn't an exercise in philosophical erudition; it's a crucial part of actively participating in the reimagining of work's core principles and practices with a view to shaping the future.

Cultural and Cognitive Metaphorical Nuances

In the following section, we explore the cultural and cognitive foundations of metaphors in more depth. Here, metaphors serve as more than linguistic tools; they offer insightful glimpses into our cultural and cognitive landscapes. They shape our perceptions and actions while reflecting the complex interplay between our cultural norms and cognitive processes. Our examination will unravel the cultural threads that imbue metaphors with their distinct meanings, considering both emic (insider) and etic (outsider) perspectives. This exploration aims to provide a layered understanding of how our cultural and cognitive frameworks jointly shape our linguistic expressions, enriching the context of Lakoff's foundational analysis, which intersects these two domains.

The Cultural Lens

Language is a rich tapestry, intricately woven with cultural motifs. Metaphors are its vibrant threads, passed down through generations, embedding themselves into our collective consciousness. Reflect on how different cultures metaphorically depict hierarchy or social relations. In societies with distinct hierarchies, terms like "pecking order" or "top of the food chain" might be prevalent. Conversely, in more egalitarian cultures, such hierarchical expressions might give way to phrases like "all hands on deck" or "every voice matters."

The metaphor "time is money," while ubiquitous in the West, might find fewer echoes in cultures with a more fluid sense of time. They may find expression in stories and values woven into our collective consciousness.

Hofstede's cultural dimensions, like power distance or masculinity versus femininity, further shape our metaphorical language. A culture emphasizing power distance might liken an organization to a "pyramid," while one valuing communal ties might see the workplace as a "family." These cultural imprints on metaphors enrich our understanding, offering a palette of insights and interpretations.

The Cognitive Lens

Metaphors, deeply rooted in culture, also emerge from the interaction between our minds and the external world. They transcend our cultural boundaries, reflecting the workings of our cognition. Cognition involves how we perceive, think, remember, and solve problems – essentially, how we make sense of the world.

Here, the interplay of universal and contextual perspectives creates a captivating dynamic. As previously discussed, the 'emic' perspective offers a deep dive into culture-specific phenomena, revealing rich, nuanced details. In contrast, the 'etic' perspective adopts a broader lens, identifying patterns that resonate across different cultures.

George Lakoff's framework distinguishes foundational from cross-cutting metaphors. Foundational metaphors are deeply ingrained in our cognitive structures, shaping how we fundamentally understand the world. Cross-cutting metaphors, on the other hand, are like the Rosetta Stones of our cognitive realm. They translate complex, unfamiliar concepts into familiar terms. Examples like 'organization as a machine' or 'business as an ecosystem' simplify and communicate intricate ideas.

This interplay of foundational and cross-cutting metaphors is not just theoretical. It is practical. These metaphors act as both compass and map. They guide our strategic thinking and directly influence outcomes. Their currents are unseen yet powerful, steering the ship of our understanding through the vast ocean of concepts.

Let's now examine some of the most commonplace metaphors we have used in connection with the world of work.

Organizations as 'Machines'

Prior to the Industrial Revolution, the nature of work was intrinsically personal, dominated by skilled artisans and craftsmen. These masters of their trades — blacksmiths, potters, tailors — not only honed their crafts but also imbued their work with a signature touch. Each piece, be it a wrought iron gate fashioned by a blacksmith or a potter's intricately designed vase, was a testament to individual skill and creativity. These products were more than mere items of trade; they were embodiments of personal artistry and cultural heritage.

For instance, a tailor, with his meticulous stitches and unique patterns, didn't just create garments; he wove stories and identities into them. His work was a reflection of both the individual and the broader cultural context, with each garment telling its own story through its design, fabric choice, and craftsmanship.

This era of work was often marked by a deep sense of pride and connection between the creator and their creation. The value of work lay not just in the functionality of the products but in their artistic expression and the transmission of tradition and expertise. This personal touch in work was a significant aspect of individual and community identity, with each crafted piece serving as a tangible link to the rich cultural and historical backdrop.

Decades after the Industrial Revolution, the allure of the craftsman's art persisted. My own experiences echo this sentiment. On my occasional visits to Hong Kong, I would seek out a highly skilled tailor who, with precise measurements and deft craftsmanship, created not just custom-made shirts with my initials but also tailored suits.

This habit continued more regularly in London, where the tradition of bespoke tailoring offered a unique blend of personalization and craftsmanship, albeit at a significantly higher price tag. These experiences transcended the mere acquisition of clothes; they were about an appreciation of artistry and personal connection inherent in each piece. As the price differential has become increasingly prohibitive, this tradition may be fading, reserved only for the very affluent. Mention tailored-made shirts to a millennial, and they may react with disbelief at this extravagant and perhaps antiquated notion.

Of course, the preference for custom-made attire extends beyond the mere contrast between craftsmanship and mass production. Consider, for instance, prestigious brands like Emporio Armani or Hugo Boss. The shirts and suits of such brands, while not 'mass-produced' in the traditional sense, still lack the personalized touch of a tailor intimately familiar with one's preferences and style. The crucial distinction lies in the personalization and the relationship between the maker and the wearer – elements often absent in larger-scale production, regardless of its overall quality or prestige. Societal priorities and preferences have indeed shifted decidedly.

In fact, I would argue that the manufactured "personality" of a brand has psychologically replaced the human relationship with an individual craftsman. Even in a mass-produced age, we still desire at least a feeling of knowing the person who makes our goods.

As previously discussed, the shift from artisan workshops to industrial assembly lines marked a significant transformation in the world of work - manifested in the scale of production but also in the nature of work itself. Workers transitioned from being craftsmen, deeply connected to the end product, to functioning as "cogs" of a larger machine performing repetitive tasks.

The assembly line scene from Chaplin's "Modern Times" is a great example of popular culture reflecting the contemporary anxieties of a changing work landscape. Chaplin is literally eaten up by the machines he works with – another potent metaphor.

This change brought about economic growth and efficiency, but it also led to a loss of personal connection and fulfillment in work – and a change in the prevailing metaphors.

Economic, Cultural and Political Dynamics

The adoption of the machine metaphor varied widely across different cultural and political landscapes, each reflecting its unique socio-economic backdrop. In the UK, USA, and Europe, this metaphor resonated with the era's emphasis on efficiency and mass production. It justified the strenuous working conditions and extended hours in the burgeoning industrial factories.

In the USA, the metaphor underpinned the 'American Dream,' suggesting success through hard work and perseverance, a mechanistic yet optimistic view of progress. Europe, on the other hand, saw the metaphor as a prompt for social reform, influencing the development of labor laws and welfare systems.

In communist societies, the official narrative, at least on the surface, starkly contrasted with that of open economies, placing a strong emphasis on collective effort and social justice. Despite this proclaimed focus, the reality often saw the ruling elite and apparatchiks exerting firm control. In these contexts, the machine metaphor served a dual purpose. On one hand, it symbolized the ideal of communal endeavor, aligning with the rhetoric of equality and shared labor. On the other, it revealed the paradox of centralized power, where despite the egalitarian discourse, a distinct hierarchy remained firmly in place.

This metaphor in such societies was complex, reflecting not just the collective efforts in production and industry but also the underlying power dynamics. While the language of unity and cooperation was prevalent, the actual implementation often glossed over the more egalitarian nuances. The machine, therefore, became a representation of both the collective aspirations and the realities of uneven power distribution. It was a symbol of the collective working together as a unified entity, yet under the guidance and often rigid control of a small ruling class.

In developing countries, the adoption of the machine metaphor likely had different connotations. It could have symbolized a beacon of modernization and economic development, a hopeful sign of transitioning from agrarian economies to industrial powerhouses. But it may also have reflected the challenges of rapid industrialization – such as urbanization, environmental degradation, and the uprooting of traditional lifestyles. In these contexts, it encapsulated both the promise of economic growth and the perils of unbalanced development.

The Organism Metaphor

The organism metaphor emerged in the knowledge economy era to capture the dynamic and adaptive nature of organizations. In contrast to the mechanistic machine metaphor, which viewed organizations as rigid and predictable systems, the organism metaphor emphasized the interconnectedness and interdependence of all organizational components.

Like living organisms, organizations are constantly evolving and adapting to their environment. They must learn from their experiences, innovate, and grow in order to survive and thrive. The emphasis is therefore on flexibility, resilience, and collaboration.

Peter Senge's concept of the learning organization and its underlying systems thinking draws on the organism metaphor. He argued that organizations must be able to learn and adapt quickly in order to keep pace with the ever-accelerating pace of change. This requires a culture of continuous learning and experimentation, where employees are encouraged to share knowledge, collaborate, and take risks.

The organism metaphor also underscores the importance of sustainability. Just as living organisms must maintain a delicate balance between their internal and external environments, organizations must also be mindful of their social and ecological impact. They must adopt sustainable practices and business models that contribute to the long-term health of the planet and society.

The Brain Metaphor

The human brain is a marvel of complexity, composed of approximately 86 billion neurons and 100 trillion synapses. These neurons are interconnected in a vast network, forming complex circuits that allow us to think, feel, and act. The brain's capacity for learning and adaptation is truly remarkable and it is this inherent ability that makes it such an aptly evocative metaphor for the modern era.

Indeed, the brain metaphor has gained currency in the age of artificial intelligence to highlight the cognitive and learning capacity of organizations. This metaphor views organizations as complex systems that are constantly processing information, learning, and adapting.

Drawing parallels with the human brain, this metaphor emphasizes the importance of collective intelligence, creativity, and innovation in organizations. It recognizes that the whole is greater than the sum of its parts, and that the best solutions often emerge from the collaborative efforts of diverse individuals with different perspectives and expertise.

The brain metaphor also highlights the importance of neuroplasticity, or the brain's ability to reorganize and form new connections throughout life. This suggests that organizations can also learn and adapt over time, becoming more agile and innovative in the process.

Just as the brain is the seat of human consciousness, organizations, when viewed through the brain metaphor, become the seat of collective intelligence, creativity, and innovation. It calls for us to embrace complexity, harness the collective intelligence of the workforce, and continuously learn and adapt.

The Family Metaphor

Organizations, especially smaller ones or startups, often liken themselves to families. This metaphor emphasizes close-knit relationships, loyalty, and a sense of belonging. Large corporations, like McDonald's (as we'll examine further in our case study for this chapter), have also adopted this metaphor to project an image of unity and warmth. In this familial setting, employees are not just workers; they're members of a close knit group, each with a unique role to play, akin to siblings, parents, or cousins.

While this metaphor can foster a sense of unity and shared purpose, it can also blur professional boundaries. There's an inherent expectation of loyalty, which can sometimes overshadow objective decision-making. Moreover, the emotional dynamics of a family can spill over, making certain discussions or decisions more challenging. However, many corporations leverage this metaphor in their narratives, emphasizing a commitment to their employees' well-being, growth, and success, much like a family would.

The Orchestra Metaphor

Navigating through the symphony of work dynamics, the orchestra metaphor strikes a compelling chord, offering an enlightening perspective derived from the world of music. Both art and music inherently embed themselves in their indigenous contexts, reverberating the distinct cultures and traditions from which they originate.

At the pinnacle of artistic and musical expression, they transcend geographical and cultural boundaries, achieving universal resonance and transforming into fitting metaphors in diverse contexts. This worldwide embrace is evident in the widespread popularity of music genres like jazz, blues, rock and roll, and hip hop. While these styles are deeply anchored in particular cultural milieus, they have flourished into global phenomena.

Employing the orchestra metaphor to dissect work dynamics, we delve into the interplay between the local and the universal within musical expression. An orchestra, a mélange of musicians from divergent backgrounds and traditions, creates a harmony that is simultaneously familiar and novel. Even as the repertoire may traverse cultural domains, each piece is amalgamated by the unique, collective sound of the orchestra.

Indeed, it's noteworthy that music, while mirroring its cultural and traditional roots, has the remarkable ability to breach cultural barriers. It connects with people globally, speaking in a language that is universally and intimately human, and resonates deeply across diverse audiences.

Another pivotal element influencing the efficacy and resonance of the orchestra metaphor is the leadership style, embodied by the conductor in a symphonic context. Take, for instance, conductors Herbert von Karajan and Leonard Bernstein, both renowned maestros yet exemplifying starkly divergent leadership styles. Von Karajan, perceived often as autocratic, preserved a discernible distance from his musicians, placing an emphasis on precision and discipline. Conversely, Bernstein, synonymous with charisma, collaboration, and emotional expressivity, nurtured a vivacious and expressive musical synthesis.

The conductor, like organizational leaders, wields significant influence over the ensemble's performance and harmony, directing not only the musicality but also shaping the emotional and collaborative climate within the orchestra. Analogously, in the metaphorical workplace "orchestra," the leader's personality and style—whether echoing von Karajan's meticulous control or Bernstein's exuberant spontaneity—mold the collective performance, dictating the efficacy with which the ensemble navigates between local and universal, individual and collective, and crafts a melody that either enchants or dissonates within the global auditorium.

The Garden Metaphor

The metaphor of the garden, when applied to organizations, traditionally paints a picture of tranquility, flourishing growth, and nurturing care. Employees, akin to diverse plants, each present unique needs and potentials for growth within this lush metaphorical imagery. The leaders, akin to attentive gardeners, are tasked with catering to these specific needs, ensuring each 'plant' receives its ideal measure of sunlight, water, and nutrients. The metaphor naturally evokes themes of growth, nurturing, patience, and an acceptance that a one-size-fits-all approach is insufficient for cultivating a thriving ecosystem of varied species.

In this realm, each member of the organization is understood to require individualized care to reach its full potential, akin to how different plants in a garden might require varying amounts of sunlight, types of soil, and hydration levels to truly flourish. Thus, the leaders or 'gardeners' must understand and respect the individual needs and potential of their 'plants', ensuring an environment that promotes holistic growth and development.

The film "Being There" eloquently plays with this metaphor, presenting Chance the Gardener, embodied by Peter Sellers, whose simplistic, literal perspectives on gardening are continually and mistakenly interpreted by those around him as profound wisdom. Chance's straightforward remarks on plant care become unintentionally imbued with deeper meaning, demonstrating that basic principles of care and nurture can inadvertently birth vibrant and healthy growth, thus spotlighting the potential depth and power latent within the garden metaphor.

Navigating through the cyclical perception of growth highlighted by Chance, "In the garden, growth has its seasons... And then we get spring and summer again," it's acknowledged that organizations, much like gardens, traverse through seasons of bounty and dormancy. With diligent care and patience, they can perennially bloom anew.

In the contemporary era, the garden metaphor takes on an additional, poignant connotation. With an enhanced societal sensitivity toward the sustainability imperative and conscious acknowledgment of the limits to growth, the metaphor naturally evolves. Thus, the embodiment of a serene and organic ecosystem now also parallels the urgency of employing sustainable practices, understanding the imperative of resource husbandry, and respecting the inherent limits imposed by the natural environment.

It is not surprising, therefore, that the concept of the organizational 'garden' begins to intertwine with notions of sustainability, advocating for an approach that ensures not only the present vitality of its 'flora' but also conscientiously preserves and enhances the 'soil' for continuous, future blooms.

This dual-faceted metaphor, embracing both the traditional and contemporary interpretations, thus offers a number of obvious possibilities to explore organizational dynamics.

The Ship or Voyage Metaphor

Imagine an organization as a ship sailing through the ever-changing seas of the business world. Just as a ship encounters different sea conditions, a company experiences varied business climates. During times of economic boom, the sailing may be smooth, but during a recession, the waters can become rough.

Leaders, like captains, guide their organizations through these changing environments. A leader like Virgin's Richard Branson, may make bold, innovative moves, venturing into various business sectors, akin to exploring uncharted waters. In contrast, a more meticulous yet cautious leader, like Tim Cook of Apple, may focus on keeping the ship on course, emphasizing operational efficiency and steady progress – while making sure the company doesn't drift from its strategic path.

This metaphor descends to us from Plato's 'Republic', where the governance of a city-state is likened to the command of a vessel. The captain of the ship is the only person fit to steer the ship and must have access to "the form of the good" – existing outside space and time, just as the ship's captain navigates a safe path through treacherous seas by use of the distant stars.

Regardless of their leadership style, all leaders must maintain and navigate the ship, keeping both the destination (business goals, customer satisfaction) and the well-being of their crew (team) in mind. For the ship to reach its destination, it must navigate external challenges while ensuring internal cohesion and effectiveness. Not an easy feat.

The Warfare Metaphor

Drawing a parallel between military strategy and business planning is nothing new. Business leaders often tap into narratives reminiscent of battlefield strategies and tactics. Consider the release of a "killer" product intended to "ambush" competitors and "conquer" market share. For instance, when Pepsi introduced Pepsi Crystal to compete with Coca-Cola, it was seen as an attempt to "invade" Coke's market space. Though it didn't work out as planned, it underscored a strategic maneuver typical of warfare.

From "The Art of War" by Lao Tzu to modern business books, the principles of warfare have been applied to strategic business planning. We frame competition as a battle, where markets are "won," competitors are "outflanked," and brands "defend" their position.

However, we must tread carefully. While warfare metaphors can illustrate strategic thinking, they can inadvertently suggest an aggressive, all-or-nothing approach which isn't always applicable in today's collaborative and sustainability-focused business world. For example, partnerships and collaborations, where businesses "ally" with each other for mutual gain, contrast starkly with a battlefield mentality.

Yet the essence is often clear: leaders navigate through varied environments, steering their teams with strategies that respond to both challenges and opportunities. Whether crossing seas or engaging in strategic 'combat', the leader's style and approach can significantly impact the organization's journey and fate, demonstrating the importance of apt metaphorical navigation in business discourse.

The Sports Metaphor

Transitioning from the battlefield to the playing field, sports metaphors offer a somewhat different shade of competition. While still emphasizing victory, they also bring forth values of teamwork, strategy, and fair play. In the US, baseball and football metaphors like "hit it out of the park," "touchdown," or "drop the ball" are deeply embedded in business jargon.

Meanwhile, in countries like India or Pakistan, cricket metaphors such as "hit a six" or "be on the back foot" serve a similar purpose. And in the rest of the world, where football (soccer) is king, we find metaphors like "golazo" (a spectacular goal) and "catenaccio" (a defensive strategy, often with negative connotations) or "build from the back" (transition from defense to offense) seeping into business conversations.

These metaphors, while culturally varied, underscore the importance of collaboration, strategy, and individual brilliance within a collective framework. They can be motivational, emphasizing teamwork, resilience, and adaptability. However, much like warfare metaphors, sports metaphors also carry a competitive edge, often highlighting a win-lose dichotomy. In an age where collaboration and win-win solutions are more sought after, it's essential to wield these metaphors judiciously.

As we have seen, metaphors are prisms that refract our understanding and interpretation of the world around us. In the workplace, metaphors have not only depicted but also actively molded organizational cultures, swayed perceptions, and steered behaviors. Rooted in the strategic aspects of warfare, the competitive spirit of sports, or the harmonious subtleties of an orchestra, metaphors offer a lens to comprehend the multifaceted nature of the workplace and trace the evolution of prevailing conceptions across different eras – but also alternative viewpoints or philosophies within the same era.

Naturally, as the landscape of work evolves, marked by rapid technological advancements and a shifting emphasis towards sustainability and collaboration, so too are our metaphors. They tend to reflect our current realities but can also be malleable enough to adapt to future trajectories. It's imperative to be discerning and mindful of the metaphors we embrace, recognizing their power in shaping both perception and action.

Sharpening our Linguistic Arsenal

As we discussed in the previous chapter, the evolution of work, from hunter-gatherers to farmers, from slaves and masters to artisans, from factory workers to knowledge workers, and now to a workforce that is increasingly enabled by AI, is a testament to our capacity to adapt and evolve. Each era, with its distinct economic system and societal structure, has shaped and been shaped by the nature and meaning of work – and has been reflected in the metaphors we use to convey its nuances.

As we venture into the uncharted territories of the future of work, the navigational tools of yore, such as the terms "domain" and "context," prove inadequate to capture the intricate dynamics and interconnectedness that imbue it with meaning. Instead, we must enrich our linguistic arsenal with terms that better reflect the fluidity, adaptability, and interdependence that underpin work's evolving dynamics.

In place of the restrictive term "domain," we may consider embracing the expansive concept of "work environment." This phrase encompasses not only the physical surroundings within which labor is performed but also the intangible elements that shape the work experience, fostering a holistic understanding of the factors that influence worker engagement and productivity.

Similarly, replacing the static term "context" with the evocative "work milieu" paints a more vivid picture of the underlying atmosphere and culture that permeates the workplace. This term highlights the shared values, beliefs, and norms that guide interactions and influence behavior, providing a lens through which we can better understand the social dynamics that shape organizational success.

To capture the intricate web of relationships within the workplace, we may also consider adopting the term "work ecosystem" – a term I use in later chapters. This phrase aptly conveys the symbiotic relationships between individuals, organizations, technologies, and processes, emphasizing the interdependence that fuels innovation and drives organizational effectiveness.

As we draw this exploration of metaphors to a close, it's evident that the language we employ in discussing organizations isn't just symbolic but richly instructive. Our voyage through metaphors, whether it be gardens nurturing growth, orchestras harmonizing diverse talents, ships navigating through tumultuous seas, or warfare that parallels strategic corporate maneuvering, reveals the multifaceted nature of our perception of work and organizations.

Indeed, they remind us that our conceptualization of work is fluid, influenced by the ebb and flow of cultural, economic, and societal tides.

As we pivot towards the future in our next chapter, let's anchor our metaphorical explorations in practical reality by examining two contrasting case studies: McDonald's and The Berlin Philharmonic.

CASE STUDY 1:
MCDONALD'S

Ray Kroc, the visionary founder of McDonald's, saw his fast-food empire as a large, extended family. This familial approach permeated every aspect of the company, from internal operations to marketing strategies.

Internally, McDonald's cultivated a sense of camaraderie and belonging by embracing the family metaphor. Employees were referred to as "family members," restaurants were dubbed "homes away from home," and generous employee benefits, such as health insurance, dental insurance, and retirement savings plans, reinforced a sense of security and belonging among the workforce.

McDonald's external marketing campaigns also heavily employed the family metaphor. Ronald McDonald, the company's iconic mascot, became a beloved symbol of friendship and family values, instantly recognizable to children and families alike. The company further strengthened its family-oriented image by sponsoring numerous events, including the Ronald McDonald House Charities, which provided support to families with sick children.

The family theme, carefully woven into the fabric of McDonald's operations, proved to be a powerful tool for building a strong sense of community and belonging among its employees and customers. Employees, feeling like valued members of a larger family, were more likely to go the extra mile for their team and customers. The family theme also resonated deeply with customers, offering a comforting respite from the stresses of daily life and providing a shared experience that could be enjoyed by families of all ages.

While some critics have raised concerns about the manipulative nature of the family metaphor and the unrealistic expectations it might create, the enduring popularity of this motif among both employees and customers suggests its profound impact on the brand itself. Indeed, the metaphor has been instrumental in shaping the brand's identity: it fostered a sense of connection and belonging that has been a key factor in the company's remarkable success.

Highlight: The family metaphor at McDonald's creates a powerful sense of community and belonging among employees who feel like they are part of something larger than themselves, and they are more likely to go the extra mile for their team and customers. The metaphor is also used to create a certain resonance with customers who want a place where they can relax and enjoy a meal with their loved ones. It evokes a sense of nostalgia and comfort, which can be appealing to customers of all ages.

CASE STUDY 2:
THE BERLIN PHILHARMONIC

The Berlin Philharmonic is one of the most prestigious orchestras in the world, known for its high level of musicianship and commitment to excellence. With a long and illustrious history, the orchestra has been led by some of the most iconic conductors in history, most notably Herbert von Karajan.

The orchestra metaphor is a powerful tool to underscore the importance of teamwork, cooperation, and execution in the workplace. Just like the musicians in an orchestra, members of an organization must work together seamlessly to produce a unified result. This requires a high level of trust, cooperation, and communication. For example, the violinists must work together to create a harmonious sound, and the percussionists must work together to keep the rhythm. Similarly, employees in an organization must work together to achieve common goals. For example, the sales team must work together to close deals, and the engineering team must work together to develop new products.

Orchestra members must cooperate with each other to ensure that they are all playing the right notes at the right time. This requires them to be aware of each other's parts and to be willing to adjust their own playing as needed. Similarly, employees in an organization must cooperate with each other to ensure that they are all working towards the same goal. For example, the marketing team must work with the sales team to generate leads, and the product team must work with the customer support team to resolve customer issues.

In addition, the orchestra spends hours rehearsing each piece of music before they perform it. This ensures that they are perfectly synchronized and that they can deliver a flawless performance. Similarly, organizations must plan and prepare carefully for any task or project. This involves setting clear goals, identifying the necessary resources, and developing a detailed plan of action. Once the plan is in place, the organization must execute it flawlessly in order to achieve its goals.

The orchestra metaphor clearly holds multiple layers of meaning in the context of the workplace. The conductor embodies the role of the leader, guiding the orchestra of employees towards a shared goal. By working together, cooperating, and executing flawlessly, employees can achieve great things and deliver exceptional results.

Yet another layer involves the diverse roles of each individual instrument. Just as the violins provide the melody, the violas contribute harmony, and the cellos and basses form the foundation, each employee in an organization plays a unique and essential part in the overall composition. Together, these individuals orchestrate workflows, ensuring that the organization's mission is fulfilled seamlessly.

Highlight: The orchestra metaphor is a powerful way of underscoring the importance of teamwork, cooperation, as well as meticulous preparation and execution. Just as an orchestra must work together harmoniously to produce a beautiful piece of music, organizations must align their efforts in ways that reflect these key organizing principles.

CHAPTER 4:
THE MEGATRENDS AFFECTING WORK

Our historical journey through the evolution of work and the changing metaphors that have defined it unveils a dynamic and ever-evolving construct. This exploration prepares us to navigate the transformative megatrends that are shaping its future trajectory.

Globalization, characterized by the expansion of businesses beyond local and national boundaries, has become a defining feature of the modern work landscape. This expansion isn't merely a result of corporate ambition; it's driven by a confluence of socio-economic factors, in tandem with technological disruption (another megatrend explored later in this chapter). These factors include:

Trade Barriers: Governments have actively reduced trade barriers, minimizing tariffs and simplifying import-export processes.

Emerging Markets: The emergence of economies like China and India has opened up vast avenues for business growth, infusing renewed dynamism into global commerce.

Transportation: Technological advancements have revolutionized the movement of goods and people, making it more efficient and cost-effective.

Corporations: Multinational corporations have played a pivotal role in technology transfer, job creation, and market expansion.

While globalization has facilitated unprecedented connectivity and diversified markets, it has also exacerbated imbalances, benefiting the wealthy and powerful at the expense of the marginalized.

Joseph Stiglitz, in his seminal work "Globalization and Its Discontents," criticizes the current trajectory of globalization, arguing that while it holds the potential to uplift nations, it is riddled with flaws: It perpetuates economic disparities, leading to job displacement, wage stagnation, increased inequality, precarious employment, and a skills mismatch. While some regions have benefited, such as China's emergence as a manufacturing hub at the expense of areas like Southern Europe, Stiglitz and other economists point to institutions like the IMF, World Bank, and WTO, suggesting they have often prioritized global finance and elite interests over the concerns of other stakeholders, particularly workers.

Martin Wolf, in "The Age of Globalization: Winners and Losers," aligns with many of Stiglitz's apprehensions. He underscores that the outcomes of globalization are not just the result of impersonal market forces but are significantly influenced by deliberate policy decisions as well as institutional frameworks. These frameworks, often designed by powerful nations and global institutions, tend to prioritize the interests of multinational corporations and financial elites over those of the broader population.

Thus, the current trajectory of globalization brings to the fore several pressing challenges, most notably inequality and environmental degradation, side effects that result from imbalances in global governance. Take trade agreements or IP rights which tilt in favor of capital rather than labor, disproportionately benefiting affluent nations at the expense of those that are less wealthy.

Moreover, the pursuit of short-term gains in the management of globalization often undermines long-term sustainability. This isn't meant as an outright critique of capitalism but rather an observation of its unchecked iterations. A prime example is environmental protection. The race for rapid economic growth often eclipses the equally crucial need for ecological preservation. It has become obvious that prioritizing short-term profit can lead to environmental harm, which, paradoxically, threatens sustained economic prosperity. This is a dilemma that market forces alone cannot rectify.

Undoubtedly, globalization has the potential to uplift societies. But its current path, influenced by a narrow set of priorities and interests, can also magnify disparities and introduce new challenges. To fully realize the benefits of globalization while mitigating its downsides, a recalibration of its governance is perhaps long overdue. This would involve a focus on sustainability and a more equitable distribution of its rewards.

From a European perspective, the complexities of globalization become even more evident. Data from 2017 underscores the benefits, with exports to non-EU countries bolstering over 36 million jobs within the EU. However, the narrative also has its shadows, especially in sectors reliant on low-skilled jobs. Europe has grappled with the repercussions of offshoring, leading to significant job losses and the decline of some industries. At the same time, agricultural subsidies in Europe and the United States have prevented African farmers from gaining a comparative advantage in the global agricultural market, even though they can produce many agricultural products at a lower cost.

Globalization has accelerated in recent years, propelled by technological breakthroughs, innovative business strategies, and shifting consumer behaviors, despite growing concerns about its consequences. Companies like Facebook, Amazon, and Starbucks exemplify this trend, transitioning from local startups to global powerhouses, skewing global systems even more profoundly as they gain market dominance.

The ubiquitous smartphone epitomizes this rapid globalization, democratizing information access but also creating regulatory challenges. Businesses now must navigate diverse regulations, cultural differences, and the digital divide.

Thomas Piketty's "Capital in the 21st Century" examines the economic imbalances exacerbated by unchecked globalization. He highlights the growing wealth gap and attributes it to factors like unrestricted capital movement and the decline of labor unions. He warns that this escalating divide could lead to societal and political unrest, threatening to undermine both economic stability and social cohesion. This could easily threaten the foundations of democratic governance.

The Interconnected Nature of Globalization

As we go deeper into the complexities of globalization, its inherent interconnection with other trends becomes increasingly evident. Technological advancements, particularly in artificial intelligence, are reshaping global interaction, breaking down socio-cultural and linguistic barriers that once seemed insurmountable. This technological revolution is not just a parallel trend; it is deeply enmeshed with globalization, facilitating and accelerating cross-border exchanges. Real-time language translation tools, for instance, transcend mere convenience, becoming pivotal in enhancing global communication and understanding. Yet, this convergence of technology and globalization is not without its challenges: concerns around privacy, data security, and the ethical implications of AI in a global context emerge, requiring a nuanced and informed approach to governance and policy-making.

Simultaneously, globalization's synergy with demographic shifts and sustainability issues (which we touch upon below) offers both challenges and opportunities. The demographic transformations brought about by global migration and cultural exchanges are reshaping societies, influencing labor markets, and altering economic dynamics. In parallel, the sustainability aspect of globalization calls for a critical examination of how global operations impact our environment and the necessity of spreading sustainable practices across borders. The interplay between these megatrends underlines the complexity of globalization — it's not a standalone phenomenon but a tapestry woven intricately with threads of technological progress, demographic shifts, and a growing consciousness towards sustainability.

Next, we will explore another significant trend: changing demographics and societal structures and their impact on the world of work.

Society & Demographics

The second major trend, society and demographics, is primarily concerned with the statistical characteristics of populations, including their size, age, location, and gender distributions, and the implications of these distributions on a range of societal issues, including work. However, this megatrend is inextricably intertwined with broader societal forces, such as urbanization, which is rapidly transforming the way we live and work. Indeed, the move from rural to urban areas is hugely consequential – having a profound impact on work, while creating new economic opportunities and challenges.

The analogy of a mighty river aptly captures the dynamic nature of this megatrend, as it persistently shifts and shapes how we conceive and structure work. Just as the flow of a river relentlessly sculpts the landscape, it dynamically reshapes how we structure our economic activities. It vividly portrays the evolving nature of populations and society, persistently molding and transforming them. It reflects the global population's growth, aging patterns, and geographical distribution, showcasing how these factors evolve over time and profoundly influence the way we work.

By 2050, the global population is projected to reach 10 billion. Accompanying this growth, we're observing an increase in aging populations and rapid urbanization but in ways that are far from uniform. For instance, rapid population growth is anticipated in Sub-Saharan Africa and a handful of low-income countries, while most high-income countries are likely to experience a slowing or even decreasing population growth post-2030.

These changes are as challenging as they are promising. This is where the notion of a "demographic dividend" comes into play. Typically, this term refers to the economic growth potential that can emerge from changes in a population's age structure, particularly when the working-age population outnumbers those not working. Essentially, a larger share of a nation's population within the working-age range means fewer dependents and more individuals producing goods and services, potentially spurring economic growth.

Gretchen Donehower, a demographer at UC Berkeley, introduces an interesting perspective - the concept of a "second demographic dividend" linked to an aging population. She argues that as the population ages, more people reach an age where they can accumulate significant capital for investment. This implies that even with a smaller working-age group, a country can still achieve higher productivity: as a population ages, the amassed wealth and resources can pave the way for greater investments in health, education, and personal development. Indeed, fewer children could mean more resources per child.

Countries with younger populations, conversely, face their unique challenges. They need to invest in education and jobs to accommodate an influx of young job seekers, managing the resultant societal and economic pressures. Failure to tackle issues like unemployment and poverty can breed discontent and impede economic growth.

Now, let's consider the demographic transformations across the globe that are shaping the future of work. Japan, for instance, had a population of 128 million in 2010 and is projected to fall below 100 million by 2050 if current trends continue. With fewer workers to support the economy and a growing elderly population, Japan faces a unique challenge, exacerbated by societal norms favoring smaller families and limited immigration.

China, the world's most populous country, offers another stark example of skewed demographics. The One-Child Policy (1979-2015) managed to control population growth but also resulted in an age and gender imbalance that proved highly problematic in a number of ways. The country's population is rapidly aging, leading to a '4-2-1 problem' where a single-child generation often supports two parents and four grandparents.

On the other hand, India and Nigeria are dealing with a 'youth bulge' - a significant increase in young job-seekers who potentially infuse considerable dynamism into their labor markets. The challenge here lies in creating enough jobs and opportunities for this expanding youth demographic, mitigating the risk of social instability and economic stagnation.

In Europe, demographic trends show a pattern that is somewhat similar to Japan's, with fewer births and an increasing number of retirees, but the severity of these trends is generally less pronounced. This shift towards an aging population is observable across the continent, including in countries such as the UK, France, Germany, Italy, and Spain. In Central and Eastern Europe, these trends are also present, though they vary in intensity and are influenced by unique regional factors.

In Eastern Europe, countries like Russia and Ukraine are experiencing their own distinctive demographic challenges. Russia, the largest country by land area, is grappling with declining fertility rates and high death rates, partly linked to alcoholism, posing significant challenges for sustaining economic growth and social welfare programs. With deaths exceeding births for the first time in Russian history, the future looks daunting. The influx of immigrants, largely from culturally Islamic regions and non-ethnic Russians, could potentially alleviate population decline but might also intensify social tensions, given the cultural differences.

Ukraine, on the other hand, is contending with additional and profound demographic disruptions due to the ongoing conflict with Russia. This naturally has had a tremendous impact on the country's population dynamics, with a falling birth rate and rising casualties among service age men. The prospective long term implications are currently still emerging, and lie outside our broader focus of the future of work.

In France, a proposal to raise the retirement age sparked widespread protests, highlighting concerns over the impact of an aging population on the country's social welfare system, labor market, and quality of life. Across countries with aging populations, there is a pressing need for strategies to employ and retain older workers, and for policies to manage demographic shifts and resultant imbalances, including social security, healthcare, and long-term care.

The United States presents a complex demographic landscape. The aging workforce has led to initiatives like the Protecting Older Workers Against Discrimination Act, safeguarding the rights of older employees. Concurrently, shifts in ethnic composition due to immigration and varying birth and mortality rates are creating a more multicultural and multiracial society, infusing dynamism into America's workforce. Thus, the aging workforce is not just a challenge, but also an opportunity for intergenerational learning and prolonged workforce engagement.

In Canada, immigration plays a significant role in shaping demographic trends. Embracing multiculturalism as a core national policy, the country has built a diverse and resilient society. This stands in contrast to countries with skewed age pyramids facing labor shortages and a shrinking tax base.

Finally, in Latin America, a region traditionally known for its youthful demographic, there is a notable shift towards an aging population. Countries like

Brazil, which now has a lower fertility rate than the United States, exemplify this trend. The decline in fertility across the region is attributed to factors such as increased education, urbanization, and changes in family planning.

This shift presents a dual challenge for Latin American countries: while it offers the potential for a demographic dividend, characterized by economic growth and better resource allocation, it also brings about challenges related to aging populations, such as the need for sustainable social security and healthcare systems.

The region, while still younger compared to more developed areas, is rapidly approaching a demographic turning point, necessitating strategic planning for future socio-economic stability and growth

Gender Dynamics

No discussion of global demographics would be complete without acknowledging the historical shifts in gender dynamics. Women have long played vital roles in families and communities, but their contributions to the workforce have become increasingly significant in recent decades, fueled by changing societal norms and economic realities.

Balancing professional aspirations with family responsibilities is indeed a tightrope. Women's participation in the workforce has enriched the workforce in multiple ways, such as by placing more emphasis on empathy and collaboration. These qualities are essential for building strong teams and creating a positive work environment as workplaces went through a general shift away from traditional "command and control" management styles towards more enabling forms of management.

The advent of flexible work arrangements and digital platforms presents an opportunity to further bridge gender disparities and create more inclusive workplaces that respect and accommodate the unique strengths of both genders.

In essence, while the nurturing role of women remains a constant, their expanding presence in the workforce's higher echelons is a testament to the evolving nature of work and society. As we look to the future, it's crucial to recognize and celebrate this duality, ensuring that our workplaces are not just diverse, equitable, and inclusive, but also infused with what we may call female traits of compassion, empathy, and collaboration.

Age Diversity: Valuing Experience

While gender dynamics in the workforce offer a lens into the evolving roles and contributions of women, it's essential to recognize that diversity isn't limited to gender alone. The demographic shifts we've explored also highlight another crucial dimension: age. Just as gender roles have evolved over time, so too have our perceptions and realities of age in the workplace as life spans increase, fueled by advances in medicine and healthcare. As a result, more and more people choose to work longer into their golden years.

Consequently, as the age spectrum in the workforce is broadening, we have on one end, the younger generations - the digital natives - bringing fresh perspectives and tech-savviness while older individuals, with their wealth of experience, continue to contribute significantly. At the same time, workplace realities help debunk the myth that productivity wanes with age.

Of course, demographics is not a 'one-size-fits-all' story. It's a multifaceted narrative with varying regional patterns and implications that are mainly socio-economic and political in nature. This narrative is rife with misconceptions, one of the most prominent being that retirement should occur at a fixed age and that aging is inherently problematic. In reality, research shows that healthy older individuals can perform just as well as their younger counterparts and bring valuable experience and knowledge to their roles.

It therefore follows that age diversity is just as important as any other form of diversity. Embracing an age-diverse workforce and debunking age-related myths are vital for building successful and inclusive organizations. Companies like Barclays and CVS Health which have implemented programs to counter ageism, have successfully leveraged the wealth of knowledge and experience older workers bring. Barclays' Bolder Apprenticeship program, for instance, is open to all ages, actively encouraging applications from those over 50. As for CVS Health's Talent Is Ageless program, it similarly aims to attract, retain, and engage mature workers.

Technological Advancements

The pulse of the future of work beats in rhythm with technological advancements – an absolutely crucial driver shaping work and a key theme of this book. We are in the midst of the Fourth Industrial Revolution, characterized by the blending of physical, digital, and biological "worlds" (see Figure 2) that is fundamentally reshaping the very fabric of our existence. As Jack Hidary, CEO of technology think tank Sandbox Industries, notes, the synergies unlocked by combining multiple breakthrough technologies make this wave truly transformative and unlike any other that preceded it.

THE BLENDING OF OUR 'WORLDS'

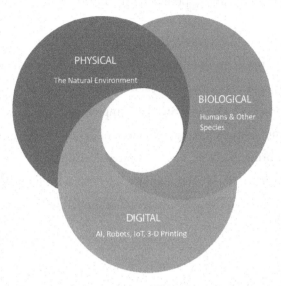

FIGURE 2: THE BLENDING OF OUR *WORLDS*

These fundamentally transformative developments are powered by advances in computing, data, and machine learning, as well as breakthroughs in interlocking domains like synthetic biology and quantum computing. Central to this technological transformation is artificial intelligence (AI), a subject we will explore in greater detail in subsequent chapters. AI's already significant potential is poised for further enhancement through advancements in fields like quantum computing.

Quantum computing, though in developmental stages, holds the promise of revolutionizing data processing with its ability to perform complex calculations at speeds far beyond the capabilities of traditional computers. This emerging technology could enable AI to extract deeper insights from vast datasets at unprecedented speed. It is important to note, however, that quantum computing is still a field of active research, with its practical, widespread application more a future prospect than an immediate reality. As such, the integration of AI and quantum computing, while potentially transformative, remains an evolving area of exploration.

In parallel to AI's growth, quantum technologies are emerging as a frontier with transformative potential across many industries, including healthcare, finance, and manufacturing. The advanced computational power of quantum computers could lead to breakthroughs in areas such as new drug discovery and materials science. Additionally, quantum sensors might develop new methods for data collection and interaction with the physical world.

The influence of AI is already evident in the services provided by tech giants like Google, Amazon, Netflix, and Spotify. By harnessing AI for tasks like refining search algorithms and curating personal user experiences, these companies enhance user satisfaction and further improve their financial performance.

Complementing AI, the Internet of Things (IoT) is forging new paradigms, with interconnected devices enabling real-time data exchange that is revolutionizing sectors such as manufacturing, healthcare, and urban transportation. Additionally, robotics has transitioned from science fiction to reality, transforming industries with applications ranging from robotic arms in factories to providing companionship for the elderly.

Complementing these technological leaps are VR and AR, revolutionizing training and education — from VR flight simulators to AR surgical training programs – and 3D printing, which has emerged to challenge the status quo across industries. Examples like Walmart's VR-based employee training and the medical applications of 3D printing demonstrate their industry-transforming potential.

The metaverse, a virtual world built on blockchain technology, alongside Web3's decentralized web architecture, is set to further revolutionize the workplace. Imagine metaverse-based training simulations offering immersive, personalized learning experiences, or Web3-enabled talent marketplaces connecting workers and employers directly, eliminating intermediaries.

Big data analytics, in its expansive scope, is steering strategic decisions by infusing them with customer-focused insights and enhancing operational efficiency. However, this vast data landscape also raises critical concerns, particularly around privacy and ethics.

The emergence of AI-driven interfaces like chatbots and digital twins, including generative AI models such as ChatGPT, Bard, and Claude, represents a significant shift. These models, which we will discuss in greater detail later, mimic human conversations and offer advanced assistance, learning, and companionship. They hold the potential to personalize learning in the metaverse or innovate customer service in Web3 applications. Their capacity to automate routine tasks also enables workers to focus on more creative and strategic endeavors.

Generative AI's multi-modal capabilities, spanning images, videos, audio, and code, are diversifying its functionalities from classification to content creation. This evolution suggests a transformative impact on various sectors - for instance, creating new forms of digital art in the metaverse or developing innovative financial services in Web3.

The widespread adoption of the internet, accelerated by the COVID-19 pandemic's push towards remote work, highlights the potential for improved work-life balance but also the challenge of maintaining clear boundaries between work and personal life.

Emerging technologies could intensify these challenges, with the risk of workers being perpetually connected to their jobs. Yet they also offer the promise of more autonomy over time and location, potentially redefining work-life balance.

As we envision the future of work, technology acts not just as a tool, but more like a conductor orchestrating a new era. This shift is redefining existing jobs while also creating new ones, such as AI engineers and VR designers. The narrative surrounding AI is not about job elimination but rather a transformation, where AI augments human capabilities, leading to new and exciting opportunities.

Of course, with these advancements comes great responsibility. As I argue throughout this book, we must address the potential for AI misuse and its tendency to exacerbate inequalities. Ensuring that the benefits of technology are both safe and equitably distributed requires a blend of proactive policies, responsible guardrails, and robust social safety nets.

The next section is concerned with another game-changer—climate change and the sustainability imperative.

Climate Change and Sustainability

For decades, we've been acutely aware of our planet's environmental limits. Early thinkers like Thomas Malthus sounded alarms about unchecked population growth, suggesting that our planet's resources would eventually be outstripped by human demands. When combined with modern industrial growth, this Malthusian warning became even more ominous.

In trying to deal with this challenge, though, we run up against "The Tragedy of the Commons" where individuals prioritize their self-interest over the collective good. Unchecked capitalism, with its relentless pursuit of growth, often leaves resource allocation to the unpredictable whims of market forces, exacerbating the negative externalities in ways that are hard to tackle through market mechanisms.

As our global population grows and consumption patterns escalate, we're teetering on the edge of several ecological tipping points. A climate 'tipping point' is a critical juncture where minor changes can trigger significant responses in the overall system, irrevocably altering its future state. Notably, the irreversible melt of the Greenland ice sheet, the dieback of the Amazon rainforest, and shifts in the West African monsoon are all now urgent concerns. Recent studies have amplified the probability of these tipping events, with their impacts being both vast and irreversible.

Specifically, when global warming reaches 1.5 °C (2.7 °F), we're likely to witness the collapse of the Greenland and West Antarctic ice sheets, tropical coral reef die-offs, and abrupt boreal permafrost thaws. The melting ice caps in Antarctica and Greenland, for instance, are causing sea levels to rise, posing existential threats to coastal communities across the globe. Entire island nations may become relics of history. Indeed, The Maldives and the Seychelles, once paradisiacal tourist destinations, now grapple with the looming specter of submersion.

These tipping points are inextricably linked to a number of phenomena that we are witnessing with increasing regularity like extreme weather events and biodiversity loss. These include wildfires in Australia and California, intensified hurricanes in the Atlantic, and other extreme weather events. Indeed, these are becoming the new norm, wreaking havoc on communities, economies, and ecosystems. At the same time, the rapid extinction of species, dubbed the 'Sixth Mass Extinction,' jeopardizes our food security, health, and overall quality of life.

Now, how do these environmental challenges intertwine with the future of work? The implications are manifold, reshaping the very fabric of work itself as well as how we manage it as organizational leaders:

Green Jobs: Combatting these environmental challenges has spurred a demand for 'green jobs.' Renewable energy, conservation science, and sustainable agriculture are burgeoning sectors, promising both employment and solutions.

Values: Companies are no longer solely profit-driven. Their environmental footprints are under scrutiny, leading to the integration of sustainability objectives and values into core corporate strategies.

Remote Work: The remote work revolution has a silver lining: reduced commuting translates to fewer emissions, making daily work routines more sustainable.

Relevant Skills: The threats posed by environmental concerns like rising sea levels necessitate expertise in coastal management, disaster response, and urban planning. As biodiversity loss looms, agricultural roles must evolve to ensure food security in changing landscapes.

Migration: The specter of "climate refugees" is becoming a reality. As communities are displaced, previously inhospitable regions might emerge as new economic hubs.

Innovation: Environmental challenges are also catalysts for innovation. From sustainable packaging solutions to advanced water conservation technologies, new industries are emerging which are driving job creation.

Finally, we must redefine our metrics of success in the future of work to be more holistic, moving beyond a narrow, short-term focus. In this evolving socio-economic environement, financial roles will increasingly integrate environmental metrics, prioritizing long-term sustainable growth over transient financial gains.

Allen Ginsberg's poem "Moloch" (1955) serves as a powerful indictment of capitalism's insatiable greed and materialism. The poem employs the image of Moloch, a Canaanite deity, as a metaphor for the relentless pursuit of wealth, and it has alarmed and inspired a generation of progressive poets, scholars, and environmental activists. In the context of the megatrends discussed in this chapter, Ginsberg's metaphor offers a stark reminder: our pursuit of growth and progress must be consciously balanced against the long-term consequences for our planet and the quality of life of future generations.

Moloch's sinister promise was, 'Cast your babes into the fire, and receive my blessing.' This chilling imagery encapsulates the essence of sacrificing the well-being of future generations at the altar of present-day greed. Ginsberg's Moloch is not merely a symbol of excess; it represents the devouring of the next generation to enrich the present one. This metaphor vividly illustrates the peril of a societal model that relentlessly pursues wealth at the expense of its own future.

This warning is echoed in a 2023 McKinsey analysis. The report shows that over the past two decades, the expansion of the global balance sheet has vastly outpaced the growth of the real economy. A staggering $160 trillion has been infused into paper wealth from 2000 to 2021, driven by soaring asset prices and low interest rates, creating an alarming economic imbalance. While this era has been lucrative for wealth accumulation, it has also stifled balanced and responsible growth and exacerbated inequality. This situation mirrors the perilous path of Moloch, threatening the well-being of our and our children's future.

As we journey towards a more sustainable and equitable future, the challenges, though daunting, are not insurmountable. This transition necessitates reimagining business not as a zero-sum game, but as fundamentally intertwined with sustainability and shared prosperity. Leaders capable of guiding this shift will significantly influence the future trajectory of work and its societal role. The responsibility for this transformation extends beyond the realm of business to society at large. Indeed, adapting to a sustainable economy opens vast opportunities for human flourishing, provided we harness humanity's nobler instincts.

The two case studies that follow illustrate how forward-looking corporations are navigating this mega-challenge.

CASE STUDY 1:
VOLVO

Volvo, a globally recognized brand, epitomizes safety, quality, and environmental care. Founded in 1927 in Gothenburg, Sweden, Volvo initially focused on automobiles but has since diversified into trucks, buses, construction equipment, and marine and industrial engines. This expansion reflects Volvo's adaptability and innovation-driven ethos.

From its inception, Volvo has been a trailblazer in automotive safety, a commitment demonstrated by early milestones such as introducing laminated glass windows in its 1944 PV model. However, its most significant contribution to vehicle safety was the invention of the three-point seatbelt in 1959, a revolutionary development that set new industry standards. These innovations underscore Volvo's longstanding dedication to vehicle safety and its role as an industry leader.

Volvo's evolution from a local enterprise to a significant global player is marked by its presence in over 100 countries and manufacturing facilities worldwide, including in Belgium, China, and the United States. This global expansion showcases Volvo's ability to adapt to market fluctuations, economic changes, and evolving industry trends.

Despite undergoing ownership changes in the 1990s and early 2000s, first to Ford Motor Company and then to Geely Holding Group in 2010, Volvo has maintained its unique brand identity and dedication to safety, quality, and environmental stewardship.

Under its vision "to be the world's most progressive and desired premium car brand," Volvo is making strides in the electric vehicle market. By 2025, it aims for half of its global sales to comprise fully electric cars, with the rest being hybrids, aligning with its commitment to sustainability and reflecting its response to the megatrend of climate change.

In tackling the megatrends of globalization, demographics, technology, and sustainability, Volvo has developed innovative strategies. The company's global expansion and adaptation to different markets showcase its response to globalization. It has embraced changing demographics by tailoring its designs to diverse customer preferences and lifestyle shifts.

Technologically, Volvo is at the forefront, integrating AI to enhance manufacturing efficiency and investing in electric and autonomous vehicles. Its focus on digital technology to improve customer experience and establish new business models is a testament to its innovative approach.

Moreover, Volvo's commitment to sustainability aligns with the pressing need to address climate change. The company's push towards electric vehicles and sustainable transportation solutions is a proactive response to this critical global challenge.

Highlight: Volvo's journey exemplifies how a company can navigate and leverage the complexities of mega-trends like globalization, demographics, technology, and sustainability, turning these challenges into competitive advantages. This case study not only reflects Volvo's resilience and innovation but also its ability to foresee and adapt to changing global conditions, setting a precedent for businesses worldwide.

CASE STUDY 2:
MCKINSEY & COMPANY

McKinsey is a global management consulting firm that provides advice and solutions to businesses, governments, and other organizations. The firm has over 30,000 employees in over 130 countries.

The firm has a long history of innovation and has been at the forefront of the adoption of new technologies in the consulting sector. In recent years, it has been investing heavily in artificial intelligence (AI). In 2023, McKinsey launched the Lilli project, an AI-powered tool that helps consultants access and leverage the firm's vast knowledge base. Lilli is a generative AI model that can summarize complex documents, identify relevant information, and generate new ideas.

Effectively, Lilli is a knowledge management platform - a centralized repository of the firm's vast knowledge and expertise.. It is available to its consultants by typing a question that scans all the knowledge sources both internally generated and those from external sources such as research papers, case studies, and expert opinions.

It identifies between five to seven of the most relevant pieces of content, summarizes key points, includes links, and even identifies experts in the appropriate fields. Indeed, as generative AI sophistication grows, knowledge management systems (far and wide the most common enterprise Generative AI use case today) will be built – powered by tools like vector databases.

Before Lilli, McKinsey consultants spent a significant amount of time searching for and retrieving information from the firm's knowledge base. This was a time-consuming and inefficient process, and it often led to consultants missing important information.

Now, the platform automates the process of searching and retrieving information from the knowledge base and by doing so frees up consultants to focus on more value-added tasks, such as analyzing data and developing solutions.

This has a number of benefits for the firm's consultants, including:

- **Productivity**: Lilli saves consultants time by automating the process of searching and retrieving information.
- **Accuracy**: Lilli can identify relevant information that humans might miss.

- **Creativity**: Lilli can generate new ideas and insights that help consultants to solve problems.

- **Collaboration**: Lilli makes it easier for consultants to share knowledge and insights with each other.

Still under development, Lilli has the potential to revolutionize the way that knowledge is created and shared within and outside the firm. It aids consultants prepare for client meetings by identifying weaknesses in arguments or anticipating questions; it also helps them self-educate on new topics and make connections across projects.

Highlight: The world's premier consulting company showcases how global companies can harness the knowledge economy and tap into AI capabilities to drive growth and competitiveness through enterprise-wide adoption of AI tools.

CHAPTER 5:

THE ROLE AND IMPACT OF AI IN ORGANIZATIONS

Artificial intelligence is reshaping the workplace and society, heralding a departure from the traditional "man as machine" metaphor of the industrial era to more dynamic human-AI relationships. This chapter examines the transformative impact of AI, tracing its historical trajectory, elucidating key concepts behind recent breakthroughs, and contemplating its future evolution, especially as it relates to organizations and their management.

We begin by charting AI's development through three distinct phases of business transformation: automation, optimization, and contextual adaptation. This journey highlights the exponential growth in AI's capabilities and its potential boundaries. We'll explore how businesses can harness AI to reimagine processes, redefine roles, and cultivate collaborative human-AI partnerships, thereby maximizing benefits and sparking innovation.

A central aim of this chapter is to provide a comprehensive overview of AI's dual nature. It serves as both a disruptive force, challenging existing business models, and a catalyst for creating new ones. We'll examine AI's influence in redefining job roles and creating new employment opportunities while addressing the ethical and societal implications of its widespread adoption.

As we explore AI's transformative potential, we'll reconsider traditional task definitions and workforce roles, pondering the fundamental nature of work in an AI-integrated world. This includes speculating on a future where work for sustenance may no longer be necessary. The implications of such a shift are profound: how might humanity adapt to a new paradigm where human fulfillment and creativity are wholly or partly disconnected from work?

To fully grasp these multifaceted impacts, we start with a historical perspective. AI's journey from conceptualization to its current state has been marked by significant milestones, each propelling the field forward and expanding its application scope.

A Brief History of AI

AI's roots trace back to the 1950s, with pioneers like Alan Turing, Marvin Minsky, John McCarthy, and Claude Shannon exploring the concept of machines mimicking human logical thinking and problem-solving. This early work at institutions such as MIT, Stanford, and Dartmouth laid the foundational groundwork for AI. Subsequent decades have witnessed continual advancements, as outlined in the timeline (see Figure 3), each contributing to the field's ever-expanding capabilities.

Time Period	Year	Milestone
1950s	1950	Alan Turing introduces the Turing Test
1950s	1956	"Artificial Intelligence" coined at Dartmouth
1960s-1970s	1965	ELIZA, early NLP program
1960s-1970s	1973	Lighthill Report criticizes AI progress
1980s	1980	Emergence of expert systems
1980s	1986	Backpropagation for neural networks
1990s-2000s	1997	IBM's Deep Blue defeats Garry Kasparov
1990s-2000s	2009	Google's self-driving cars
2010s	2015	AlphaGo defeats Go world champion
2010s	2018	OpenAI's GPT-2 released
2020s	2021	GPT-3 and other advanced models revolutionize various apps

FIGURE 3: AI DEVELOPMENT TIMELINE

In the 1960s, Joseph Weizenbaum created ELIZA, an early natural language processing system that simulated human conversation using pattern matching and basic rules. The system was able to fool many people into thinking they were talking to a real person (passing the Turing test), but it was ultimately limited by its rule-based approach.

By the mid-1970s, the limitations of rule-based AI were becoming apparent. While they are good at following explicit rules, these systems are not able to learn or adapt to new information. This makes them brittle and prone to failure in unexpected situations.

In 1973, James Lighthill published a report that critiqued the lack of progress in AI research. He argued that AI researchers were overselling their capabilities and that it would be many years before machines could achieve human-level intelligence. The report led to a period of reduced funding and pessimism about the future of AI, known as the "AI winter."

Expert Systems and Machine Learning

During the so-called AI winter, the flame of innovation burned lower as public interest waned, but dedicated scholars kept the field of artificial intelligence alive. They focused on expert systems, which encapsulated human expertise within computer programs. These systems showed promise in specialized areas like medical diagnosis and financial planning, yet they stumbled when asked to venture beyond their narrow confines or to learn from new data.

Simultaneously, machine learning began to develop, where computers could learn from data without explicit instructions. This held the key to solving more complex problems that eluded the rigid rule-based systems of the past.

The renaissance of AI began with a resurgence of interest in deep learning in the 1980s. Neural networks, modeled loosely after the human brain, began to demonstrate their potential. These networks, composed of layers of interconnected nodes, learned to recognize patterns by adjusting the weights of these connections through a process known as training. Once trained, they could make predictions or decisions on new data, a capability that would soon revolutionize the way machines understood the world.

The Deep Learning Breakthrough

Deep learning's prowess was proven beyond doubt when AlphaGo, a program developed by Google's DeepMind, defeated Go champion Lee Sedol in 2016. This victory was a triumph of computing power but also a clear signal that machines could match and even surpass human intellect in certain complex, rule-based tasks. It effectively dispelled the myth that intricate reasoning and strategy were exclusively human faculties.

As the new millennium unfolded, AI, driven by deep learning, transitioned from an academic curiosity to mainstream technology. It matured to give rise to systems capable of creating realistic images, translating languages in real-time, and autonomously navigating vehicles. This technological advancement extended beyond the digital realm, with industries from healthcare to finance beginning to harness AI's unparalleled data analysis and pattern recognition capabilities.

Redefining Intelligence: Beyond Anthropocentrism

Our perceptions of artificial intelligence (AI) are shaped by captivating cultural representations, such as the enigmatic HAL 9000 from "2001: A Space Odyssey" or the sophisticated hosts of "Westworld." These fictional portrayals, while undeniably captivating, can lead to a distorted understanding of the true nature and potential of AI. To fully grasp the trajectory of AI, we must move beyond these cinematic stereotypes and engage in deeper analysis and reflection that is likely to lead us to scenarios previously unimagined.

AI, fundamentally, is about creating machines that can exhibit intelligent behavior. But this basic definition barely scratches the surface. In many (and perhaps ultimately all) aspects, machines have the potential to outpace human capabilities. For example, while humans are adept at pattern recognition, AI can analyze vast datasets at speeds that are orders of magnitude faster than human cognition. It's like juxtaposing a bird's flight with a rocket's propulsion; both achieve movement, but through vastly different magnitudes and mechanisms.

Since its inception, the field of artificial intelligence (AI) has been deeply rooted in anthropocentrism, the belief that humans are the central or most important element of existence. This mindset has driven the ambitious pursuit of replicating the functionalities of the human brain, the pinnacle of biological intelligence.

The human brain, with its intricate network of approximately 86 billion neurons and trillions of synapses, orchestrates our thoughts, emotions, and actions through complex electrochemical processes. It operates at remarkable speeds while consuming relatively little energy – roughly 20 watts, equivalent to a low-power lightbulb.

The brain's sheer complexity and our limited understanding of its inner workings make it an enigmatic masterpiece. This is further complicated by the role of elusive concepts such as consciousness and the brain/mind distinction, which delve into the nature of our subjective experiences and the relationship between the physical brain and the intangible mind.

Despite significant advancements in neuroscience, fully understanding and emulating the brain's exact functions remains a distant, if not elusive, goal. The brain's adaptability, flexibility, and ability to learn and evolve through experience continue to pose formidable challenges for replicating its capabilities in artificial systems.

While the anthropocentric approach has yielded impressive progress in AI, it has also exposed its limitations. The pursuit of replicating human intelligence has led to narrow AI systems, designed to perform specific tasks, but lacking the generality and adaptability of human cognition.

This realization has led to the emergence of alternative approaches to AI, such as artificial general intelligence (AGI) and neuromorphic computing, which aim to develop AI systems that are more human-like in their ability to learn, adapt, and reason.

These new approaches, while still in their early stages, offer promising avenues for advancing AI beyond its current limitations. They hold the potential to create AI systems that are not only capable of solving complex problems but also capable of interacting with and understanding the world in ways that are more akin to humans.

The Mainstreaming of AI

The introduction of generative AI models such as ChatGPT, Bard, and Claude represents a significant milestone in AI's mainstream integration. These models, though still evolving, have demonstrated a remarkable ability to generate creative content and simulate human reasoning. Their swift ascent to prominence, while it might seem to align with the typical patterns of Gartner's hype cycles, is grounded in tangible capabilities rather than mere expectations.

While it's true that new technologies often undergo a phase of heightened expectations followed by a period of recalibration as limitations emerge, it's important to recognize the substantial advances these AI models have already made. They are not merely experimental but are actively transforming industries. In customer service, for instance, AI-driven solutions are redefining efficiency and effectiveness, demonstrating the practical utility of these technologies.

Nevertheless, it's also crucial to acknowledge that as we push the boundaries of what current generative models can achieve, we may encounter the limits of their existing architectures. This realization points to the necessity of exploring alternative AI architectures beyond the current language-based models. The future of AI, therefore, lies not just in refining current models but in pioneering new ones that can surpass the limitations of present-day technologies.

In this context, the story of generative AI is one of real progress coupled with an understanding of its potential and limitations. This balanced view acknowledges the susceptibility to hype but also emphasizes the genuine advancements and the ongoing need for innovation in AI architectures.

This growing awareness has spurred interest in developing models that integrate a more comprehensive, multimodal, and multisensory understanding of the world. These models represent the next frontier in AI research and development, combining generative and multimodal AI to interpret and create content using diverse data types like text, images, and audio. The potential of generative AI to enhance its processing and output capabilities with such varied data is substantial.

As AI continues its evolution, the focus is on crafting ethically sound, diverse, and representative models to avoid perpetuating biases or stereotypes. The future of AI, deeply integrated into our daily lives, is envisioned as an era of collective intelligence, where the full potential of AI is harnessed alongside human ingenuity to advance humanity.

The widespread integration of AI across various industries underscores its growing acceptance and effectiveness. In healthcare, AI aids in diagnostics and medical imagery analysis, at times surpassing the expertise of seasoned professionals. In the finance sector, AI is instrumental in fraud detection and automated trading, capitalizing on its rapid data processing capabilities. Similarly, in manufacturing and transportation, AI contributes significantly to predictive maintenance and logistics optimization.

It's important to recognize that while AI's form of 'creativity' differs from human creativity, this difference does not diminish its role but rather complements human capabilities. AI, driven by data and algorithms, brings a unique set of strengths to problem-solving and innovation, distinct from the depth of human intuition and emotion. As AI models continue to evolve, they are poised to become as integral to our lives as foundational technologies like the internet or electricity. This integration heralds a future where AI and human intelligence synergistically collaborate, combining their respective strengths to tackle complex global challenges.

The Evolutionary Trajectory

As we examine the evolutionary journey of AI, we find ourselves at a pivotal point where AI's influence is permeating areas once thought to be exclusive domains of complex human thought and ingenuity. The current phase, highlighted by the advent of generative AI models, showcases an unprecedented capacity to produce content that is beginning to rival human quality.

These generative models have demonstrated their prowess in creating text, images, music, and more, achieving a level of sophistication that blurs the line between machine-generated and human-created content. Yet, while they excel in mimicking human-like output, these models are not without their limitations. They occasionally exhibit flaws such as a lack of deep understanding of context, occasional generation of nonsensical or biased content, and challenges in capturing the nuanced subtleties of human emotion and creativity.

Despite these imperfections, the trajectory of AI development points towards continuous improvement and refinement. As generative AI models evolve, they are progressively closing the gap in areas where they currently fall short. This journey reflects a broader trend in AI evolution – one where the boundaries of what AI can achieve are constantly being pushed further, reshaping our understanding of the interplay between human creativity and machine intelligence.

Indeed, as I've already argued, while their 'creativity' differs from human creativity, being more a product of data-driven algorithms than emotional depth and experiential nuances, these models are unlocking a plethora of possibilities. Millions of users are beginning to experiment with platforms such as ChatGPT, Bard and Claude, learning to use various prompt methods to generate content (see Figure 4).

Type	Description	Example
Reductive	Reduces the size and complexity of data.	Summarizing a long article, identifying key points from a large dataset, extracting relevant information from a document.
Transformative	Changes the format or meaning of data.	Converting a text document to speech, translating languages, generating different creative text formats, like poems, code, scripts, musical pieces, email, letters, etc.
Generative	Creates new content or ideas.	Generating new text, translating languages, creating images, writing music, designing creative content.
Latent	Reveals hidden information or patterns in data.	Identifying hidden connections between data points, uncovering previously undetected trends or relationships, extracting insights from complex data.
Emergent	Creates or discovers new things that were not explicitly programmed.	Generating new ideas, formulating original hypotheses, discovering new scientific phenomena, solving open-ended problems in unexpected ways.

FIGURE 4: THE PATH TOWARDS EMERGENCE

Consequently, today's generative AI models largely break the mold of the typical initial stage of a hype cycle. They exhibit a broad spectrum of capabilities, surpassing preliminary expectations. While they offer only preliminary insights into the more advanced applications – those requiring a holistic understanding of the world beyond language-based models – their current capabilities are considerable. Acknowledging this is vital in appreciating the strengths of current AI technology and recognizing its potential for further development.

Simplifying Complex Information (Reduce): LLMs excel at distilling complex information into more understandable forms. They can summarize lengthy articles, abstract scientific papers, and extract key points from extensive discussions. This simplification capability makes them invaluable in fields like education and research, where clarity and brevity are essential.

Adapting and Reimagining Content (Transform): These models adeptly translate text across languages, tailor content for new audiences, and creatively adapt existing works. LLMs can rejuvenate content, creating various text formats, engaging marketing copy, and educational resources. They also extend their versatility to programming, translating ideas into efficient code, thereby streamlining software development.

Generating New Creative Works (Generate): A key capability of LLMs is generating new content, from ideation to creative composition. They can develop original narratives, musical pieces, and innovative concepts. However, it's important to understand that this 'creativity' is a reflection and reassembly of human-generated inputs, not an extension beyond the realm of human imagination. Nevertheless, their abilities open new possibilities in fields like marketing, entertainment, and education.

Hidden Insights from Data (Uncover): Beyond content creation, LLMs possess the ability to reveal hidden insights in large datasets. They can detect anomalies, forecast trends, and suggest new theories, proving invaluable in areas like fraud detection, risk management, and scientific exploration. This analytical capability underscores their role in enhancing decision-making and fostering innovation.

Extending Innovation (Emerge, Evolve): The emergent capabilities of AI point to a future where it can contribute to creative thought and problem-solving. Advanced AI systems are beginning to self-design, self-learn, and apply knowledge across various contexts. While their potential might seem to surpass human capabilities, it's more accurate to view them as augmenting and complementing human intelligence, creating new opportunities for innovation and problem-solving.

Towards Complex Reasoning & Problem Solving

AI visionaries like Geoffrey Hinton have emphasized that AI's true potential might not lie in mere replication of human intelligence but in carving out its unique capacities. Drawing an analogy with the Wright brothers' pioneering work in aviation, AI can learn from biological intelligence but also forge its own distinct path.

The Wright brothers, inspired by the flight of birds, did not attempt to mimic every aspect of avian flight. Instead, they harnessed aerodynamics in a way that was distinct from birds' flapping mechanisms, creating fixed-wing aircraft that revolutionized travel. They were inspired by what they understood, but they also realized the limits of excessive replication.

Similarly, AI's recent foray into generative models, while still far from achieving Artificial General Intelligence (AGI) capabilities, marks remarkable progress. Chatbots like ChatGPT, Bard, and Claude showcase an impressive ability to understand and generate human-like text.

Nevertheless, complex reasoning and contextual adaptation are still nascent. Early designs are often limited by the ways users interact with them, which can sometimes lead to responses that lack context and depth. But these are still early days, and with each new version, capabilities improve vastly.

The binary categorization of AI as either "narrow" or "general" is a reductionist view of a much more intricate range. The true essence of AI lies in understanding it as a spectrum, with varying degrees of complexity and capability (see Figure 5).

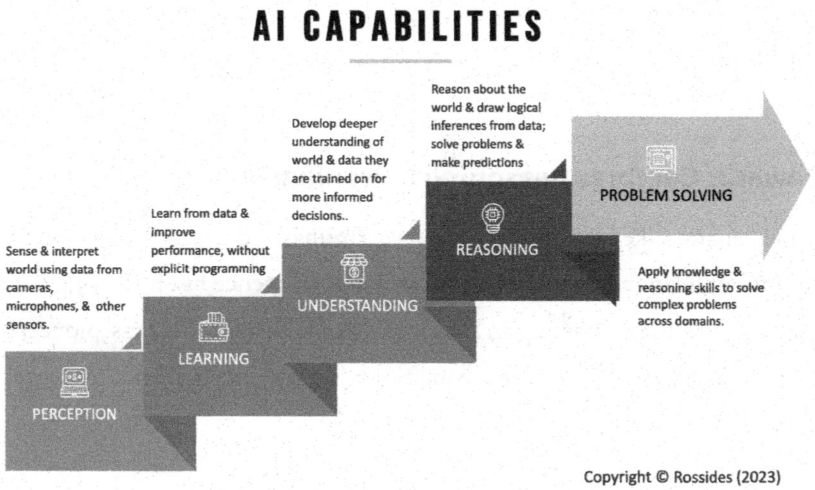

AI CAPABILITIES

FIGURE 5: THE AI CAPABILITIES SPECTRUM

The journey of artificial intelligence (AI) can be visualized as a ladder with perception at the bottom rung and reasoning and problem-solving at the top. Each rung represents a distinct stage of AI development, marked by unique capabilities and ethical considerations.

At the lower end of the spectrum reside rule-based systems, the foundation of AI. These systems, like autopilots and business software, excel at consistent execution, adhering to pre-programmed rules and instructions. Their perception is rather limited, relying on predefined data inputs including from cameras, microphones, and other sensors.

Context-aware systems climb a rung higher, exhibiting an ability to understand situational information and adapt accordingly. They can analyze and interpret data, forming a more comprehensive understanding of their environment. Customer service chatbots, for instance, personalize responses based on user input, enhancing customer interactions.

Domain expertise systems transcend the limitations of rules, employing strategizing and learning capabilities. They can analyze vast amounts of data, identifying patterns and relationships to make generalizations and predictions. AlphaGo, a landmark AI system, mastered the intricate game of Go by analyzing gameplay data and honing its strategy.

Reasoning algorithms, a more advanced breed of AI, exhibit early signs of understanding intent and logic behind content, not just raw data. They can analyze and interpret natural language, paving the way for more nuanced human-AI interactions.

Artificial general intelligence (AGI), the pinnacle of AI aspirations, aims to replicate and surpass human cognition. AGI would have the ability to perceive, learn, understand, reason, and solve problems in a way that is indistinguishable from humans.

Management & Business Implications

As AI capabilities evolve, the implications for management and business become increasingly profound and complex. AI's spectrum of capabilities, extending beyond discrete categories, opens a multitude of possibilities for business operations and strategic decision-making.

At the fundamental end of the spectrum, narrow AI systems, like chess-playing computers, demonstrate potential applications of strategic game theory in business contexts. Their precision and reliability can be harnessed to formulate competitive strategies, aiding businesses in outmaneuvering competitors for market advantage.

Moving up the spectrum, we encounter systems with limited memory, such as chatbots. These AI constructs interact with customers, providing consistent, adaptive responses within their programmed scope. Their deployment in customer service streamlines interactions and improves satisfaction, while also offering valuable consumer behavior insights, enabling businesses to more effectively tailor services and marketing strategies.

Advancing towards the higher end of the spectrum, we find AI systems capable of modeling human mental states, facilitating more intuitive interactions. This capability can revolutionize customer relationship management by anticipating needs, responding to unexpressed customer sentiments, and proactively resolving issues. Deep customer engagement fostered by these systems can enhance loyalty, potentially increasing revenue and market share.

At the zenith of AI development, the pursuit of artificial general intelligence (AGI) promises a future where AI could replicate the versatility of human cognition. For management, this represents an ultimate tool in overcoming bounded rationality—the cognitive limitations constraining decision-making.

AI systems are able to process and synthesize vast amounts of information, far surpassing human capacity, and provide decision-makers with an expansive view of complex data. This enhanced understanding of market trends, consumer behavior, and competitive dynamics facilitates the identification of patterns and insights that might otherwise remain undiscovered, leading to more informed decision-making.

The synergy between foundational AI technologies like machine learning, and applied domains such as natural language processing and computer vision, is particularly relevant to marketing. These technologies enable the analysis of consumer sentiment across social media platforms and provide real-time feedback on product, campaign, and brand reception. Businesses leveraging these insights can adapt their strategies, optimize messaging, and proactively address emerging trends or concerns.

In essence, AI acts as a catalyst, amplifying human intellect within the business realm. It expands cognitive boundaries, helps mitigate inherent biases, and refines decision-making processes. Deeper integration of AI into business operations promises gains in efficiency, productivity, and customer satisfaction, and provides strategic clarity by transcending cognitive limitations.

The spectrum of AI capabilities should not be viewed as a linear progression but as a multifaceted field with varying degrees of development and application. Each capability opens new avenues of potential; however, the trajectory of these advancements is not predetermined. Businesses should remain agile, embracing AI's exploratory nature and its transformative potential as it evolves.

The Frontiers of the Metaverse & Web3

As the business landscape continues to evolve, we are ushered into the cutting-edge realms of the Metaverse and Web3, each representing groundbreaking shifts in digital interaction and internet infrastructure.

The Metaverse, characterized by its immersive virtual environments enabled by extended reality technologies, offers a new frontier for human interaction. This digital realm extends beyond traditional digital experiences, allowing users to engage in a fully immersive and interactive digital world. In the Metaverse, businesses can create unique, engaging environments for meetings, collaborations, and even virtual events, transforming how we connect and conduct business.

Web3, often mentioned alongside the Metaverse but distinct in its core concept, is a paradigm shift towards a decentralized internet. It is built on blockchain technology, which is essentially a distributed ledger that maintains a secure and decentralized record of transactions. This technology allows for a more democratized internet where users have greater control over their data, and transactions are secured without the need for central authorities. Web3's architecture enables new forms of online interactions and transactions, characterized by enhanced security, privacy, and user autonomy.

As we stand on the brink of significant digital transformation with the advent of the Metaverse and Web3, it's essential to navigate these waters with both enthusiasm and caution. While these technologies promise revolutionary changes in the way we work and interact online, they bring their own set of challenges and controversies.

The promise of the Metaverse and Web3 extends beyond mere technological advancement; they offer new paradigms for digital interaction and business operations. However, their association with the volatile and often speculative domain of cryptocurrencies introduces a layer of complexity. The world of digital currencies, while offering opportunities for new financial models, is also fraught with risks such as market volatility, regulatory uncertainties, and security vulnerabilities. As managers in this evolving landscape, it is imperative to be well-informed and cautious, especially when it comes to integrating these technologies into business models or financial operations.

Workplaces: Decentralized, Virtual & Immersive

Web3, with its emphasis on decentralization, brings a radical shift in digital platforms and tools. This shift has profound implications for managers, especially in areas like hiring and collaborative work. Decentralized platforms can transform traditional workflows, offering more autonomy and control over data to both companies and employees. For instance, in a Web3-enabled workplace, managers might find themselves navigating decentralized recruit-ment platforms where candidates have greater control over their data and credentials. This can lead to more transparent and efficient hiring processes but also requires managers to adapt to new ways of accessing and evaluating candidate information.

Moreover, Web3's potential for enhancing collaborative work cannot be overstated. By utilizing decentralized platforms, teams can collaborate in environments that are secure, transparent, and free from the constraints of centralized data control. This can empower employees to take greater ownership of their work and foster an environment where data security and privacy are prioritized. For managers, this means adapting to new tools that facilitate such collaboration while ensuring that team dynamics and produc-tivity are maintained.

The integration of Web3 and the Metaverse into business operations is not just about adopting new technologies; it's about embracing a new digital culture. Managers play a crucial role in this transition, guiding their teams through the complexities of these technologies while leveraging their poten-tial to create more dynamic, equitable, and efficient workplaces. As these technologies continue to evolve, they hold the promise of fundamentally altering the nature of work, making it more data-empowered, decentralized, and driven by individual autonomy and collaboration.

The Interplay of Automation and Augmentation

Understanding AI's role in the future of work involves exploring how auto-mation and augmentation are interconnected rather than parallel strategies. Insights from Schad, Lewis, Raisch, and Smith's 2016 study in the *Academy of Management Annals* highlight how these two aspects of AI can coexist and complement each other in business and societal contexts.

Automation in AI refers to technology performing tasks without human intervention, crucial in environments where consistency, speed, and error reduction are key. In manufacturing, for example, AI-driven robots can assemble parts with precision and efficiency, surpassing human capabilities.

Augmentation, in contrast, involves AI assisting and enhancing human skills and decision-making. In healthcare, AI-driven diagnostic tools aid doctors by analyzing medical data to suggest possible diagnoses, which doctors then review and confirm based on their expertise and patient interaction.

Beyond Dichotomy: Complementarity

It might initially seem that automation and augmentation are in conflict – one replacing human effort, the other enhancing it. However, when viewed as complementary elements, they offer a holistic approach to AI in the workplace.

For instance, in customer service, chatbots (automation) can handle routine inquiries, freeing human employees to focus on complex, nuanced customer interactions (augmentation). This not only improves efficiency but also the quality of service, as employees can dedicate more time and attention to cases where their human judgment and empathy are crucial.

The challenge for organizations is to navigate the balance between automation and augmentation. An overemphasis on automation risks job displacement and the loss of valuable human skills, while ignoring automation could mean missed efficiency gains.

A balanced example is seen in the retail industry, where automated inventory systems streamline stock management, and augmented reality (AR) applications enhance the shopping experience by allowing customers to visualize products in their homes before purchasing. This synergy optimizes operational efficiency and customer engagement.

In sum, understanding the interconnected nature of automation and augmentation can enhance efficiency while enriching the human aspects of work, promising a future where AI not only transforms how we work but also reinforces the value of human contribution – a testament to AI's dual roles in enhancing operational efficiency whilst also providing innovative platforms for building businesses.

AI as Business Enabler & Multisided Platform

Artificial Intelligence (AI) stands at the forefront of a paradigm shift, transforming not just business workflows but redefining entire industries. Its influence extends far beyond mere technological advancement, positioning AI as both a formidable business enabler and a foundational element of innovative multi-sided platform business models. This dual role of AI – as a powerful tool streamlining and enhancing traditional business processes, and as a central cog in the wheel of complex, interconnected business ecosystems – is reshaping the landscape of industry and commerce.

In understanding AI's transformative impact, we must explore how it navigates this duality, serving as a versatile assistant, a strategic manager, and a collaborative partner while also driving the dynamics of multi-sided platforms that connect and empower various stakeholders in a dynamic business ecosystem.

AI as Assistant, Manager, and Collaborator

In the ever-evolving landscape of modern business, AI is playing increasingly diverse roles. Far from being a mere technological tool, AI has become an indispensable assistant in decision-making, a strategic manager of complex tasks, and an innovative collaborator in various workplace activities. This transformation transcends industry boundaries, profoundly reshaping roles and responsibilities across sectors from healthcare to legal services.

Central to AI's transformative potential in the workplace is its capacity to extend beyond human limitations in processing complex information. This capability enables us to overcome the challenge of bounded rationality – the cognitive limitations that restrict our ability to make optimal decisions in complex situations. AI aids in this by automating repetitive tasks, providing deep insights from large datasets, and simulating diverse scenarios, thus enhancing our decision-making abilities under the constraints of limited time and information.

For instance, in the medical field, AI systems can swiftly analyze millions of records to identify diagnostic patterns that would be imperceptible to human doctors. In business strategy, AI's ability to simulate numerous scenarios helps in making informed decisions about critical operations, such as identifying the most advantageous locations for new business establishments.

As AI systems become more advanced, their role in the workplace is also evolving. They are transitioning from tools that automate tasks and analyze data to becoming collaborative partners, assistants, and managers, reshaping the dynamics of teamwork and leadership.

Who AI Works With & Where AI Works

The relationship between humans and AI in the workplace has developed into a complex interplay of roles. AI systems are increasingly seen not just as replacements for human tasks but as collaborative partners, capable assistants, and even managers, changing the traditional dynamics of various professions.

In the healthcare sector, the collaboration between radiologists and AI stands as a prime example, where their combined efforts lead to more accurate diagnoses than either could achieve independently. In the legal realm, AI algorithms are transforming the labor-intensive process of due diligence during mergers and acquisitions by swiftly analyzing vast quantities of documents. This shift allows legal professionals to focus on higher-level tasks that require human judgment, critical thinking, and the balancing of complex criteria.

The influence of AI extends to altering how we work and are managed. As indicated by research from Brookings, AI now plays a managerial role in many companies. A notable example is Uber, where algorithms are heavily relied upon for assigning rides, setting wages, and monitoring performance.

Advanced AI applications have even expanded to physical task management, such as providing haptic feedback to guide warehouse workers based on motion sensors. This expansion of AI into managerial and supervisory roles marks a significant shift in our understanding of workplace leadership and guidance. It heralds the advent of innovative AI-driven platforms and interfaces that offer unparalleled flexibility and efficiency, redefining conventional notions of management and workspace organization.

AI Across Business Functions: Transforming Enterprises

AI has evolved from being a highly promising yet unproven technological novelty to a ubiquitous force in modern business workflows. As we've delved into the three waves of AI transformation, it's evident that AI's influence is not confined to automation—it's foundational.

From predictive analytics, personalized customer experiences and improved customer engagement to fine-tuning distribution logistics and dynamic pricing models, AI's imprint is profound and pervasive.

Predictive Analytics: Leveraging vast data troves and advanced machine learning, AI empowers granular predictive modeling in marketing. As White (2019) highlights, techniques like sentiment analysis provide insight into customer preferences. Chatbots garner real-time feedback. Content personalization engines refine recommendations based on usage patterns. This data-driven approach allows brands to anticipate consumer needs and pinpoint high-value opportunities. Additionally, predictive analytics can forecast market trends, allowing businesses to preemptively adjust their strategies and ensure they remain ahead of the curve.

Customer Acquisition & Experience: AI is transforming the way businesses acquire and retain customers. From personalized promotions to AI-generated product recommendations, AI is making marketing more customized and two-way. At the same time, AI-powered chatbots and predictive analytics are enhancing customer experience and helping businesses stay competitive.

AI is revolutionizing customer acquisition by harnessing vast reservoirs of user data. Machine learning algorithms can now tailor marketing campaigns to individual preferences, ensuring messages resonate on a personal level. For example, platforms like HubSpot use AI to segment audiences, ensuring content reaches those most likely to engage. AI-driven chatbots can also provide real-time customer support, enhancing user experience and brand loyalty.

AI is also transforming the customer experience. For example, Sephora's AI-powered recommendation engine helps shoppers discover new products aligned to their preferences. The beauty retailer reported increased sales and engagement after implementing this tool.

Content Creation: Consider the vast forms of content creation: from blog posts, social media snippets, and ad copy to long-form articles, video scripts, and even poetry. Each requires a unique touch, tone, and texture. While AI can provide the structure, the depth, nuance, and soul come from human insight. What is more, AI's role isn't limited to content generation. It's an invaluable brainstorming partner.

For instance, when faced with writer's block or seeking fresh perspectives, professionals can engage in a creative dialogue with AI provided that they provide appropriate prompts. By posing questions, challenging AI-generated ideas, or even seeking inspiration from its suggestions, content creators can discover novel angles, innovative themes, or even unexpected twists in narratives. In essence, the future of content creation isn't about AI replacing human creators but amplifying them. It's about harnessing the computational prowess of AI while infusing it with the irreplaceable creativity, emotion, and soul that only humans can provide. This symbiotic relationship between AI and human professionals promises not just efficiency but a renaissance of authentic, impactful, and soulful storytelling.

Pricing for Value Perception: Pricing isn't just about numbers; it's a nuanced dance of understanding market dynamics, gauging customer perceptions, and positioning oneself amidst competitors. AI elevates this dance to an orchestrated ballet. Platforms such as Pricefx harness AI to delve deep into market trends, competitor pricing strategies, and real-time customer feedback. But it doesn't stop there. By analyzing customer sentiment and purchase behaviors, these platforms can predict how pricing changes might resonate with target demographics. This ensures businesses aren't just reactive but proactive, setting prices that encapsulate both tangible costs and intangible values, such as brand equity and customer loyalty.

Synthetic Data: In the quest for competitive advantage and innovation, synthetic data emerges as a key enabler. This unique form of data not only simulates real-world scenarios but also draws upon actual data elements, effectively bridging gaps in situations where real data collection is impractical or sensitive. Generated through sophisticated algorithms and simulations, synthetic data replicates the complex patterns and relationships inherent in authentic datasets.

This blend of simulated and real data elements makes synthetic data particularly valuable in fields like predictive analytics, directly influencing the performance of AI systems. By employing synthetic data, organizations can develop AI models that are both robust and ethical, well-tuned for real-world complexities.

Synthetic data's primary advantage lies in its ability to circumvent the challenges associated with collecting real-world data, especially in contexts involving sensitive or private information. This artificial data can be generated abundantly, freeing AI development from the constraints of scarce or biased real-world datasets.

Moreover, synthetic data offers superior control over data quality and consistency. Real-world data often suffers from noise, incompleteness, or biases, potentially skewing AI training. Synthetic data, however, can be meticulously crafted to avoid these pitfalls, ensuring high-quality, unbiased training for AI models.

One of the most notable aspects of synthetic data is its customizability. Developers can tailor it to specific scenarios, including rare or edge cases often underrepresented in real data. This versatility allows for the creation of AI models that are not only more robust but also broadly applicable across different situations.

Synthetic data's applications are diverse, encompassing:

Training AI Models: It can replace the need for real-world data, which might be costly or difficult to obtain, in training AI models.

Data Augmentation: Synthetic data can enhance real-world datasets, adding variety and depth necessary for comprehensive AI training.

Privacy Protection: It serves as a tool for anonymizing data, replacing sensitive real data with synthetic versions to uphold privacy.

Edge Case Testing: Synthetic data is invaluable for testing AI models against rare or unusual scenarios not typically found in real datasets.

Therefore, while synthetic data is not a perfect substitute for real-world data, its advantages make it an indispensable tool in the development of AI. It addresses real-world data limitations, offers enhanced control over data quality, and allows for greater customization. This adaptability empowers researchers and developers to create AI solutions that are robust, generalizable, and respectful of privacy considerations.

Supply Chain Management: In the realm of supply chain management, AI acts as a strategic orchestrator. Platforms like Llamasoft employ AI to analyze a multitude of variables – from inventory levels to geopolitical factors – optimizing the entire supply chain. This application of AI ensures efficient product flow, anticipates potential disruptions, and adapts to changing demands, keeping businesses agile and resilient.

Performance Monitoring: AI transforms performance monitoring by turning complex data into insightful, actionable intelligence. Tools such as Tableau, infused with AI capabilities, democratize data analytics by visualizing data trends in an understandable format. This enables businesses to track customer behaviors, forecast market trends, and make evidence-backed strategic decisions.

Change Management and AI Integration

The integration of AI into business processes requires thoughtful change management. Successful AI adoption hinges on a company's ability to navigate the complexities of technological and human factors. It involves preparing and training the workforce, aligning AI initiatives with business objectives, and fostering a culture of innovation and adaptability. Managers play a crucial role in guiding their teams through this transition, ensuring that the integration of AI is smooth, efficient, and beneficial for all stakeholders.

Cost-Benefit Analysis of AI Implementation

The implementation of AI within business functions represents a significant investment, making it essential for managers to conduct a thorough cost-benefit analysis to fully understand the financial implications. This analysis goes beyond the direct costs associated with AI technology, such as acquisition and training. It also encompasses potential savings and revenue enhancements that AI can bring over the long term. For instance, while AI systems may require substantial upfront investments, their deployment can lead to long-term savings through improved operational efficiency, enhanced decision-making capabilities, and increased sales.

To effectively conduct this analysis, managers can employ strategic frameworks like Return on Investment (ROI) analysis or the Balanced Scorecard approach. These frameworks are instrumental in quantifying the financial benefits of AI projects, providing a clear picture of the investment against anticipated gains. They facilitate a comprehensive evaluation that considers both direct financial outcomes, such as cost reductions and revenue increases, and indirect benefits, including improved customer satisfaction, employee efficiency, and a strengthened competitive position in the market.

A critical aspect of this process involves addressing common challenges such as underestimating the costs associated with AI integration or overestimating its benefits. To mitigate these risks, managers should engage in thorough market research and benchmarking against similar AI implementations within their industry. This approach ensures a realistic and grounded understanding of AI's potential financial impact, enabling informed decision-making.

By leveraging these analytical frameworks, managers can develop well-rounded strategies that maximize AI's benefits while mitigating risks, ensuring that investments in AI align with the broader strategic objectives of their organizations and yield tangible, long-term advantages.

Now that we've explored AI's growing role as an internal enabler for businesses, let's examine how it is also assuming the function of a central multi-sided business platform.

AI as the Business Core & Platform

As we've recognized AI's evolving role as an internal business enabler, it's clear we're on the brink of an even broader transformation. AI is stepping beyond supportive functions to become the heart of business models, especially as a multi-sided platform. In these dynamic ecosystems, AI transcends its traditional role, acting as the driving force that connects and empowers a diverse array of stakeholders, marking a paradigm shift in our approach to technology in business.

No longer confined to auxiliary tasks, AI in some enterprises has become central, often manifesting as a multi-sided platform that forms the core of their business model. This evolution from a supportive tool to a central system represents a significant shift in business strategy and operations.

Platforms like Uber and Airbnb have demonstrated the power of connecting diverse stakeholders. AI elevates this concept, linking data providers, algorithm developers, businesses, and end-users in a more integrated and intelligent manner. This synergy not only maximizes AI's potential but also fosters a vibrant ecosystem where innovation flourishes and industries discover new synergies.

Industry Transformations Through AI Platforms

Artificial Intelligence is not just reshaping individual businesses; it's revolutionizing entire industries. By creating interconnected platforms, AI is enabling unprecedented collaboration, efficiency, and innovation. These platforms are not just technological breakthroughs; they represent a new way of orchestrating business processes, connecting diverse stakeholders, and driving growth. As AI becomes central to these industries, it creates opportunities and challenges for managers, demanding new strategies and a rethinking of traditional business models. Let's explore how AI platforms are transforming key industries:

Healthcare: Integrated Networks for Enhanced Care

In healthcare, AI platforms are transforming the landscape by creating integrated networks that connect medical researchers, clinicians, patients, and pharmaceutical companies. This interconnectedness facilitates the sharing of real-time data, driving advancements in predictive analytics and personalized medicine. For healthcare managers, this means overseeing a more data-centric approach to care delivery, where AI-driven insights inform treatment plans, improve patient outcomes, and optimize operational efficiency. Managers must navigate the challenges of integrating AI into existing systems, ensuring data privacy, and managing the transition towards a more collaborative, data-driven healthcare model.

Finance: Securing and Personalizing Financial Services

In the finance industry, AI is reshaping how financial entities interact and operate, enhancing efficiency and security at multiple levels.

Major financial institutions are employing AI to transform traditional processes. For instance, JPMorgan Chase uses machine learning algorithms to analyze loan applications more efficiently, reducing the time and cost of credit assessments while maintaining accuracy. This AI-driven approach enables quicker loan processing and a better customer experience.

In fraud detection, AI is proving invaluable. Banks like HSBC are leveraging AI to monitor transactions in real-time, identifying and preventing fraudulent activities with unprecedented accuracy. This not only protects the bank and its customers from financial losses but also enhances trust in the institution.

Algorithmic Decision-Making in Risk Management

Integrating AI into risk management is a key focus for financial managers. Companies like Goldman Sachs are utilizing AI to analyze market data and predict trends, helping managers make more informed investment decisions and manage risks more effectively. The challenge lies in balancing AI's insights with human expertise to optimize decision-making processes.

Enhancing Customer Experience with AI

AI is also transforming customer service in finance. Wells Fargo, for example, uses AI-driven chatbots to provide personalized banking assistance to customers, offering convenient and efficient customer support. Similarly, financial advisory services are increasingly incorporating AI to offer personalized investment advice based on individual financial goals and risk profiles.

Innovations like these demonstrate AI's growing influence in the finance sector. They highlight how AI is not just automating processes but also enabling more personalized, secure, and efficient financial services. For finance managers, this shift towards AI-driven operations presents opportunities to enhance customer experiences, streamline operations, and improve risk management – all crucial aspects in the ever-evolving world of finance.

Retail: Tailoring Customer Experiences

In the retail sector, AI platforms are redefining the way businesses engage with customers. By offering personalized recommendations and optimizing supply chain operations, AI is instrumental in creating a retail environment that is both responsive and customer-focused. For retail managers, the integration of AI tools is essential for captivating customers and boosting sales. The key challenge lies in seamlessly incorporating AI to not only understand and anticipate customer preferences but also to manage inventory with efficiency and provide an effortlessly smooth shopping experience.

AI's role in enhancing supply chain efficiency is particularly noteworthy. By monitoring the movement of goods and pinpointing potential delays, AI offers retailers a clearer view of their operations, allowing for streamlined processes, quicker delivery times, and, ultimately, heightened customer satisfaction. A prime example of AI's transformative impact in retail is Visenze. com. This AI-powered product recommendation platform delves deep into customer data, including past purchases, browsing habits, and even subtle visual cues from product images. By doing so, it generates personalized product suggestions that align closely with individual consumer preferences.

Moreover, Visenze.com's advanced deep learning capabilities give it a unique ability to interpret the visual language of products. It comprehends nuances in color, style, and texture, enabling it to suggest products that resonate not just with expressed customer preferences but also with their unarticulated desires and aesthetic inclinations. This sophisticated approach exemplifies how AI in retail goes beyond conventional methods, tapping into a level of personalization that truly reflects the evolving desires and tastes of customers.

Manufacturing: AI-Driven Production and Efficiency

In the manufacturing sector, AI is fundamentally altering production processes and operational efficiency. AI-driven platforms are revolutionizing the industry in several key areas:

Predictive Maintenance: AI platforms utilize data from sensors and machine learning algorithms to predict equipment failures before they occur. This predictive approach drastically reduces downtime and maintenance costs. For example, Siemens uses AI in its gas turbines to predict malfunctions, allowing for timely maintenance that avoids costly interruptions.

Optimized Production Schedules: AI systems analyze production data to optimize schedules, ensuring maximum efficiency. They can adapt in real-time to changes in demand, supply chain disruptions, or resource availability. An example is BMW's use of AI to optimize its assembly line sequences for car production, which significantly reduces the time and cost of manufacturing.

Supply Chain Management: AI enhances supply chain transparency and responsiveness. It can forecast demand, manage inventory levels, and identify the most efficient routes for logistics. For instance, AI-driven logistics in Amazon's warehouses have streamlined their supply chain, reducing delivery times and operational costs.

Quality Control: AI tools are increasingly used for quality control, employing vision systems and machine learning to detect defects with greater accuracy than human inspectors. General Electric, for instance, uses AI-driven robotic arms to inspect and analyze materials with precision, ensuring high product quality.

For managers in manufacturing, the integration of AI means adopting a more data-driven approach to oversee production. This integration is not without challenges, especially in balancing the technical aspects of AI with workforce adaptation. Managers must ensure that employees are adequately trained to work alongside AI systems, understanding their benefits and adapting to new operational paradigms.

A significant challenge is also ensuring that the workforce understands and embraces AI. Effective communication about the benefits of AI, combined with training programs, can ease the transition and foster a collaborative environment where human skills and AI tools complement each other.

Education: A Dual Revolution in Learning and Teaching

The educational landscape is undergoing a significant transformation, driven by AI's dual impact on both learners and educators.

AI-powered platforms are revolutionizing student learning by offering personalized educational experiences. For instance, the Khan Academy utilizes AI algorithms to provide customized learning paths across various subjects, adapting to each student's progress and learning style. This approach enables students to master topics at their own pace, ensuring a deeper understanding of the material.

At the university level, institutions like Stanford and MIT are pioneering the use of AI in education. Stanford's "AI in Education" initiative uses machine learning to analyze student learning patterns, tailoring course materials and assessments to optimize learning outcomes. Similarly, MIT's AI applications help create dynamic course content that adapts to student feedback, ensuring courses remain relevant and engaging.

Educators can now leverage AI to enhance their teaching methodologies and operational efficiency. Automated grading systems, like the one developed by the University of Michigan, use AI to evaluate student assignments, significantly reducing grading time while maintaining accuracy. This allows educators to devote more time to student interaction and personalized teaching.

The advent of massive open online courses (MOOCs) marks a pivotal transformation in higher education, with prestigious institutions like Harvard University at the forefront. Leveraging AI-driven platforms, these universities are providing personalized learning experiences to a global student body. These advanced platforms streamline course content management, student engagement, and grading processes while also enhancing them - ensuring efficiency without compromising the critical human element in teaching. Such innovations represent a significant leap forward, democratizing access to quality education and tailoring it to individual learner needs.

The leveragoing and integration of AI in educational institutions like Khan Academy, Stanford, MIT, Harvard, and the University of Michigan exemplifies a trend towards more adaptive, efficient, and personalized education. It represents a collaborative approach where AI complements human-led teaching, paving the way for an educational environment that is more inclusive, effective, and tailored to individual learning needs.

Ecosystem Effects of AI Platforms

AI platforms are not just technological marvels; they are catalysts for a new era of business, creating powerful ecosystem effects that exponentially expand value as more participants join. For instance, a platform connecting doctors and researchers becomes richer and more insightful with each contribution of diverse expertise and data. This leads to a virtuous cycle of continuously improving AI systems, fueled by growing data and engagement.

Nevertheless, as these ecosystems expand, they also present challenges, including data privacy and the need for standardization across platforms. Addressing these concerns is crucial, requiring businesses to adopt ethical practices and robust security measures, ensuring data integrity and user trust. The balance between leveraging the power of AI and maintaining ethical and secure operations is a key consideration for businesses in this evolving landscape.

Leading AI Platform Companies

Companies like OpenAI, DeepMind, and NVIDIA are not merely participants in the AI revolution; they are its architects. Their business models don't just leverage AI; they are fundamentally built upon it, driving innovation and setting new standards across industries. These companies exemplify how integrating AI at the core can transform operational capabilities and market strategies.

While these giants lead the way, there is also significant scope for smaller businesses and startups to make their mark in the AI ecosystem. They can collaborate with larger companies, leverage open-source AI technologies, or focus on niche areas where they can offer specialized AI solutions. This inclusive environment ensures that the benefits of AI are not confined to industry leaders but are accessible to a broader range of participants, fostering a diverse and dynamic AI landscape.

A New Epoch of Innovation and Progress

As AI continues to advance, it reshapes not only tasks and workflows but also the very fabric of industries and workforces. Businesses face the dual challenge and opportunity of embracing AI's transformative potential. This means strategically navigating the AI-augmented landscape, harnessing its capabilities across various domains, and aligning them with ethical standards and security best practices.

The imperative for managers and business leaders is clear: adapt and innovate within this AI-driven landscape. Embracing AI's duality as a tool for operational efficiency and a platform for groundbreaking business strategies is essential. This era of AI-driven business models demands strategic thinking, operational agility, and responsible leadership.

As we prepare to explore specific case studies, these examples will highlight how innovative companies are leveraging AI platforms to transform their industries. These narratives will provide practical insights into the application of AI, illustrating the balance between technological advancement, ethical considerations, and security imperatives in real-world settings.

CASE STUDY 1:
PATHAI

PathAI, a Boston-based healthcare company, developed an AI platform that revolutionized medical diagnostic accuracy by fostering collaboration among stakeholders: medical professionals, researchers, developers, and patients. This collaborative approach enabled continuous refinement of algorithms, elevating diagnostic precision beyond the capabilities of either humans or machines alone.

The company's vision extended beyond diagnosis, aiming to predict disease trajectories and personalize treatment plans. PathAI's platform demonstrated the transformative power of AI while simultaneously fostering essential collaboration and continuous learning, all aimed at improving patient outcomes.

The platform addressed the critical challenge of diagnostic errors, which had become prevalent due to overwhelming caseloads and clinician fatigue. With the increasing volume of medical imagery, pathologists struggled to maintain consistent accuracy.

PathAI's solution went beyond utilizing AI as a tool; it integrated it as a core component within a multi-faceted ecosystem. This ecosystem became a hub where medical professionals, researchers, AI developers, and patients could converge, each stakeholder contributing their unique perspective.

The deep learning algorithms, trained on massive datasets, excelled at anomaly detection, enabling constant dialogues between humans and AI. The AI system often identified subtle details that might escape the human eye. As more professionals engaged with the platform, the AI system continuously refined its diagnostic capabilities, creating a highly valuable feedback loop.

The company's vision extended beyond diagnostics, envisioning a future where their platform could predict disease trajectories, empowering medical professionals to tailor therapeutic interventions to individual patient outcomes. Disease identification was of course important but so was the understanding of the disease's likely evolution.

PathAI's multi-faceted platform approach has had a profound impact. Diagnostic wait times have plummeted, accuracy rates have soared, and the platform now serves as a testament to the immense potential of AI.

Highlight: PathAI's multi-sided platform approach has revolutionized healthcare diagnostics by seamlessly integrating AI's analytical power with human expertise. The platform addresses the immediate challenges of diagnostic errors but also aims to predict disease trajectories. What is more, it created a dynamic ecosystem where continuous learning and feedback loops enhance diagnostic precision and patient outcomes.

CASE STUDY 2:
OPENAI

OpenAI is a San Francisco-based artificial intelligence research laboratory that aims to promote the open and responsible development of AI technologies.

The company, with its foundational ethos of open collaboration, has always sought to democratize the AI landscape. Their commitment was not just a declaration of a lofty ideal; it was a practical strategy to ensure that the benefits of AI didn't remain confined to elites.

OpenAI's platform emerged as a vibrant hub, connecting AI researchers, developers, businesses, and end-users. This wasn't just a space for transactional interactions; it was a crucible of innovation, where each stakeholder could both contribute to and benefit from the collective wisdom.

The platform's open collaboration ethos meant that research and findings were shared, not hoarded. This transparency accelerated AI advancements and promoted a culture of collaborative problem-solving.

Tailored AI solutions, catering to diverse sectors from healthcare to finance, began to emerge from this collaborative space. Each solution drew on diverse expertise, from industry veterans to AI novices.

But the company's platform went beyond technological advancements and embraced the notion of responsible innovation. Ethicists, regulators, and AI developers come together to ensure that the AI solutions being developed are ethical, transparent, and beneficial.

Highlight: OpenAI's commitment to democratizing AI is powered by its vibrant multi-sided platform. By connecting a diverse array of stakeholders, from researchers to end-users, OpenAI has accelerated AI advancements while ensuring they remain transparent and accessible. The platform's ethos of open collaboration and responsible innovation has positioned the company as a leader in the AI revolution.

CHAPTER 6:
THE METAMORPHOSIS OF WORK & THE WORKFORCE:

New Management Paradigms

We stand at a historic inflection point in work's evolution. The four dominant megatrends discussed in Chapter 3, particularly technology, are profoundly disrupting old paradigms across industries. They are reshaping how organizations operate, collaborate, and create and capture value.

This transformation is not just a tale of technological progress; it's also a narrative of our evolving relationship with work itself. As we probe deeper into the realms of AI and digital technologies, we witness a growing detachment from the physical world of work – a detachment that has significant implications for how we perceive, value, and engage in labor.

The Nature of Work ('What')

In the modern era, the nature of work is undergoing a significant transformation. Static, predefined job roles are evolving into fluid, modular workflows, marked by a transition from rigid positions to adaptable skills and agile team structures. Amidst these changes, there's a growing risk of losing the tangible essence of labor – the hands-on, direct engagement with materials and processes that epitomize tactile mastery and true craftsmanship.

The insights of Robert M. Pirsig, through his work 'Zen and the Art of Motorcycle Maintenance,' and Matthew B. Crawford's 'Shop Class as Soulcraft,' are increasingly relevant in this context. They draw our attention to the profound satisfaction and intrinsic value found in hands-on work, a critical aspect often overshadowed by digital abstraction and society's gravitation towards certain types of knowledge work.

These authors explore the essence of finding fulfillment and meaning in work. They highlight how the division of labor, as exemplified by Henry Ford's assembly line, created a dichotomy between thinking and doing. This separation leads to existential dissatisfaction – manual workers are deprived of intellectual autonomy, and knowledge workers are alienated from the tactile fulfillment of craftsmanship. Despite the coexistence of both kinds of work, each group experiences a sense of detachment from the full spectrum of their potential.

In contemporary professional settings, this pattern often repeats itself. The allure of corporate jobs sometimes masks the reality of mundane, repetitive tasks, where individual creativity and a sense of accountability can be diminished, leading to a disconnect from the real impact of one's work.

Crawford, in particular, challenges our prevailing education and work paradigms, critiquing the perception of manual labor as inferior or suited only for those less intellectually inclined. He sheds light on the intricate intelligence involved in manual work and the deep satisfaction derived from seeing its tangible outcomes. His call to reevaluate career choices is especially pertinent in an era where societal norms and educational systems often undervalue skilled trades, steering many towards a uniform path of college education and office-based careers.

Pirsig and Crawford thus urge us to reexamine the often-ignored virtues of skilled manual labor - its ability to engage both mind and body, the joy found in multisensory tasks, and the gratification of producing tangible results. They encourage a balanced appreciation of both intellectual and physical work, recognizing the dignity and intelligence in all forms of labor. In the spirit of Socrates' wisdom, 'The unexamined life is not worth living,' examining our approach to work and career paths becomes crucial for a more fulfilling and meaningful professional life.

The Composition of the Workforce ('Who')

The evolving composition of the workforce is as significant as the nature of the work itself. The traditional, full-time employee model is increasingly giving way to a more diverse array of work arrangements. This includes part-timers, freelancers, gig workers, and crowdsourced talent, each bringing unique skills and perspectives. This shift raises critical questions about inclusivity, equity, and the dynamics of power and control in the workplace.

As we embrace this diversity, it's essential to consider how we're equipping this multifaceted workforce for a future that demands both digital proficiency and, as Crawford emphasizes, the skillful art of physical work. Are our educational and training systems adapting fast enough to this new reality? How are we ensuring that all workers, regardless of their employment status, have access to the learning and development opportunities they need to thrive in this changing landscape?

Moreover, this diversification of the workforce is reshaping organizational cultures and work dynamics. Companies must navigate the complexities of managing a more fluid workforce while maintaining a cohesive, inclusive, and productive work environment. This includes addressing the challenges of communication, collaboration, and community-building in a workforce that is more dispersed and varied than ever before.

Geo-Centric Offices Dissolving ('Where' and 'How')

The 'where' and 'how' of work are also undergoing a paradigm shift. Traditional office spaces, once the hubs of professional activity, are increasingly being replaced by remote and hybrid work models. This transformation, catalyzed by the Covid pandemic and enabled by digital technology, is redefining the concept of the workplace.

This shift to virtual workspaces offers clear benefits in terms of accessibility, time, and resources saved from commuting. It opens up opportunities for a more diverse workforce, including those who may have been previously marginalized due to geographical constraints or physical disabilities. Additionally, the flexibility of remote work can lead to improved work-life balance and increased productivity.

However, this transition also presents its own set of challenges. One significant concern is how to maintain a tangible connection to our work in an environment where physical presence is increasingly rare. This is especially crucial in professions where hands-on interaction with materials, products, or people is integral.

The move away from geo-centric offices also raises questions about collaboration and creativity. While digital tools facilitate communication, there's a need to assess how remote and hybrid environments impact teamwork, idea generation, and innovation. The challenge lies in determining whether digital interactions can fully replicate the creativity and spontaneity often sparked by in-person exchanges.

Moreover, the blurring of lines between home and work life poses challenges in maintaining a healthy work-life balance and managing stress. The integration of work into personal spaces can lead to difficulties in disconnecting, potentially impacting mental and emotional well-being. As such, organizations and individuals are exploring new strategies to establish healthy boundaries and promote well-being in an increasingly digital and flexible work environment.

Organizational Structures & Processes

As we delve deeper into understanding how AI is reshaping organizational structures and processes, it's crucial to consider the nuanced roles AI plays within this context. The IMF's 2023 report highlights three significant areas of uncertainty that are pivotal in understanding AI's impact on organizations and labor markets:

A Substitute or Complement to Human Labor: The ongoing debate about AI either replacing human workers or augmenting their capabilities is fundamental. The reality is that AI's role varies widely. In some industries, like manufacturing, AI and automation technologies have replaced certain repetitive tasks. However, in sectors like healthcare, AI acts more as a complement, enhancing human decision-making and efficiency. For instance, AI in diagnostic imaging supports radiologists but doesn't replace the need for their expert interpretation.

Global Disparity in AI Exposure: The disparity in AI adoption between Advanced Economies (AEs) and Emerging Markets (EMs) is stark. AEs, with greater access to technology and resources, are rapidly integrating AI into various sectors, potentially widening the economic gap with EMs. This disparity also raises questions about global competitiveness and the equitable distribution of AI's benefits.

Internal Economic Disparities Due to AI: Within countries, AI's impact differs across demographic groups and skill levels. For example, low-skilled jobs in sectors like retail and customer service face a higher risk of automation, whereas jobs requiring complex problem-solving skills are less susceptible. This varying impact of AI could exacerbate income inequalities and necessitate targeted educational and policy interventions.

The IMF report emphasizes the need for comprehensive strategies to manage AI's impact on the workforce, including upskilling programs, policy reforms, and international cooperation to bridge the AI divide between nations.

Further insights from the Global Partnership on Artificial Intelligence (GPAI, 2020) highlight five ways AI affects workers: from potential job displacement to enhancing creative and social skills. This spectrum of impact illustrates the varied implications of AI, underscoring the importance of adaptive workforce strategies.

Predictions about AI's impact on jobs are diverse. The Economist (2022) points to significant potential for automation, while the World Economic Forum (2022) views AI as a driver of new job creation and roles centered around efficiency. These varying viewpoints reflect the complex and multi-faceted nature of AI's influence on the workforce.

As we consider AI's integration into organizational structures, understanding the limits of automation becomes essential. The current capabilities of AI define the boundaries of automation and have significant implications for the future trajectory of work and human labor. For example, while AI can process data at unprecedented speeds, it lacks the innate human capabilities of empathy, creativity, and complex judgment. Recognizing these limitations is key to strategically integrating AI into organizational processes, ensuring that it complements rather than replaces the unique strengths of the human workforce.

Blending Human Creativity with AI

As we delve deeper into the impact of AI and technology on work, revisiting the insights of MIT economist Frank Levy, articulated in 2014, proves incredibly instructive. At a time when AI was in a relatively nascent stage,

Levy offered a critical perspective that has shaped subsequent debates and understanding of AI in the workplace.

Levy posited that understanding AI's role is not merely about determining if a service can be delivered electronically but hinges more crucially on whether the service is rules-based or relies on intuitive judgment. This distinction, pivotal at the time, has since evolved and become more nuanced as AI capabilities have advanced. Originally, rules-based tasks were seen as more susceptible to automation, while jobs requiring intuitive judgment were considered safe from AI disruption.

However, the rapid evolution of AI has somewhat blurred these lines. Advanced AI systems now demonstrate capabilities in areas previously thought to rely solely on human intuition and judgment. For instance, in fields like healthcare, AI systems are not only handling diagnostic procedures, which are largely rules-based, but are also aiding in more intuitive aspects such as patient care plans, though they still require human oversight.

The interlocking and complementary nature of AI with human skills has become more apparent. AI systems excel at processing vast quantities of data and identifying patterns, a task challenging for humans, while human workers provide the nuanced understanding and emotional intelligence that AI currently lacks. This synergy is reshaping job roles and workflows, prompting a reevaluation of how we perceive tasks as either rules-based or intuition-driven.

Levy's early insights thus serve as a foundation for understanding AI's role in the workplace, but they also highlight the dynamic nature of this technology. As AI continues to evolve, it not only automates tasks but also transforms them, creating new collaborations between human and machine capabilities. This ongoing evolution underscores the need for continuous learning and adaptation in the workforce, ensuring that human skills evolve alongside AI advancements to harness the full potential of this technological synergy.

In considering the interplay between AI and human expertise, let's reflect on a scenario involving a skilled auto mechanic using computerized equipment to diagnose a transmission issue. The equipment, relying on algorithms and rules, indicates no problems. However, the mechanic, through experience and intuition, discerns a discrepancy – the transmission shifts at the wrong engine speed. This scenario underscores what Frank Levy referred to as 'creativity' – the ability to navigate situations where there are no definitive rules, or where existing rules fall short.

This example echoes our earlier discussions about the enduring value of craftsmanship, hands-on skills, and creativity in the age of AI. It illustrates how attempts to replace the nuanced, intuitive judgments of skilled professionals with algorithmic processes can lead to a devaluation of work. AI and technology, as 'intellectual technologies,' often try to supplant human intuition with data-driven decision-making. However, as seen in fields as diverse as auto mechanics, carpentry, and medicine, there remains a domain of human expertise resistant to complete AI takeover – the realm of intuitive judgment and creative problem-solving.

As we formulate new management paradigms, it's crucial not only to integrate AI into our workflows but also to preserve and value the intuitive and creative aspects of work. The goal should be a balance where AI handles primarily rules-based tasks, while human expertise navigates areas where these rules are inadequate or non-existent. Such an approach promotes a work environment that values both the efficiency of algorithms and the irreplaceable insights derived from human experience and creativity.

Recent AI advancements are indeed beginning to encroach upon tasks that extend beyond rule-based activities. However, the distinction between human and machine roles, while evolving, remains significant. An overly simplistic emphasis on automation risks overlooking the nuanced interplay between AI capabilities and human skills. The future of work is not solely about machines supplanting human roles but about machines and humans collaborating, each amplifying the other's strengths.

This synergy may eventually lead to a paradigm shift where human work is decoupled from economic necessity. In the near future, though, the collaboration between humans and machines promises an ecosystem that capitalizes on the unique strengths of both entities. AI's transformative potential, therefore, lies in its ability to catalyze shifts across various continuums – production, transactions, and interactions – redefining how we perceive and engage with work.

Economic Domains: Production, Transactions & Interactions

When analyzing economic activity, it's useful to examine it through three different lenses or domains of activity: production, transactions and interactions (see Figure 6).

AI & Economic Activity

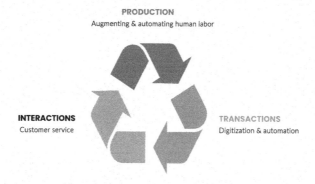

PRODUCTION
Augmenting & automating human labor

INTERACTIONS
Customer service

TRANSACTIONS
Digitization & automation

FIGURE 6: AI & DOMAINS OF ECONOMIC ACTIVITY

The turn of the last century marked a pivotal shift in the domain of **production**, as detailed in Chapter 2. The Industrial Revolution was a new era, bringing machines into factories and augmenting human capabilities. Innovations like the spinning jenny and the steam engine began automating manual tasks, boosting production rates, and reducing human errors.

While not all aspects of production have been or can be fully mechanized, we can draw parallels from trades like carpentry or plumbing to fields integral to organizational contexts, such as engineering, architecture, and design. In these disciplines, the concept of craftsmanship manifests in the precision of engineering, the creativity of architectural design, and the innovation of product development. These fields require a deep, nuanced understanding and interaction with both the physical and conceptual world, showcasing a form of craftsmanship that is as intricate and valuable as that found in more traditional trades.

As we ventured into the AI era, we witnessed machines and AI-powered robots taking on increasingly complex tasks. This technological evolution underscores a crucial question about the delicate balance between machine efficiency and human skill. In fields like engineering, architecture, and design, the craftsmanship lies not just in the execution of tasks but in the creative and critical thinking that drives innovation and problem-solving. These skills embody the essence of craftsmanship in a modern organizational context, resisting full automation due to their complexity and need for human insight.

Parallel to these advancements in production, the realm of **transactions** underwent its own remarkable evolution. The shift from paper-based records to digital formats, fueled by the rise of computers in the late 20th century, marked a significant transition. This digital shift didn't just streamline processes; it fundamentally transformed them, reducing errors and increasing efficiency.

The advent of the internet further revolutionized transactions, giving rise to e-commerce platforms that enabled online shopping and digital payments – this made transactions instantaneous and borderless. Modern systems have taken this a step further by automating various transactional processes, from inventory management to billing, enhancing the speed and accuracy of business operations.

However, despite these technological strides in production and transactions, the domain of **interactions**, particularly in customer service, remained less affected by technological advancements. Early technological interventions, such as automated phone systems and rudimentary chatbots, often fell short of effectively replicating the nuances of human interaction, leading to user frustration and a longing for human touch.

Now, however, we are witnessing a significant transformation in this domain too. New generative AI models are reshaping customer service. These advanced systems are capable of engaging in meaningful conversations, answering complex queries, and assisting in intricate problem-solving tasks, all while closely mimicking human behavior.

This leap in technology is not about entirely replacing human agents with machines; instead, it's about augmenting human capabilities and enhancing the customer experience. The AI-powered interactions of today are more intuitive, responsive, and personalized, bridging the gap between the efficiency of technology and the empathetic understanding of human service.

The implications of these advancements are profound. They signify a shift towards a more integrated approach where technology complements human skills, rather than replacing them outright. In customer service, this means combining the efficiency and scalability of AI with the emotional intelligence and creative problem-solving abilities of humans. This synergy promises a future where businesses can provide more effective, efficient, and personalized services, meeting the evolving expectations of their customers.

In summary, the journey from the automation of production to the digitization of transactions, and now to the AI-driven transformation of interactions, illustrates a broader narrative. It's a story of technological progress that, while bringing efficiency and scale, increasingly seeks to retain and enhance the human elements of empathy, creativity and intuition, which remain at the heart of meaningful customer experiences.

Retaining a Connection to the Real World

In our journey through an era increasingly dominated by AI and technology, revisiting the insights of Robert M. Pirsig and Matthew B. Crawford becomes crucial. Their works delve into the importance of maintaining a tangible connection to the real world, a theme that gains even more relevance today.

Pirsig and Crawford eloquently underscore the value of manual labor, but their exploration goes beyond this. They illuminate how tactile engagement with our surroundings deepens our understanding of both the world and ourselves. This interaction isn't just about performing physical tasks; it's a pathway to a more profound mindfulness and presence. In an era where digital interactions can often obscure our sense of the tangible world, these grounding experiences become essential for our mental and emotional health.

Furthermore, the emphasis on tactile experiences — the direct, hands-on interaction with the physical realm — starkly contrasts with virtual or abstract intellectual activities. The significance here extends beyond the satisfaction derived from physical work; it's about how such engagement fundamentally shapes our cognitive and emotional landscapes. Engaging physically with our environment nurtures essential human qualities, fostering a deepened sense of empathy and a richer connection to both our surroundings and our communities.

As virtual realities and automated processes become increasingly commonplace, recognizing and preserving this balance between technology and tactile experience is crucial. We must strive to integrate technology in ways that enrich rather than eclipse our physical experiences. This approach not only promises more sustainable and gratifying lifestyles but also champions a society that appreciates diverse forms of intelligence and skill, bridging the gap between intellectual and manual work.

In embracing AI and digital advancements, it is imperative that we also consciously reaffirm our ties to the tangible, real world. This balance is vital, not just for preserving our humanity amidst rapid technological changes but for fostering a society that values comprehensive development, mental health, and the full spectrum of human experience. Ensuring this balance means our progress into the future is not only technologically advanced but also deeply rooted in the essential qualities that define us as human beings.

The Human-AI Partnership

The rapid advancements in artificial intelligence (AI) have sparked intense debates about what is to come. Automation, often perceived as an unstoppable force, is likely to displace workers in numerous industries. This view echoes fears from past industrial revolutions, which, in retrospect, created more opportunities than the jobs they eliminated. While these concerns are valid, they call for a balanced perspective on AI's transformative potential, acknowledging that this technological revolution might bring about unprecedented effects. The experience of past revolutions may not be entirely relevant, as the current confluence of forces may mean that AI could potentially become "the last human invention."

Until recently, it was assumed that AI would be limited to 'narrow' applications, excelling in specific tasks but lacking the broader general intelligence required for a wide array of human activities. However, the development of sophisticated Large Language Models (LLMs) like OpenAI's GPT-4 and Google AI's LaMDA challenges this view. These breakthroughs have demonstrated impressive capabilities in natural language processing, problem-solving, and creative tasks, blurring the lines between narrow AI and artificial general intelligence (AGI). This suggests that large-scale job displacement may occur more rapidly than anticipated.

Recognizing both the current limitations and the growing capabilities of AI is critical. The implications for the future of work are profound, making it essential to understand AI's evolving role.

Beyond AI's Current Reach

While AI has achieved remarkable advancements, there remains a spectrum of tasks that are, for the moment, distinctly human. These tasks are characterized by their inherent complexity, nuance, and demand for creative thinking — elements that defy easy automation. They require attributes such as human judgment, empathy, and social intelligence, areas where AI is still catching up.

In therapeutic roles, for instance, the subtle understanding and emotional depth required are uniquely human traits. Similarly, in complex negotiations or creative arts, the finesse and intuition of humans remain unmatched. High-stakes decision-making, especially those involving ethical dilemmas, and personalized education, where an understanding of diverse individual needs and backgrounds is essential, are predominantly human endeavors. Additionally, service roles in industries like hospitality and caregiving still heavily depend on genuine human empathy and connection.

These domains not only underscore the irreplaceable value of human skills but also highlight the complementary nature of human and AI capabilities. In an increasingly AI-integrated world, it is these human attributes that continue to stand out as essential, defining elements of numerous professional and personal interactions.

Economics: The Cost-Benefit Equation

The decision to automate extends beyond technical feasibility; economic viability is equally critical. While automation is beneficial for repetitive, time-intensive, or physically demanding tasks, the costs can sometimes outweigh the benefits. This aspect is often overlooked in discussions about AI's impact on jobs. For instance, automating tasks like fruit harvesting or assembling intricate electronics could be technically feasible, but the high investment in sophisticated machinery and ongoing maintenance costs may not be economically justifiable compared to human labor. Additionally, the variability and delicate nature of these tasks might require adaptability and finesse beyond current AI-driven machines' economic reach in most scenarios. This economic calculus often favors human labor in certain sectors, despite the technical possibilities for automation. Yet, in other industries, automation has proven economically advantageous, highlighting the diverse economic landscapes shaped by AI.

Societal Barriers: Ethical and Regulatory Quandaries

Technical and economic aspects aside, societal norms and regulations significantly shape AI adoption. Safety, privacy, and ethical concerns pose substantial barriers. For example, despite advancements in autonomous vehicles and AI-assisted surgery, these domains remain predominantly human-operated due to regulatory constraints and societal wariness. Reluctance to entrust life-critical tasks to machines arises from a complex mix of ethical considerations, liability concerns, and cultural attitudes towards risk and trust in technology.

These societal and regulatory factors necessitate a cautious approach to deploying AI in sensitive areas, mirroring a broader dialogue about technology's role and limits in our lives. As AI capabilities improve and societal trust grows, perceptions and regulatory guardrails will undoubtedly evolve.

Shift in Management Paradigms

The metamorphosis in the way we go about conducting work, the composition of the workforce and the modalities of executing it, have inevitably led to profound shifts in management thinking.

Indeed, historically, work was viewed primarily through the lens of "jobs" (as the central organizing principle) while the workforce was viewed dichotomously: employers versus employees. As I've already argued, these perspectives are being replaced by a vibrant mosaic of work processes as well as talent models, both external and internal.

Evidence shows this transformation is well underway. A global executive survey by Sloan Management Review and Deloitte (conducted in 2021), found that a significant majority of global managers (87%), consider not just employees but other contributors — contractors, service providers, gig workers, marketplace sellers, and even bots — to be part of their workforce. The survey also found that a substantial percentage of companies, 63%, cite access to specialized skills as a key driver for incorporating external talent.

Despite the expanding workforce, organizational systems frequently lag, predominantly catering to formal, internal employees. This presents a significant challenge for contemporary management, tasked with addressing the paradox where organizational structures and practices are yet to fully adapt to the increasingly diverse and broadened workforce.

Work's digital transformation reflects notable yet subtle societal shifts. Sociologist Pierre Bourdieu spotlights social capital - the value derived from networks and relationships. In decentralized digital workspaces like Upwork and Mechanical Turk, social capital may be pivotal in accessing opportunities without traditional offices. Networking and forging connections online become critical for tapping into opportunities.

It is perhaps useful to revisit Bourdieu's four key forms of capital, namely economic, cultural, social, and symbolic. Of these, social capital becomes especially relevant in digital work environments and can be further broken down into *bonding* (tight-knit groups), *bridging* (looser affiliations) and *linking* (associations across power differentials). (See Figure 7).

Bourdieu's Forms of Capital

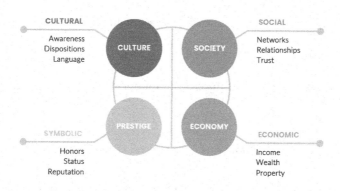

FIGURE 7: BOURDIEU'S FORMS OF CAPITAL

So this transformation isn't just locational but social. By recognizing this, companies can attempt to build equitable digital work ecosystems - thoughtfully integrating external talent into their operating systems.

Fluidity and Adaptability

Our evolving work environment is inherently fluid - dynamic, responsive, and adaptable. This liquid workforce thrives on versatility, harnessing diverse capabilities to advance organizational goals. Such agility is a strategic advantage, driving innovation amidst shifting business conditions.

Independent contractors like gig workers and freelancers exemplify this fluidity. They both offer organizations flexible work arrangements, although freelancers typically work on longer projects compared to gig workers' shorter engagements.

Some argue that freelancers have more autonomy than gig workers over work arrangements although others contend that these categories are more similar than distinct - since both operate independently and without traditional employment.

Regardless, organizations can derive real benefits by strategically utilizing gig economy talent:

Agility: Gig workers provide flexibility to meet short-term needs. Freelancers offer specialized expertise.

Access to talent: Organizations can curate optimal external talent for specific projects.

Cost savings: Variable labor costs can be lower than permanent hires.

Innovation: External perspectives inject new ideas and specialized skills.

Therefore, the gig economy can be seen as a reflection of a deeper societal shift towards valuing autonomy, flexibility, and specialization even as it comes with downsides: job security and long-term employment.

What is more, this new workforce, driven by digital platforms and an on-demand culture, is redefining the boundaries between employers and employees, creating a mosaic of opportunities and challenges.

Decentralized Work: Psychological Dynamics

Decentralized work introduces complexities that extend beyond mere logistics, encompassing nuanced psychological dynamics such as trust and communication. Traditional management models, designed for more centralized environments, often struggle in this new landscape.

Consequently, new strategies are necessary to strike a balance between organizational objectives and personal goals, although addressing these psychological challenges is just the beginning of adapting to a decentralized work structure.

It has become quite clear that as we navigate these challenges, AI's integration into the workforce plays a critical role. The Brookings Institute helps us articulate this challenge by identifying three distinct roles of AI in this context:

AI-as-Assistant: Here, AI augments human performance, like the use of VR in training, enhancing the capabilities of employees.

AI-as-Peer: In this role, AI collaborates with humans, leveraging complementary strengths. A prime example is in medicine, where radiologists and AI systems work together to improve diagnostic accuracy.

AI-as-Manager: AI assumes decision-making duties traditionally reserved for human managers, overseeing logistics or providing digital supervision.

In these roles, AI is not just a tool but a significant influencer in tasks, decisions, and development. The imperative now is to align human aspirations with AI's capabilities, fostering a positive societal impact. This calls for agility and adaptability in management, echoing the insights of Peter Drucker (1985) on the importance of shaping change proactively.

AI and Workflow Transformation

As we probe deeper into AI's impact, we observe its transformative effect on workflows, transitioning from traditional job structures to a focus on tasks and skills.

This shift from jobs to tasks and skills is creating work environments that are moving managers' focus away from static job roles and departmental silos to a dynamic landscape shaped by several key factors:

Codification: Converting tasks into formats for AI automation, like algorithms managing complex data entry.

Modularization: Deconstructing workflows into flexible components for agile reconfiguration.

Hybrid Roles: Merging human skills with AI capabilities, creating roles like "data detectives" who combine data analysis with innovative thinking.

Cloud Computing: Enabling decentralized collaboration, breaking down geographical and functional barriers.

Continuous Learning: Prioritizing ongoing skill development, as seen in AT&T's commitment to employee training.

This shift from rigid roles to a focus on adaptable skills and tasks is fundamental to the evolving work landscape. The next chapter will delve deeper into the workforce implications of this transformative shift, highlighting the increasing importance of adaptability and versatility.

Digitalization, AI, and the Workforce

Digitalization and AI are driving shifts in work paradigms, dissolving the boundaries of traditional workplaces defined by static roles and structures.

McKinsey's research (2020) provides insight into this transformation, highlighting how digitization is altering workplaces and challenging our conventional understanding of their purpose and function. It underscores the potential of global digital platforms like Toptal or Upwork as strategic tools for organizations to source top talent for critical projects, based on flexible workflows – thereby redefining and expanding the workforce ecosystem.

I refer to this phenomenon as the "liquid workforce" – a dynamic, adaptable group, unconstrained by rigid roles or locations. It's not a predefined workforce but a rich mosaic of skills and technologies propelling organizational goals amidst shifting business landscapes. This agility offers strategic advantages, fostering innovation. However, it also brings challenges related to job security, the need for continuous reskilling, and existential uncertainty about the future.

While the traditional 9-to-5 model persists, organizations are increasingly adopting flexible talent strategies. This diversification creates both opportunities and obstacles, requiring a delicate balance. We lack established formulas from the past, necessitating real-time calibration.

Sebastian Matthee explores this in "The Gig Economy: The Rise of the New Workforce" (2020), suggesting that the gig economy reflects a societal shift towards valuing autonomy, flexibility, and specialization. He argues that the gig economy offers alternatives to traditional employment and actively reshapes the fabric of work itself: it redefines work culture and expectations. For example, it allows freelancers to focus on and develop niche skills, catering to specific market needs – which in turn can lead to higher job satisfaction and opportunities for professional growth.

Of course, Matthee also acknowledges the challenges inherent in gig work, such as the lack of job security, benefits, and the potential for income instability. Clearly, new labor laws and management practices need to address these issues.

An important consequence of this transformation is the change in workforce goals (see Figure 8) which are now shaped by a diverse set of factors: digitalization, flexible work, forward-looking management practices, and labor laws.

FIGURE 8: WORKFORCE GOALS

This new workforce, driven by digital platforms and an on-demand culture, is creating a mosaic of opportunities and challenges for management. And the balancing act is far from straightforward. Organizations are tasked with the intricate challenge of seamlessly integrating varied talent models, ensuring they align cohesively with overarching organizational strategies and values.

It's a dance of achieving balance, and where possible, inclusion, but more than that, it's about sculpting an ecosystem that values and nurtures talent diversity while at the same time leveraging it for sustainable success.

Adaptive Workflows

Static workflow models struggle to adapt to today's dynamic environments, which require dynamic workflow models that can evolve and respond to real-time data and changes. Adaptive workflows are flexible, immediate, and collaborative, making them ideal for these new work arrangements.

AI and machine learning enable adaptive workflows and are therefore central to evolving organizational capabilities. AI can provide predictive insights, identify and eliminate bottlenecks, and facilitate seamless virtual collaboration. Integrated platforms can also coordinate tools into cohesive environments.

Adaptive workflows also require human adaptability, beyond the purely technological considerations. Employees need flexible mindsets, a commitment to continuous learning, and openness to communication. This often requires an alignment with their organization's vision - essential for psychological buy-in and motivation.

The potential benefits of adaptive workflows are apparent: increased productivity, improved employee engagement, and enhanced agility. But at the same time, organizations must balance flexibility with structure and address workers' perceptions and fears to realize these benefits.

Those that can nimbly incorporate adaptive workflows while keeping their workforce engaged will be well-positioned to thrive in the digital age. They will be better equipped to deal with change, adapt to new challenges, and seize new opportunities.

Sectoral Variations in Adaptive Workflows

When examining adaptive workflows, the importance of granularity cannot be overstated, whether we're considering entire sectors or individual companies. The dynamics that shape a call center, for instance, are markedly different from those influencing a consulting firm or a healthcare provider. While the foundational principles of adaptive workflows are universally applicable, their practical implementation varies significantly across different sectors. This diversity necessitates a tailored approach, recognizing the unique challenges and opportunities inherent in each field.

The transformative potential of adaptive workflows is undeniable, offering significant benefits in terms of efficiency, innovation, and responsiveness. But adopting a one-size-fits-all approach is ill-advised. Such a templated strategy risks overlooking the nuanced needs and specificities of each sector and can lead to suboptimal outcomes. Instead, a customized approach, sensitive to the particularities of each industry, is essential.

This approach ensures that the adoption of adaptive workflows is not just a superficial change but a deep, meaningful transformation that truly enhances the sector's unique operational dynamics. Therefore, the key lies in skillfully adapting the core principles of adaptive workflows to the distinct rhythms and requirements of each sector as well as company culture and capabilities.

Each industry—and indeed, each firm within that industry—must sculpt its adaptive strategy, mindful of its unique challenges and opportunities. This nuanced approach ensures that adaptability doesn't just become a buzzword but aligns seamlessly with the goals and constraints intrinsic to each sector and an organization's unique context.

Healthcare: In this critical sector, adaptive workflows can streamline patient care pathways. For instance, the Cleveland Clinic utilizes real-time data analytics to predict patient inflows and optimize bed allocations. However, with the rise of telemedicine and digital health records, ensuring data privacy and maintaining the human touch in patient interactions become paramount challenges.

Manufacturing: Companies like Toyota have long embraced adaptive workflows with their 'Just-In-Time' production, adjusting manufacturing processes based on real-time demand. However, as Industry 4.0 introduces more automation and AI, there's a pressing need to upskill workers and ensure that machines enhance human roles rather than replace them. Leading companies such as Toyota have adapted their workforce learning and development programs to address this pressing need.

Finance: Fintech startups like Robinhood have exemplified the power of adaptive workflows, offering real-time stock trading insights and democratizing access to financial markets. Another notable innovation in finance is the use of decentralized exchanges (DEXs), especially those powered by Bitcoin. These platforms allow users to trade cryptocurrencies without traditional intermediaries, like banks or exchange platforms, by utilizing smart contracts on blockchain technology.

The case of Sam Bankman-Fried and his cryptocurrency exchange, FTX, provides a poignant illustration of both the potential and pitfalls of these financial innovations. FTX's rapid ascent in the crypto world was a testament to the power of agile and adaptive workflows in finance. The platform's ability to quickly scale and diversify its offerings, from standard trading services to intricate financial products, underscored the centrality of agility and innovation in fintech's adaptive workflows.

Yet the issues and controversies that later engulfed the company highlight the need for more robust regulatory frameworks and risk management strategies in decentralized finance. The FTX saga serves as a cautionary tale, emphasizing the necessity of a balanced approach in fintech innovations – one that harmonizes the drive for innovation with the imperatives of stability and trust.

Education: Platforms like Coursera and Khan Academy, leveraging adaptive learning algorithms, are redefining the domain of education. These platforms dynamically adjust to each learner's pace and style by analyzing performance in real-time, offering a truly personalized educational experience. For instance, a student struggling with a math concept might receive additional exercises or explanatory videos, catering to their specific learning needs. This approach not only makes education more accessible but also more effective, accommodating diverse learning preferences.

Nevertheless, the digitization of education brings to the forefront a crucial societal challenge: ensuring equitable access to these resources. Beyond just providing the necessary technology and internet connectivity, it's imperative to address the nuances of diverse learning contexts. These contexts should support critical thinking and ethical values, catering to students from varied socio-economic backgrounds with additional support structures. Bridging this digital divide is essential to avoid exacerbating educational inequalities in the era of online learning.

Retail: In the retail sector, Amazon's recommendation system is a prime example of adaptive workflows. By analyzing customer data, including past purchases and browsing habits, Amazon's algorithms dynamically tailor product recommendations, enhancing the shopping experience and potentially increasing sales.

Similarly, Netflix's adaptive algorithms for content recommendation offer a personalized user experience. By analyzing viewing histories and preferences, Netflix curates its homepage to align with individual tastes, enhancing engagement and content discovery.

However, with the digitization of retail supply chains, caution is necessary. Over-reliance on predictive algorithms can lead to significant issues, like stock imbalances. Inaccurate predictions can result in excess inventory or stock shortages, underscoring the need for a balanced approach that combines algorithmic efficiency with human oversight and market awareness.

Extended Workforce Ecosystems

As we embrace extended workforce ecosystems enhanced by AI, the opportunities are immense, yet the balancing act is complex. Understanding what fuels and engages the diverse categories within these ecosystems is crucial. This understanding must be both sector-wide and specific to individual firms, delving into the granular aspects of each entity.

Extended Talent Models

The multifaceted talent spectrum calls for adaptable management strategies that acknowledge that value creation now depends not only on formal employees but also "off-balance sheet" talent.

Effectively, these varied talent pools now require flexible, strategic approaches to rapidly harness in-demand skills - regardless of their source. The challenge for managers is to create environments where all contributors feel valued and able to thrive. Companies which manage this feat stand to reap the benefits of enhanced productivity and competitiveness. For this, we need to recalibrate people management's key pillars: attraction, development, and retention. An effective talent management framework needs to address each of these (as we shall further elaborate in Chapter 9):

Attraction: Attracting the right talent requires a deep understanding of the organization's needs and the skills and experience of the available talent pool. Organizations need to use a variety of channels to reach potential candidates, including online job boards, social media, and employee referrals.

Development: Once talent is onboarded, it is important to invest in their development. This includes providing them with training and opportunities to learn new skills. It also includes creating a culture of continuous learning and growth.

Retention: Retaining talent is essential in today's competitive environment. Organizations can retain talent by providing competitive compensation and benefits, creating a positive work environment, and offering opportunities for advancement. It therefore follows that adopting such a strategic talent model allows firms to acquire, develop, motivate, and retain the blend of talent needed to succeed today. This would require several conceptual pivots:

Empowered Teams: Top-down hierarchies are transforming into fluid, cross-functional teams. Pioneering technology firms have embraced this shift, forming "squads" of diverse experts that work autonomously.

Leadership has evolved in parallel from commanding managers to enabling coaches. Companies like Shopify enculture inclusive, consultative decision-making to amplify employee empowerment.

These flatter organizational structures are not just about reducing layers; they signify a shift in managerial paradigms. The emphasis has transitioned from rigid command-and-control mechanisms to facilitative leadership styles that prioritize enablement, coaching, and empowerment. In this new paradigm, leaders act as enablers, fostering environments where innovation thrives and teams can autonomously meet challenges head on.

Remote Collaboration: Rethinking Workspaces and Tools

The landscape of workspaces is undergoing a significant transformation as geo-centralized offices give way to virtual work environments. This shift is facilitated by mobile tools and technologies that support collaboration across geographically dispersed teams. Companies like Twitter, for instance, have embraced "work from anywhere" policies, effectively utilizing video conferencing and cloud-based workflow applications to maintain productivity and connection among remote employees.

This paradigm shift not only promotes work-life balance but also widens the pool of global talent accessible to companies. However, maintaining an engaged and cohesive organizational culture becomes a critical challenge in these virtual settings. An illustrative example is InVision, a company specializing in digital product design. To foster a sense of community and mitigate feelings of isolation among its remote workforce, InVision employs Donut - a digital tool integrated within communication platforms like Slack. It randomly pairs employees for virtual meetups or coffee breaks, encouraging informal interactions and personal connections that are often missing in remote work settings. This initiative exemplifies how companies can use creative digital solutions to cultivate a sense of belonging and teamwork, even when employees are not co-located.

The Broader Transformation of the Workplace

The decentralization of traditional office models through remote and hybrid arrangements represents just one facet of the changing work landscape. Alongside these locational shifts, there is also a rapid evolution in approaches to employee training and development. As workspaces become more digital and less centralized, training methods are adapting to be more flexible, personalized, and accessible, reflecting the broader trends in how work is being redefined in the modern era.

New Organizing Principles

The shift from predefined jobs to modular project teams enables the tactical deployment of talent based on evolving initiatives. Agility and continuous skill development are essential.

Individuals must cultivate versatility to fulfill shifting project needs. Firms need to remain nimble, calibrating workforces to sync with project demands. Consulting firms like Bain exemplify this agile project-based approach.

It is therefore evident that this metamorphosis represents a wholesale reimagining of work. Embracing these changes helps organizations build engaging cultures that empower employees to thrive amidst uncertainty while driving impact through purposeful projects.

As I've already argued, in this emerging paradigm, work is no longer confined to static job descriptions as a key organizing principle. Instead, it revolves around specific yet adaptable workflows and projects. This ensures that workers are strategically positioned, leveraging their unique skills and expertise for optimal performance. At the core of this paradigm lie agility, adaptability, and an enhanced opportunity for worker autonomy.

Making Better & Faster Decisions

In today's dynamic business environments, refining decision-making processes is crucial for organizations to keep pace with evolving work environments, empowered teams, and integrated talent ecosystems. The ability to make quality decisions quickly is especially critical in fast-paced and complex business settings.

Overcoming Cognitive Limitations

Rationality in decision-making, traditionally understood as the process of making choices that align optimally with one's objectives and values, has long been a cornerstone concept in understanding human behavior and choices. Classical economic theory's 'rational economic man' makes decisions that maximize self-interest, an assumption that implies flawless information processing based on complete information about options and consequences.

However, our understanding has evolved to recognize that human rationality is limited by our cognitive abilities, particularly in terms of the volume of information we can access and the speed of processing it. Nobel Laureate

Herbert Simon's concept of "bounded rationality" suggests that humans often use 'satisficing' strategies, settling for 'good enough' solutions due to limitations in information and cognitive capacity. This means that decisions are frequently made based on intuition or gut feelings, rather than robust evidence, leading to potentially sub-optimal outcomes.

AI systems can effectively address these limitations. They excel at rapidly analyzing large datasets, uncovering hidden patterns, and providing predictive insights. This data processing capability positions AI as a valuable tool in decision-making. Furthermore, emerging technologies like metaverse simulations offer innovative ways to test decisions by creating detailed virtual environments. These simulations can model complex scenarios, allowing decision-makers to explore outcomes and impacts in a controlled, yet realistic setting.

By leveraging the strengths of both humans and AI, organizations can significantly enhance decision-making across various areas, from hiring and training to product development and operations. However, it's crucial to approach this integration with caution, particularly in mitigating potential biases inherent in AI systems. Ensuring that AI's data-driven insights are tempered with human discernment and ethical considerations is key.

Incorporating AI into decision-making processes doesn't mean replacing human judgment; rather, it's about augmenting it. AI can provide comprehensive data analysis and predictive modeling, while humans bring contextual understanding, ethical considerations, and creative problem-solving to the table. This symbiotic relationship between human intuition and AI's analytical prowess can lead to more informed, efficient, and effective decision-making.

In essence, the future of decision-making in organizations lies in a balanced approach that harnesses AI's computational power and human cognitive strengths. This synergy can help organizations navigate the complexities of modern business landscapes, making decisions that are not only faster but also smarter and more aligned with long-term strategic goals.

The Metaverse in Decision-Making & Workforce Development

As technology continues to evolve, the metaverse emerges as a groundbreaking development with significant implications for decision-making processes in the modern workforce ecosystem. This expansive virtual realm offers a unique platform for interaction within digital environments, presenting novel opportunities for organizations.

In the metaverse, AI-powered simulations provide an unparalleled environment for testing various business strategies and training employees in sophisticated skills. This immersive approach to professional development and strategic planning can significantly enhance an organization's capabilities, leading to improved decision-making processes and operational efficiency. For instance, a company could use metaverse simulations to virtually onboard and train new employees, allowing them to interact with digital representations of their future workspaces and colleagues.

The potential applications extend to critical business areas such as hiring, performance management, product development, and operational optimization. For example, product teams can use the metaverse to collaboratively design and test new products in a virtual space, reducing costs and accelerating development cycles.

Yet while AI systems aid in overcoming certain cognitive limitations, their susceptibility to bias remains a concern. These systems, often trained on datasets reflecting human prejudices, can replicate and reinforce societal biases. To address this, proactive bias mitigation strategies are essential. One effective approach is the implementation of diverse training datasets and continuous monitoring for bias. For example, IBM has implemented AI Fairness 360, a toolkit that helps developers detect and mitigate bias in AI models, ensuring more equitable decision-making processes.

Therefore, the metaverse offers exciting opportunities for advancing decision-making and workforce development although the integration of AI in these virtual environments necessitates a careful approach; one that ensures that ethical guardrails and bias mitigation measures are firmly in place.

Now let's turn to our case studies (Lego and Buffer), casting a light on how they are reshaping the diverse workforce paradigm.

CASE STUDY 1:
LEGO

LEGO, the iconic toy brick company, faced a significant downturn in the early 2000s as digital entertainment gained popularity. Children were spending more time playing video games and watching TV, and less time playing with physical toys.

In response to this challenge, LEGO undertook a major transformation of its business model and product offerings. The company embraced digital technology, integrating digital elements into its core products and services. This included introducing video games, mobile apps, and even a successful movie franchise. LEGO also embraced digital design tools for its product development, allowing for rapid prototyping and testing of new brick designs.

The digital transformation paid off handsomely. The company's revenue and profits have grown steadily in recent years, and the company is once again one of the most popular toy brands in the world.

The metamorphosis of work is not just about changing job roles or organizational structures; it's also about how traditional companies can reinvent themselves by integrating digital elements into their core offerings. LEGO's transformation demonstrates that companies can achieve significant benefits by embracing digital technology, such as increased agility, faster product development cycles, and expanded market reach.

Highlight: LEGO's case exemplifies the importance of a culture of innovation and willingness to take risks. The company was not afraid to experiment with new products and services, even if they were outside of its traditional comfort zone. This willingness to experiment has been key to LEGO's success in the digital age.

CASE STUDY 2: BUFFER

Buffer, a prominent social media management platform, embarked on a mission to radically redefine its work environment, focusing on greater flexibility and support for its team. In a striking departure from convention, Buffer abandoned the traditional physical office setup in favor of a fully digital workspace. This pivot included investing in robust digital communication tools and prioritizing asynchronous communication, enabling effective collaboration across different time zones and tapping into a global talent pool.

A key initiative in Buffer's transformation was its bold commitment to transparency. The company took the pioneering step of openly sharing salary information and decision-making processes with all employees. This approach played a pivotal role in creating a more horizontal power dynamic within the workforce, breaking down traditional hierarchies and fostering a culture rooted in trust and inclusivity.

Buffer's transition to a remote-first workplace has been met with resounding success. The shift has not only enabled Buffer to attract and retain exceptional talent globally, but it has also led to increased employee happiness and productivity. This case is a powerful endorsement of the potential of remote work to revolutionize traditional workplace models.

The Buffer story is emblematic of a significant shift in the work landscape: the movement from rigid, location-bound structures to flexible, fluid work arrangements. As remote and hybrid work models gain traction, the importance of nurturing a supportive and inclusive culture, regardless of physical location, becomes increasingly evident. Buffer's experience highlights that remote work is not merely an alternative to traditional models but can be a highly effective strategy for businesses of all sizes.

Highlight: Buffer's journey underscores the profound impact of granting employees autonomy over their work. By allowing team members the freedom to work from anywhere and offering flexible scheduling, Buffer has successfully cultivated an empowering and productive environment. This strategy has not only maintained the company's competitive edge but also set a new standard for how modern organizations can excel in today's digital and interconnected landscape.

CHAPTER 7:

SKILLS AND COMPETENCIES FOR THE NEW ERA

As we delve into the evolving landscape of work, transformed by the rise of AI and automation, it becomes essential to precisely define and distinguish the terms 'skills' and 'competencies,' often used interchangeably but distinct in their essence and application.

Skills refer to specific capabilities developed through training and practice. They are tangible, measurable, and often technical, acquired through education, experience, or certification. For example, coding in a particular programming language is a skill that can be learned, practiced, and assessed for proficiency. Skills serve as the foundational elements or 'ingredients' of a job, indicating the basic requirements needed to perform specific tasks.

In contrast, competencies encompass a broader spectrum. They integrate not only skills but also include knowledge, behaviors, motivations, and traits necessary for successful job performance. Competencies are multifaceted, encapsulating how a job is performed rather than just what is performed. They can be likened to a 'recipe,' which involves not only ingredients (skills) but also the method and manner of combining and applying these ingredients to achieve the desired outcome. For instance, the competency of problem-solving involves analytical thinking (a skill), creativity (an attitude), and adaptability (a behavior), all working in concert.

As we advance into a new era of work, it's imperative to understand and cultivate both skills and competencies. Skills provide the technical foundation necessary for job performance, while competencies guide the application of these skills in a dynamic, real-world context. This chapter aims to explore and define the critical skills and competencies needed in the AI-driven workplace, offering a holistic view of what it takes to thrive in this rapidly changing environment.

As we probe deeper into the distinction between skills and competencies, it's pertinent to reexamine the enduring value of physical work, particularly in trades and crafts, from a philosophical perspective. In an era increasingly dominated by digital technology, certain skills and their broader set of competency categories like 'Physical Dexterity and Craftsmanship' might appear secondary.

However, they hold a profound and lasting significance. Indeed, they tend to encompass a blend of specific skills, knowledge, and the adept use of hands, reminding us of the critical balance between digital acumen and tangible, creative craftsmanship. They represent a synergy of the human spirit with the physical world, a balance that tends to be lost as we operate in an AI-dominated world.

Our comprehensive competency framework, encompassing eight key areas, thoughtfully integrates both technical skills and human-centric competencies. The advent of AI in reshaping job roles brings to the forefront the necessity for skills that extend beyond the realm of automation, such as creative problem-solving, emotional intelligence, and adaptability. The new managerial environment calls for a transformative approach to training and development programs, emphasizing the cultivation of these human-centric skills in tandem with technical know-how.

In adapting to these changes, workforce management strategies must also evolve, fostering continuous learning and agile adaptability. This approach is crucial for navigating the dynamic interplay between human capabilities and machine efficiency. Such a strategy ensures the development of a workforce that is not only proficient in technological applications but also deeply perceptive of the intricacies and nuances of a modern, AI-integrated work environment.

In addressing the practical shifts in workforce management and skill requirements prompted by technological advancements, it is imperative to underscore the impact of AI and automation in redefining job roles and the associated competencies. As AI takes over routine tasks, the demand escalates for uniquely human skills — those that AI cannot easily replicate — such as creative problem-solving, emotional intelligence, and adaptability.

This pivotal shift necessitates a comprehensive reevaluation of training and development paradigms, aiming to nurture these human-centric competencies alongside technical prowess. Moreover, it calls for an evolution in workforce management practices, advocating for more flexible, team-centric structures that promote continuous learning and adaptability amidst rapid technological advancements. Embracing this approach prepares the workforce not only for imminent challenges but also equips them with the resilience and diverse skill set required to deal with future uncertainties.

For our analysis, we have adopted an integrated competency framework, spanning eight key categories, which seamlessly blends macro-level competencies with micro-level skills (see Figure 9). This framework offers a multi-dimensional perspective, encompassing the diverse prerequisites essential for success in today's fluid and rapidly evolving work environment.

COMPETENCIES & SKILLS

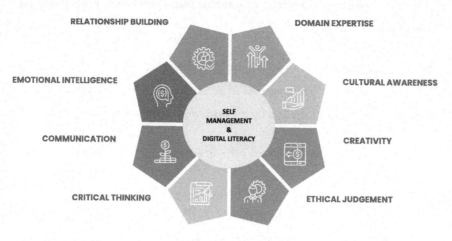

FIGURE 9: COMPETENCIES & SKILLS

Anchoring this framework are two foundational competencies:

Self-Management is the linchpin competency, providing stability that enables the effective application of other skills. It refers to one's ability to regulate their emotions, beliefs, and behaviors across diverse situations. This includes managing time efficiently, overcoming procrastination, persisting through setbacks, and maintaining composure under stress.

Consider a manager who, when faced with a sudden project delay, adapts swiftly, rallies their team, and steers them towards timely resolution with poise and determination. Or the lifelong learner who proactively seeks growth opportunities to stay relevant amidst rapid technological shifts affecting their industry. Qualities like perseverance, self-discipline, resilience, and methodical working are paramount.

Digital Literacy emerges as an equally vital foundation in an era where nearly every professional role has a digital component. This goes beyond mere proficiency with digital devices and platforms. It encompasses the ability to understand, evaluate and appropriately leverage technology to enhance workflows, while also grasping the broader ramifications of the digital realm - from cybersecurity threats to ethical considerations around topics like AI and automation.

For instance, while a radiologist must hone their medical expertise, they also need digital literacy to harness AI in enhancing diagnostic accuracy rather than resisting technology and facing potential obsolescence.

Surrounding this robust base there are a number of other essential competencies:

Critical Thinking involves the ability to logically analyze information, apply appropriate frames to structure data, discern what is relevant from what is extraneous, make connections between disparate concepts, and synthesize insights to arrive at reasoned, evidence-based decisions. This competency empowers professionals to effectively filter through information overload, ask probing questions, overcome confirmation bias, and extract meaningful signals from noisy data. Consider a manager and data analyst collaborating to sift through a mountain of data, leveraging logic and critical thinking to uncover key patterns and actionable insights without resorting to hasty, preconceived notions.

Communication, both written and verbal, serves as the conduit for clearly conveying ideas, insights, and instructions between diverse teams and stakeholders. Whether it's a CEO articulating a bold strategic vision to rally an organization or a software developer explaining a complex algorithm to a non-technical audience, the capacity for precise self-expression and careful listening is paramount. Here, the ability to distill complexity into lucid narratives, tailor communication to audiences, and avoid ambiguities is crucial. Harvard's Steven Pinker in his book "The Sense of Style" warns of 'the curse of knowledge' where experts, overly immersed in a subject, fail to explain concepts accessibly to laypeople. Such pitfalls can severely impede effective communication.

Emotional Intelligence involves understanding and managing one's own emotions and recognizing, appreciating and influencing the emotions of others. At an intrapersonal level, it is the ability to be aware of, control, and express one's emotions appropriately. Interpersonally, emotional intelligence enables sensing others' unspoken feelings, responding empathetically, and providing support even during disagreement. For example, a team leader diplomatically guiding a heated meeting to a constructive outcome demonstrates emotional intelligence, as does the colleague who lends a compassionate ear to someone coping with professional or personal struggles.

Relationship Building revolves around initiating, cultivating, and nurturing strong connections throughout diverse networks. This competency stems from the fact that humans are inherently social creatures, and our individual success relies heavily on our ability to collaborate and build trust. Consider the common 'lone wolf' metaphor, which often proves ill-suited to the team-oriented nature of modern work. A more fitting conceptualization is that of a 'networked node', emphasizing professional success through developing robust reciprocal relationships. Those who excel at establishing rapport and radiating approachability often outperform even domain experts who remain isolated or apathetic towards relationship building.

Domain expertise, particularly in the early stages of one's career, is fundamental in shaping professional trajectories. While interpersonal skills are increasingly valued, deep knowledge and skill in one's chosen field remain crucial. This expertise encompasses not only intellectual understanding but also the practical dexterity and craftsmanship in various trades, resonating with the perspectives of thinkers like Matthew B. Crawford.

For example, an investment banker's proficiency in financial regulations, an AI researcher's command of the latest technological advances, or a physician's adeptness with contemporary treatment methodologies, all illustrate the importance of specialized knowledge in different professions. Additionally, we must also appreciate the expertise of craftsmen and artisans. Consider a master woodworker who possesses an intricate understanding of wood properties and the precision required in their craft, or a mechanic whose intuitive grasp of engines allows them to diagnose and fix issues that evade computerized diagnostics.

In any profession, it is imperative to continuously enhance one's core technical skills with supplementary multidisciplinary knowledge. This approach not only broadens one's expertise but also ensures its relevance in the ever-evolving professional landscape. Acknowledging the value of both intellectual acumen and physical skill is key — the former often lauded in contemporary professional settings and the latter, as Crawford argues, equally deserving of esteem and recognition.

Therefore, domain expertise in its various forms is a cornerstone for professionals. It serves as the foundation upon which they build and adapt their careers amidst the dynamic shifts brought on by AI and automation. Be it in finance, AI, medicine, or craftsmanship, maintaining and expanding upon this expertise is essential. This might involve a banker staying abreast of evolving financial regulations, a bio-medical researcher leading groundbreaking projects, or a physician integrating new technologies into their practice. Professionals should aim to continually enrich their primary skills with cross-disciplinary knowledge, thus securing and future-proofing their roles in the workforce.

Cultural Awareness has become an invaluable skill in our interconnected, globalized world. It involves understanding and appreciating diverse cultural contexts and navigating cross-cultural interactions with tact. Edward

T. Hall's distinction between high-context and low-context cultures illustrates this well. The former relies on non-verbal cues and shared contextual understanding, while the latter emphasizes explicit verbal communication. Mastery in interpreting these varied communication styles is crucial to avoid misunderstandings in international teams. Moreover, an appreciation of differing cultural perspectives on individualism, power distance, and other societal norms facilitates smoother intercultural collaboration.

Creativity, essential across various fields, acts as a launchpad for innovation. It is nurtured at the intersection of domain expertise, openness to new ideas, and a willingness to venture into unexplored territories. Creativity's relevance extends beyond the typical realms of marketing or engineering to the tactile world of craftsmanship and skilled trades. Whether it's a master woodworker or a sculptor, creativity in these fields emerges from a profound understanding of materials and techniques, akin to the creative processes in more traditional corporate roles.

Organizations aiming to foster a holistic creative environment should encourage experimentation in all domains, from the boardroom to the workshop floor. Such a culture values failures as learning opportunities and encourages free knowledge exchange, allowing inspiration to flow from both intellectual and physical experiences. By embracing this comprehensive view of creativity, we recognize that innovation can arise from any quarter, be it digital marketing, engineering, or traditional craftsmanship.

Ethical Judgment and Integrity: In an era where corporate actions are under intense moral scrutiny, ethical judgment and integrity are indispensable. A sound moral compass is crucial for success, as seen in timeless ethical philosophies. Aristotle's concept of "eudaimonia," or flourishing through moral virtue, and the Stoic emphasis on wisdom, courage, justice, and temperance, provide enduring frameworks for professional excellence. These ancient principles remind us that ethical judgment remains the foundation of personal and institutional integrity, even in today's complex world.

Multidimensional Competencies: A Strategic View

This multidimensional competency framework – encompassing technical expertise, interpersonal skills, and ethical judgment – is essential for unlocking human potential and guiding organizations through turbulent times. As we turn our focus to organizational strategies for nurturing these competencies, we recognize the importance of preparing workforces to not only survive but thrive in the dynamic landscapes of today and tomorrow.

In the rapidly evolving landscape of work, organizations must be diligent and proactive in formulating strategies that align with their overarching vision and unique industry context. This necessitates a keen understanding of existing skills gaps within their workforce, embracing future-focused learning approaches, and harnessing the power of AI and technology to enrich life-long learning experiences. Essentially, a shift towards a more fluid, skills-first approach is imperative for long-term resilience.

Labor Market Trends and Skills Mismatches

Recent research by the International Labour Organization and reports by consultancies like McKinsey shed light on a pressing concern for today's business leaders: ensuring a smooth labor market transition for workforces in the face of seismic shifts in required skill sets across geographical regions. Amidst the ebb and flow of job churn spurred by automation and other factors, one concerning trend has prominently emerged – a noticeable skills deficit within the younger talent pool vying to enter the workforce. This gap represents a significant roadblock for companies seeking to remain competitive within their respective industries.

For example, ManpowerGroup's 2021 Talent Shortage Survey revealed that around 70% of US companies reported difficulty filling open job roles, with the most acute talent shortages in highly skilled trades, information technology, engineering, and manufacturing. Their analysis indicates over 8 million vacant positions remain unfilled within the US job market alone owing to this skills mismatch.

Similarly, a 2021 McKinsey survey on Europe's skills gap suggested that by 2030, 16% of the European workforce could be significantly under-skilled while 10% could be over-skilled for their assigned roles, pointing to a severe asymmetry between available talent and required competencies.

The disconnect between mainstream educational institutions and the skill requirements of employers is a widespread issue. In the UK, for instance, a significant proportion of employers believe that secondary education falls short in preparing students for the workforce. This gap encompasses not just technical skills but also extends to foundational competencies crucial in today's job market, such as effective communication, collaboration, creative thinking, and problem-solving.

This disparity is particularly pronounced in STEM fields. The UK Commission for Employment and Skills (UKCES) has identified that more than half of the job vacancies in STEM are difficult to fill due to the shortage of applicants with the required qualifications and skills. This indicates a serious mismatch between the output of educational programs and the actual demands of the job market.

The challenge is not confined to Western countries. For example, in China, despite producing a high number of engineering graduates — reportedly triple the number of the United States — there are concerns regarding the relevance and applicability of their skills. The Chinese education system's robust emphasis on STEM education succeeds in quantity but sparks debate over the quality of these graduates. For instance, while Chinese universities excel in theoretical teaching, there is often a gap in practical, hands-on experience that is critical for engineering roles in the global market. This discrepancy highlights the need for educational reforms that balance theoretical knowledge with practical industry-aligned skills.

Thus, the pattern of skill deficits is not exclusive to developed nations but extends to emerging economies as well. Even in developed nations, like Japan for instance, there is a growing need for skills that support technological innovation and digital transformation, yet educational institutions often lag in updating their curricula to reflect these new industry trends.

In the coming decades, these skill gap issues are expected to resonate globally, impacting both established and developing economies. The central challenge lies in not only producing a high number of graduates but also ensuring that their skills are attuned to the evolving requirements of a rapidly changing global workforce. This necessitates a reevaluation of educational curricula, a greater emphasis on practical skills, and closer collaboration between educational institutions and industry to ensure that graduates are equipped with the skills that are in demand.

The volatile dynamics of technological disruption and automation in job roles risks exacerbating these geographic mismatches between local talent availability and employer needs – an asymmetry which often leads to persistent unemployment in certain demographics, while simultaneously, other areas face continuous job vacancies. This can hamper productive job creation and workforce participation.

The exponential increase in remote work and flexible job models has provided some relief from these geographical talent mismatches. By enabling companies to access a wider talent pool regardless of location, remote work has mitigated, to an extent, the challenges posed by localized talent shortages.

Nevertheless, the impact of this shift varies significantly across different nations, reflecting disparities in technological infrastructure, cultural norms, and economic conditions. This underscores the need for nuanced, region-specific strategies to effectively address the imbalance.

In addressing these challenges, a multifaceted approach must account for the evolving nature of work, the geographical distribution of skills and opportunities, and the quality of educational outputs. The aim is to cultivate a global workforce that is adaptable, skilled, and capable of meeting the demands of an increasingly dynamic and interconnected world economy.

The Shortening Half-Life of Skills

The concept of the 'half-life' of skills, akin to the half-life in nuclear physics, speaks to the rapidly evolving nature of the contemporary workforce. It suggests that the amount of time it takes for half of the knowledge or competencies underpinning a particular skill to become obsolete is shrinking. This metaphor highlights the urgency for continuous learning and development, especially in fields heavily impacted by technological advancements.

However, it's important to acknowledge that this phenomenon applies less to certain professions that maintain a strong, physical connection to the real world. Trades such as plumbing, electrical work, and various forms of artistry, often rooted in deep-seated skills and craftsmanship, experience a different dynamic in terms of skill obsolescence. In these areas, the foundational skills and techniques tend to have a longer half-life, owing to the more enduring nature of the physical principles and materials they work with.

This is not to say that these fields are immune to change – technological advancements and new materials do influence them. Nevertheless, the core skills, often honed through years of hands-on experience and intuitive understanding of materials and processes, remain valuable over a longer period.

This contrasts with the more rapid obsolescence seen in many categories of knowledge work, where the onslaught of technological change can render skills outdated in a relatively short time.

The relentless pressure for continuous reskilling is indeed more acute in areas deeply intertwined with technological and operational upheavals. In the past, learning a skill or trade could set an individual up for a lifetime of employment, but today skills in many fields need regular updating to stay relevant.

For both managers and individuals, recognizing this varied landscape of skill obsolescence is key to navigating the contemporary business environment.

Here are some specific strategies managers can employ to address the specter of skills shorter half-lives:

- Conduct periodic skills gap analysis to objectively identify areas where employees' existing capabilities diverge from those needed to perform their roles effectively.
- Develop structured learning and development frameworks tailored to bridge identified skills gaps, empowering employees to gain must-have capabilities.
- Provide on-the-job learning opportunities through mechanisms like job rotation, internships, mentorship, and challenging project assignments to enable experiential development.
- Focus on nurturing portable transferrable skills like communication, emotional intelligence, and critical thinking that retain relevance across varied job functions.
- Remain open to modifying traditionally rigid hiring criteria and job descriptions to accommodate emerging skills and roles.

Alongside managerial strategies, individuals also carry responsibility for their own lifelong learning and skills maintenance:

- Consistently set aside time for professional development by reading, listening to podcasts, taking online courses, and attending seminars or workshops.

- Actively network with fellow professionals to remain updated on industry developments.

- Embrace opportunities to gain new capabilities by volunteering for unfamiliar projects and assignments.

- Maintain updated resumes and professional profiles that accurately reflect current skill sets.

- Consider pivoting into alternate career pathways when existing skills plateau in usefulness.

But circling back to the organizational level, let's take a typical example of Mary - a manager of a team of software developers. She knows that the software industry is constantly changing, and that her employees' skills need to keep up.

Mary conducts a skills gap analysis to identify both the skills that her employees have and the skills that they need. She then develops a training and development plan based on the results of the analysis that identifies specific opportunities for learning new skills on the job. At the same time, she encourages them to attend workshops and conferences to stay up-to-date on the latest trends and developments.

Mary also focuses on developing the transferable skills of her employees – as she knows that transferable skills, such as communication, problem-solving, and teamwork, will be important for them to succeed in any role.

Organizational Learning and Development

As specialized skills become outdated quickly, continuous learning is now imperative. Online education platforms have proliferated in response, offering diverse upskilling courses.

Data-driven talent management systems additionally enable personalized learning aligned to evolving career goals and dynamic industry demands. Organizations like AT&T focus on embedding learning within corporate cultures.

The vital significance of continuous learning, upskilling and reskilling in today's disruptive business landscape simply cannot be overstated. In fact, this skills imperative has profound ramifications for corporate learning and development philosophies moving forward.

AI and machine learning are playing increasingly prominent roles in enabling more personalized and adaptive adult education models that ultimately benefit both the organization and the worker. Here, educational content and instruction are dynamically customized based on an individual learner's strengths, needs, and preferences. For instance, AI-powered tutors can continually adjust presented problems and recommendations to align with a working professional's evolving mastery and progress within a skill domain.

Such granular personalization can dramatically boost learner engagement, motivation and outcomes. AI algorithms can also provide automated, real-time assessment by scoring learning activities and providing corrective feedback to hone competency.

As managers guide their workforces through this transitional period of increasing integration of AI in corporate training, a renewed emphasis on continuous education and a culture of learning will be pivotal. Specifically, managers must underscore how AI-enabled learning allows professionals to gain specialized skills to collaborate productively and thrive in symbiosis with intelligent systems.

Insights from experts highlight how forward-thinking organizations that make learning and development central to their talent strategies find themselves far better equipped to tackle disruptive challenges and harness emerging opportunities. Let's look at some researched, strategic approaches needed to ensure robust L&D frameworks:

External Expert Opinions: Management consultancies like McKinsey and Deloitte that work closely with major companies have underscored the urgency for business leaders to reimagine learning. McKinsey stresses getting in front of the curve when it comes to skill gaps, while Deloitte emphasizes adaptive mindsets and cultivating a culture of learning across entire workforces. Some firms have also created future-focused corporate learning programs, like Microsoft's LEAP, which exemplify structured approaches to capability building underpinned by data and behavioral science.

Personalized Learning Pathways: Given varying needs and preferences, a one-size-fits-all approach to training is suboptimal. Organizations must move towards tailored pathways, where data and AI guide professional development based on employee profiles, role requirements, and aspirations. For instance, machine learning algorithms help create customized learning journeys, ensuring individuals build capabilities most relevant to their objectives.

Blended Learning: While digital learning enables flexibility and scale, face-to-face interactions remain invaluable for comprehension and engagement. A balanced blend of online courses along with in-person workshops, coaching and collaborative assignments provides a rich development experience. This hybrid approach is endorsed by experts like McKinsey.

Mentorship and Peer Learning: Beyond formal methods, informal mechanisms like mentorship programs and peer learning help weave capability building into organizational culture. New recruits learn the ropes quickly from experienced staff. Knowledge flows freely through peer collaboration.

Embracing Microlearning: In an era of compressed attention spans, microlearning delivers focused learning in bite-sized segments. This technique aligns with McKinsey insights on more agile, project-based application of knowledge. Short modules are digestible and actionable.

Continuous Feedback Loops: Learning is a two-way street. Regular input from employees provides insights into L&D effectiveness and areas for improvement. This iterative approach keeps initiatives aligned to evolving individual and organizational needs.

Integrating Digital Technologies: From virtual reality simulations to AI-based education platforms, technology is elevating learning. Organizations must keep pace by adopting innovations, as suggested by McKinsey and Deloitte. Gamification, adaptive learning through AI, and immersive technologies provide rich experiences.

Growth Mindset: An underlying culture valuing continuous growth is crucial. Managers should promote a mindset where challenges represent opportunities to learn and expand capabilities. 3M's long-standing innovation ethos captures this: "Improve our products. Improve ourselves."

So amidst tectonic shifts in work, a strategic approach to L&D becomes paramount. Firms that view learning as an investment in their most valuable asset - their people – will have a higher chance of leading in the future of work. Continuous learning is the cornerstone of resilience and competitiveness in the digital age - and specialized skills and competencies provide a robust foundation to achieve that.

Leadership Capabilities for the New Era

As organizations adapt to the evolving work landscape, the capabilities required of leaders are also transforming. While foundational skills like strategic thinking remain vital, the new context demands that leaders embrace change, empower teams, and seamlessly integrate AI and emerging technologies. Some key leadership capabilities include:

Change Management: With continuous disruption the norm, leaders must become adept change agents, able to guide their organizations through transformations smoothly. This requires resilience, emotional intelligence, and strategic clarity.

Digital Acuity: Technology literacy is now imperative, requiring leaders to understand concepts like AI, data analytics, and cybersecurity. They must spot opportunities for digital transformation while ensuring human-centric design.

Cross-Boundary Collaboration: Innovation often emerges from diversity. Leaders must foster collaboration across hierarchies, functions, and geographies. This entails cultivating global mindsets and building partnerships.

Cross-Cultural Dexterity: As work becomes more globally integrated, leaders require cross-cultural sensitivity to bridge geographic and linguistic divides. This involves understanding varied cultural contexts, leading diverse teams, and fostering inclusivity across global organizations.

Coaching and Empowerment: Command-and-control leadership falters today. Leaders must enable autonomous teams, acting as coaches and facilitators. Fostering agility and nurturing talent become vital.

Experimentation and Learning: Leading amid complexity requires openness to experimentation, learning quickly from failures, and continuously honing strategies based on emerging trends.

Purpose and Ethics: With growing scrutiny, leaders must exemplify strong values and ethics. They need to ensure organizational purpose aligns with societal needs, communicating transparently around topics like sustainability and digital ethics.

This leads us to the vital themes of motivation, engagement, and meaning addressed in the next chapter. But before we transition, let's explore how two tech giants, LinkedIn and Google, exemplify the pivotal role of a systematic approach to the development of skills and competencies.

While LinkedIn serves as a platform that facilitates skill development and acquisition, Google stands as a prime example of a company that effectively utilizes systematic approaches to cultivate and nurture the skills of its workforce.

CASE STUDY 1: LINKEDIN'S SKILLS GRAPH

Picture this. It's 2002. Reid Hoffman, a serial entrepreneur, gathers a small team in his living room. They're not there for a casual get together. Rather, they're intensively brainstorming the blueprint for what would soon become the world's largest professional networking platform.

At its essence, LinkedIn aimed to be far more than just another job-hunting board. It sought to map the complex web of professional connections spanning the globe, transforming cold outreach into warm introductions between mutual contacts. It was about amplifying the power of relationships and community to shape careers through moments of serendipitous discovery.

Over the years, several of LinkedIn's innovations profoundly transformed professional networking:

Endorsements and Recommendations: Remember the joy of endorsing a colleague for their mastery of "Project Management" or penning a heartfelt recommendation? These features evolved LinkedIn from a static digital resume to a dynamic representation of one's professional journey, vouched for by peers.

LinkedIn Learning: Recognizing professionals' need for continuous skills development amidst digital disruption, LinkedIn acquired online learning platform Lynda.com and integrated it as its learning service. This positioned the company as a one-stop platform to both demonstrate and develop skills.

News Feed and Thought Leadership: The introduction of LinkedIn's news feed transformed static profiles into hubs for the exchange of ideas. Industry veterans shared insights alongside new graduates narrating their first job experiences. A culture of mutual learning emerged organically.

Leveraging the Power of Professional Data

With over 700 million members actively updating profiles, sharing posts, and making connections, LinkedIn evolved into a goldmine of professional data and insights. But the true value lay not just in aggregating volumes of data - instead, it was about identifying meaningful trends related to skills in demand, emerging job roles, career transitions, and global talent migration patterns. LinkedIn's annual "Emerging Jobs Report" established itself as a credible crystal ball for forecasting the future of work.

Yet amidst all its digital prowess, the platform never lost sight of the human element underpinning professional networking. Features like the "Open To Work" badge not only helped job seekers signal their availability but also fostered a sense of community and support during challenging economic times.

Highlight: Today, as the world's largest professional networking platform, LinkedIn serves as the living, breathing pulse of global talent - not just as a tool for hunting jobs but for discovering purpose and meaning in one's work. The Skills Graph creates a common language around skills to help us all better understand the skills that power the global workforce. It also drives relevance and matching across LinkedIn – helping learners find content more relevant to their career path; helping job seekers find jobs that are a good fit; and helping recruiters find the highest quality candidates. The platform provides a transparent and fair job matching process that drives better outcomes for employers and employees.

CASE STUDY 2:
GOOGLE'S PROJECT ARISTOTLE

In 2012, Google's People Analytics division embarked on an ambitious research initiative nicknamed "Project Aristotle." Its objective was to decode the traits, habits and norms underpinning the most successful teams within Google's sprawling organizational landscape and global footprint. Put simply, the goal was to identify key factors that reliably differentiated top-performing teams from the rest at Google.

After rigorously analyzing troves of performance data from scores of teams, Project Aristotle revealed several common competencies and practices shared by Google's highest-achieving teams. Surprisingly, purely technical prowess or individual star players took a backseat. Instead, competencies like psychological safety, dependability, structure and clarity rose to the forefront as the strongest predictors of team excellence.

Specifically, psychological safety - described as the degree of confidence team members feel that the team is a safe space for risk-taking without fear of embarrassment or rejection - emerged as foundational. Google researchers concluded this climate of trust enabled the conditions for collaboration, innovation and speaking up that underpinned stellar results.

Meanwhile, other influential competencies included:

- Dependability - ability to be counted on to complete quality work on time.
- Structure & Clarity - having clear goals, roles and plans.
- Meaning - finding purpose and value in the team's work.
- Impact - belief that the team's work matters.

The Project Aristotle research strongly highlighted that while technical expertise is indispensable, the "soft" competencies have exponential impact on team success. Furthermore, managers and leaders played pivotal roles in actively nurturing the conditions and climate to amplify these competencies.

Highlight: Google's Project Aristotle underscores the outsized influence of blending technical know-how with human-centric competencies - especially when these competencies are actively cultivated through supportive management practices. This case study provides empirical evidence that technical skills, while necessary, are not sufficient. Mastering the human elements of work is vital for organizations to unleash their full potential.

CHAPTER 8:
MOTIVATING AND ENGAGING THE WORKFORCE

Thriving in today's ever-evolving work environment demands a deep understanding of its dynamic nature, shifting organizational structures, and the emergence of a new managerial ethos. In this era, where knowledge is the pivotal fulcrum of the economy, we are witnessing a significant departure from the Taylorist model of management, characterized by its command-and-control approach, towards a style of management that is more facilitative and empowering.

This paradigm shift responds to the transition from a manufacturing-based economy to one that is predominantly knowledge-based. In this new economy, talent management has become paramount. The adage "You can copy processes, but not people" aptly underscores the vital role human capital plays in any organization's success. In an age marked by rapid technological innovation and widespread replication, it is the unique talent, creativity, and commitment of individuals that emerge as irreplaceable and inimitable assets.

Consequently, traditional methods of fostering motivation and engagement, designed for a bygone era and a different economic context, are proving increasingly inadequate. These methods fall short in addressing the nuanced and complex needs of the contemporary workforce. Despite this recognition, moving away from entrenched paradigms remains a challenge.

Motivation and Engagement Defined

In this chapter, we explore the notions of motivation and engagement as vital interconnected aspects of a comprehensive workforce management strategy. In the large array of business challenges that leaders confront, understanding and leveraging the synergy between motivation and engagement is indeed crucial for organizational success.

In the following sections, we will explore the theoretical underpinnings of motivation and engagement, examine how these concepts have evolved in the new world of work, and suggest strategies for leveraging them to unlock the full potential of your workforce in the digital age.

Our exploration begins with motivation - the driving force that propels individuals towards their goals. It can be intrinsic, fueled by the innate satisfaction derived from task completion or new experiences, or extrinsic, tied to tangible rewards such as salary increments or recognition. Acting as the 'why' behind our actions, motivation is nourished by personal interests, ambitions, and the quest for external validation. What is more, translating that to high performance requires the addition of two key elements: skill (capability) as well as opportunity.

Motivation has a rich theoretical history, from Maslow's hierarchy of needs (Maslow, 1943) to Herzberg's two-factor model of intrinsic and extrinsic motivation (Herzberg, 1959). While motivation can ignite an individual's desire to act, it is engagement that sustains this drive in the long term through mechanisms that are triggered by a range of causal factors or antecedents. Most scholars espouse a variant of the view that engagement represents a deep emotional and psychological connection to one's work, characterized by vigor, dedication, and absorption, as supported by the highly influential Utrecht Work Engagement model (Schaufeli et al, 2002) – one which focuses on 'work engagement' (as opposed to 'organizational engagement').

In my book, Engaging the Workforce: The Grand Management Challenge of the 21st Century (Rossides, 2021), I describe engagement as "a positive and fulfilling state of mind towards one's work and organization, characterized by vigor, dedication, and absorption, complemented by a willingness to expend discretionary time and effort," and propose a systematic framework for its implementation within organizations addressing both the intertwined elements: towards the work itself and the organization.

Crucially, from the perspective of "psychological affect," engagement nurtures positive emotions such as energy, enthusiasm, and a sense of fulfillment (see Figure 10).

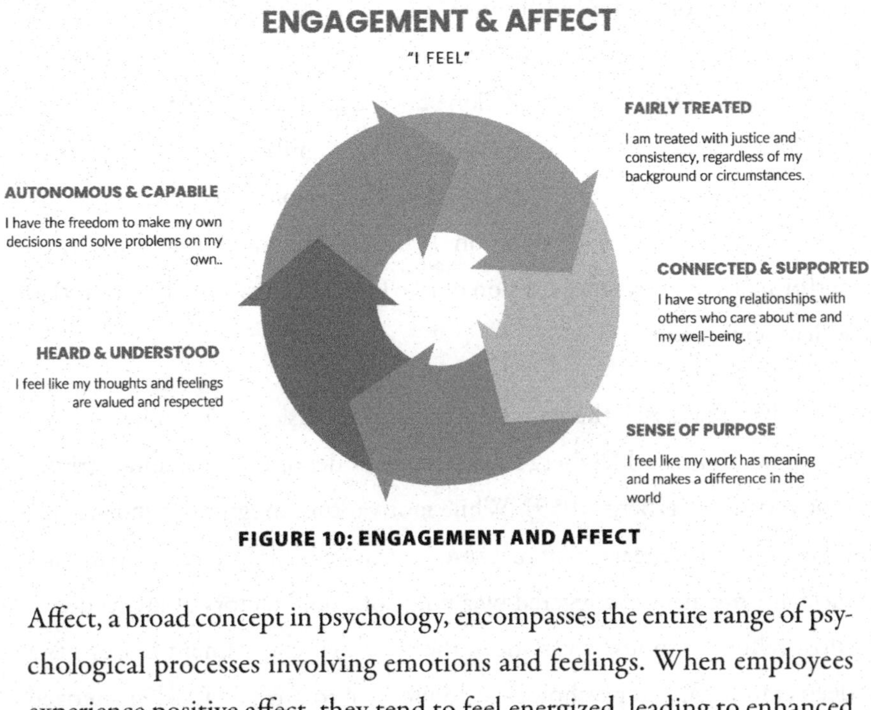

ENGAGEMENT & AFFECT
"I FEEL"

FAIRLY TREATED
I am treated with justice and consistency, regardless of my background or circumstances.

AUTONOMOUS & CAPABLE
I have the freedom to make my own decisions and solve problems on my own..

CONNECTED & SUPPORTED
I have strong relationships with others who care about me and my well-being.

HEARD & UNDERSTOOD
I feel like my thoughts and feelings are valued and respected

SENSE OF PURPOSE
I feel like my work has meaning and makes a difference in the world

FIGURE 10: ENGAGEMENT AND AFFECT

Affect, a broad concept in psychology, encompasses the entire range of psychological processes involving emotions and feelings. When employees experience positive affect, they tend to feel energized, leading to enhanced productivity. This positive emotional state also encourages creativity, innovation, and collaboration. In contrast, when employees experience negative affect, they are more likely to disengage, lose motivation, and experience reduced productivity. As I elaborate in my book, engagement is a complex and multifaceted phenomenon, intricately interwoven with our emotional, cognitive, and behavioral processes.

Turning to the managerial implications of fostering engagement, it's crucial to recognize that there are no universal, one-size-fits-all solutions. While our models provide validated causal frameworks that offer clear directionality and are undoubtedly useful, the effectiveness of organizational interventions hinges significantly on context-specific calibration. Just as a medical diagnosis and treatment plan must be tailored to the individual patient, considering their unique health profile and circumstances, so too must engagement strategies be customized to the distinctive environment of each organization. Basic directionality, akin to a general diagnosis, can guide us towards understanding underlying issues, but it is the nuanced, context-specific application that leads to effective solutions.

Interventions can be adjusted at two fundamental levels: first, at the level of work itself, where practices like 'job crafting' allow employees to personalize aspects of their roles to better fit their strengths and interests. Second, adjustments occur within the broader organizational context, through the implementation of policies that enhance perceptions of fairness and organizational support.

The key lies in tailoring managerial interventions to meet the specific needs and dynamics of each organization, much like how a doctor personalizes treatment to each patient's unique health situation. This bespoke approach ensures that strategies are not only theoretically sound but also practically effective in the specific organizational setting.

But before we go further, let us briefly review the evolution of the concept of employee engagement and how we got to our current understanding. Indeed, the notion has been used in management for several decades, replacing the outdated model of measuring employee 'satisfaction'. The latter, primarily focused on assessing employee contentment, was criticized for its narrow focus and limited utility in driving organizational performance.

So, let's unpack this idea a bit further. Imagine you're dining at a restaurant, and at the end of the meal, the server asks, "Were you satisfied with your meal?" You think back to the food that was decent, the service that was passable, and the ambiance that was comfortable. Yes, you were satisfied. But, if a new restaurant opens across the street offering a unique menu, exceptional service, and a vibrant atmosphere, your 'satisfaction' with the previous restaurant might not hold you back from trying the new place. So while you were 'satisfied' at the moment, it doesn't necessarily mean you are committed to returning.

Or consider a slightly different example. Suppose you purchase a brand new car. You're asked, "Are you satisfied with your car?" At first glance, it's a beautiful car, drives well, and you've had no issues. So, you reply, "Yes, I'm satisfied." However, six months later, it starts breaking down. Your 'satisfaction' at the time of purchase was based on a moment in time and did not predict future performance or commitment to the brand.

So, in the search for a deeper understanding of employees' relationship with their work, the transient concept of 'satisfaction' proved to be insufficient. It merely offered a superficial snapshot of employee sentiment at a specific point in time, failing to predict future behavior or elicit a sense of loyalty. In the quest for more profound insights, scholars turned to more comprehensive constructs such as commitment, engagement and experience.

While 'commitment' and 'engagement' as constructs emerged around the same period, it was the concept of 'engagement' that arguably became more widely adopted in both academic discourse and organizational practice. The introduction of the term 'engagement' by William Kahn in 1990 marked a significant shift in the conversation about employee motivation and performance. His foundational work positioned engagement as a complex construct, representing the "harnessing of organization members' selves to their work roles." This notion emphasized a deep, multidimensional connection between an employee and their work, encompassing emotional, cognitive, and physical investment.

As for commitment, John Meyer and Natalie Allen introduced it as part of their "Three Component Model" of Commitment (1991):

- **Affective** commitment (a strong emotional attachment to the organization).

- **Continuance** commitment (an awareness of the costs associated with leaving the organization).

- **Normative** commitment (a feeling of obligation to remain with the organization).

Although there are overlaps in these two models (engagement and commitment, especially affective commitment), the engagement construct managed to dominate the broader organizational discourse. It became dominant in the relevant literature, underscoring the need for a holistic view of what drives employee performance. The concept of fully engaging oneself—emotionally, cognitively, and physically—in one's work has garnered widespread acceptance.

Since Kahn's seminal work, the engagement discourse has not just expanded within academic circles but has also permeated the realm of organizational practice. Numerous studies have dissected its various dimensions, such as the different facets of organizational justice, its 'proximate' and 'distal' consequences, and its intersections with related constructs such as the employee experience.

In the array of proposed approaches and instruments for measuring engagement, the Utrecht Work Engagement Scale (UWES) stands out. It has been validated in numerous contexts, and the resultant engagement metric it offers is best predicted by job resources, including autonomy, supervisory coaching, performance feedback, and personal resources such as optimism, self-efficacy, and self-esteem (Schaufeli & Bakker, 2004).

Engagement has also seen a significant boom in the consulting business, with an array of models which, while sometimes deficient in a strong theoretical grounding, are focused on practical application within organizational contexts. Among these, Gallup's Q12, backed by substantial longitudinal data, allows for effective benchmarking (Harter et al, 2002). Alongside this are various off-the-shelf solutions from major consultancies such as Hays, Deloitte, PwC, and others. In the last few decades, the measurement and management of engagement has grown into a robust industry that is generating substantial revenues.

The focus for managers has evolved from the question 'does engagement matter?' (it unequivocally does) to 'which precise management practices should be implemented, and how?' Engaged employees extend beyond mere motivation; they embody the organization's values and goals, going beyond their contractual obligations in what is termed "extra-role behaviors." And that feeds a virtuous cycle of improved outcomes across the board, especially through improved service quality which in turn leads to loyal customers (see Figure 11).

THE VIRTUOUS ENGAGEMENT CYCLE

The Dividends Of Engagement

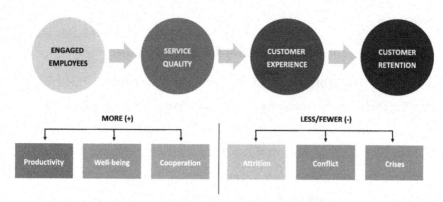

FIGURE 11: THE VIRTUOUS ENGAGEMENT CYCLE

Numerous factors influence engagement, including psychological states, job-person compatibility, job-organization compatibility, leadership quality, organizational support, working relationships, and perceptions of organizational justice. Importantly, engagement originates from the fulfillment of basic psychological needs: autonomy, mastery, relatedness, and meaningfulness.

Investing in employee engagement yields significant returns, positively impacting task performance, commitment, discretionary effort, and overall organizational performance. This investment goes beyond boosting immediate productivity; it fortifies long-term outcomes such as corporate reputation and brand strength (Schaufeli et al. 2016; Rossides, 2021). The impact of heightened engagement is evident at multiple levels. 'Proximal' effects include improved work rate, productivity, and extra-role behaviors. More 'distal' effects extend to broader organizational achievements like increased profitability, enhanced reputation, and stronger brand equity.

As for the relationship between motivation and engagement, they are deeply symbiotic, with each element reinforcing the other. A motivated employee is invariably more engaged in their work, contributing to a dynamic and productive workplace. This synergy is crucial for effective management, enabling organizations to cultivate a workforce that is not only driven but also deeply connected to their roles and the company's mission.

The Metaverse: A New Frontier for Engagement

The advent of technologies like the metaverse opens up unprecedented opportunities to elevate employee engagement and revolutionize customer interactions. This immersive and interactive digital realm offers a novel platform for creating virtual environments that foster a sense of belonging, provide personalized learning experiences, and facilitate real-time collaboration. Within the metaverse, businesses can design experiences that are both engaging and surreal, offering new ways for employees to connect with their work and for customers to interact with brands.

The metaverse presents an opportunity to reimagine traditional workspaces and customer engagement strategies. It enables organizations to create a more immersive and engaging environment, enhancing both internal collaboration and external brand interactions. This technological advancement is not just a new tool; it's a paradigm shift, offering innovative ways to deepen engagement and reshape the interaction landscape in the business world.

The Unfolding Metaverse

The concept of the metaverse, once a staple of science fiction, is rapidly becoming a tangible reality thanks to advancements in virtual and augmented reality (AR/VR) technologies. Originating from Neal Stephenson's 1992 novel "Snow Crash," the metaverse concept has evolved from a speculative idea to a viable digital ecosystem.

Key developments have marked the journey toward realizing the metaverse. In 2016, Microsoft's HoloLens and the Pokémon Go phenomenon illustrated the potential of augmented reality to create shared, interactive experiences. IKEA's 2017 Place app revolutionized retail by enabling customers to virtually place furniture in their homes. Apple's introduction of advanced AR capabilities in its devices in 2020 further expanded these possibilities.

Facebook's 2021 rebranding to Meta and the subsequent launch of Horizon Workrooms in 2022 underscored the corporate world's growing interest in the metaverse. These platforms offer virtual spaces for collaborative work, allowing digital avatars to interact in ways previously confined to physical offices.

The metaverse presents unprecedented opportunities to redefine how businesses operate and engage with customers. In this virtual realm, employees can collaborate across borders in immersive environments, undergo personalized training via simulations, and participate in interactive team-building activities that transcend physical limitations.

For retailers, the metaverse opens doors to revolutionary customer experiences, like virtual try-ons and interactive product demonstrations, offering an engaging blend of physical and digital shopping experiences.

However, as businesses explore these virtual frontiers, they must navigate challenges around data privacy, accessibility, and maintaining a healthy work-life balance. There's a risk that without proper management, these technologies could exacerbate workplace issues like harassment or surveillance.

To realize the metaverse's potential responsibly, organizations must balance its integration with the human aspects of work. Virtual interactions should complement, not replace, the need for face-to-face connections that nurture trust and team cohesion.

As we explore this new paradigm, crucial questions arise: How do we balance virtual and in-person interactions effectively? How can leadership qualities and team dynamics be maintained in a digital realm? And importantly, how do we ensure ethical and inclusive access to these technologies?

The future of the metaverse in business is a blend of virtual and physical worlds, offering new ways to connect, collaborate, and engage. By navigating its challenges thoughtfully, organizations can harness the metaverse as a tool for enriching workplace experiences and customer interactions, ensuring it enhances rather than diminishes our fundamental human needs for connection and authenticity.

Shifting Workforce Dynamics and Engagement Strategies

As we've already argued, the landscape of employment is experiencing a profound transformation, redefining our understanding of 'work', the 'workforce', and the 'workplace'. This evolution requires a reevaluation of engagement, motivation, and holistic talent management strategies.

The move towards more modular, 'task-based' workflows offers organizations the agility to blend permanent and contingent employees with AI-driven automation and augmentation. While this approach introduces operational fluidity, it also challenges traditional role definitions and career progression paths. These changes have far-reaching implications for employee motivation and engagement, necessitating innovative approaches to sustain workforce morale and productivity.

The reconfiguration of 'workplaces' into more flexible environments presents both opportunities and challenges. On one hand, it grants employees unprecedented flexibility, allowing them to tailor work-life balance to their individual needs. On the other hand, this dispersion of physical workspaces, often spanning multiple time zones, introduces complexities in fostering a sense of belonging, maintaining team cohesion, and ensuring effective communication. These factors are critical in keeping engagement levels high and promoting a healthy work-life balance.

Furthermore, as the 'workforce' becomes more diverse and geographically dispersed, it demands a nuanced approach to manage, motivate, and engage a varied talent pool. This diversity necessitates adaptable management styles and engagement tactics that recognize and cater to the unique needs of a heterogeneous workforce.

A critical aspect requiring further exploration is the evolution of the traditional psychological contract — the unspoken expectations and obligations between employees and employers. The transition towards more flexible work arrangements is reshaping employee expectations and perceived obligations. This shift calls for a renegotiation of this psychological contract, fostering a new dynamic that aligns with these changing expectations while ensuring sustained engagement and motivation.

Organizations must navigate these shifting dynamics carefully. The challenge lies in creating a work environment that not only adapts to these changes but also thrives within them. This entails developing strategies that maintain motivation and engagement, ensuring a harmonious and productive workforce in a rapidly evolving work landscape.

We also need to re-examine the concept of organizational climate, which encapsulates the collective mood, morale, and shared perceptions of the work environment. The shift towards remote, flexible, and project-based work has significant implications for the organizational climate (see Figure 12). A number of tricky questions arise: How can we assess and manage this climate when physical co-location isn't the norm? What strategies are needed to foster trust, inclusivity, and motivation when team members may be dispersed across geographies and time zones?

ORGANIZATIONAL CLIMATE

For Workforce Engagement

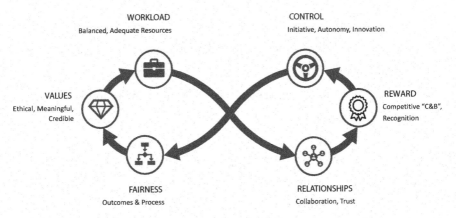

FIGURE 12: ORGANIZATIONAL CLIMATE

Finally, we need to explore the wider and more profound concept of organizational culture, encompassing shared values, beliefs, norms, and practices. In this evolving landscape of diverse and fluid working arrangements, how does culture adapt and evolve? How can leaders shape a resilient and adaptable culture that instills a sense of belonging and purpose, especially when interactions may be virtual, and the workforce transient?

Given the profound shifts in work dynamics, organizations must deeply understand how the psychological contract, organizational climate, and culture influence employee motivation and engagement. Organizations can then adopt tailored strategies, such as robust learning and development programs and job crafting, to foster a more engaged and productive workforce.

Balancing Productivity and Motivation

As I've argued above, AI has the potential to automate many routine tasks, freeing up workers to focus on more creative and strategic work. Nevertheless, there is a risk that managers may become too focused on increasing productivity and efficiency through automation, neglecting other factors important for employee motivation, such as autonomy, competence, and psychological safety.

Drawing on engagement and motivation literature (Rossides, 2023) here are some tips for managers on how to achieve a balance between productivity and motivation:

Empower employees with autonomy: Grant employees ownership over their work, allowing them to determine task priorities and execution methods, fostering a sense of ownership and engagement.

Foster employee competence through training and support: Provide comprehensive training and support to enhance employees' confidence and proficiency in their roles, enabling them to tackle challenges with greater expertise.

Nurture a risk-tolerant environment: Create a supportive space where employees feel empowered to take calculated risks and learn from their missteps, fostering innovation and growth while minimizing fear of failure.

Celebrate and reward employee contributions: Recognize and commend employees for their efforts and accomplishments, reinforcing their value and stimulating continued engagement.

Enhance organizational support: Provide adequate resources, infrastructure, and tools to ensure employees have the necessary support to excel in their roles. This encompasses access to technology, equipment, and administrative support.

Ensure fairness in both process and outcomes: Demonstrate impartiality and transparency in decision-making processes, ensuring employees feel their contributions are valued and their efforts are rewarded fairly. This fosters a sense of equity and trust within the organization.

Balancing Flexibility & Engagement

Remote and hybrid work have become increasingly popular in recent years, offering a number of advantages for both employers and employees. However, it is important to be aware of the potential downsides of these arrangements, particularly when it comes to the social needs of employees and their uneven access to required resources.

While flexibility in the workplace can enhance motivation and engagement, it is essential to approach it with caution to avoid unintended consequences, such as job insecurity, unpredictable work hours, and lack of access to social protection or benefits. In addition, remote and hybrid work can lead to feelings of isolation and disconnection from colleagues and managers, especially those living in less than ideal housing conditions.

Given the importance of social connection to our well-being, it is crucial for organizations to implement remote and hybrid work arrangements in ways that prioritize relatedness. This may involve creating opportunities for virtual social gatherings, providing employees with the tools and resources they need to collaborate effectively, and fostering a culture of trust and support.

Here are some specific strategies that organizations can use to boost motivation and engagement while also supporting the social needs of remote and hybrid workers:

- Create opportunities for virtual social gatherings. This could include regular team meetings, coffee chats, happy hours, or even just casual watercooler chats.
- Provide employees with the tools and resources they need to collaborate effectively. This includes things like video conferencing software, project management tools, and communication channels.

- Foster a culture of trust and support. Encourage employees to reach out for help when they need it and to support each other.

- Recognize and reward employees for their contributions. This will help employees to feel valued and appreciated.

Therefore, as we move towards more flexible work arrangements, largely driven by technological advancements and changing worker preferences, we need to approach it with studious caution. While offering numerous advantages for both employers and employees, it does come with its own set of challenges as I've argued above. And it is especially apparent in non-standard forms of employment.

The Non-Standard Employment Conundrum

Recent trends, as highlighted by the International Labour Organization (ILO), show an uptick in non-standard forms of employment (NSE) across both developed and developing economies. NSE encapsulates a wide spectrum, including temporary positions, part-time roles, short-term agency contracts, and dependent self-employment.

While these non-traditional employment formats offer certain advantages, they also come with a host of challenges and concerns that may make motivation and engagement strategies harder to implement:

Challenges for Workers: For many individuals in NSE roles, job security remains elusive. These forms of employment, by their very nature, can offer less stability than traditional full-time positions. Consequently, many workers find themselves grappling with unpredictable working conditions, reduced benefits, and the looming uncertainty of their employment status.

Short-Term Gains vs Long-Term Impacts for Employers: While employers might initially benefit from the cost savings and flexibility that NSE provides—especially if they can bypass standard social security contributions and other benefits—the long-term picture may not be as rosy. As indicated by research by management scholars, such as that by Aleksynaka and Berg (2016), the immediate financial perks may ultimately be offset by dips in productivity. This decline can be attributed to the erosion of firm-specific skills, which are integral to adapting to changing market dynamics.

Managerial Complexities: As organizations increasingly adopt NSE, they must also brace themselves for the enhanced managerial demands these employment formats bring. If a significant chunk of an organization's workforce falls under NSE, navigating the nuances of managing such a diverse and transient team can be taxing. It requires a rethinking of management strategies, communication protocols, and engagement initiatives.

Given these considerations, organizations must proceed with caution. While the flexibility and potential cost savings associated with non-standard forms of employment (NSE) might seem attractive, we need to keep in mind that there are hidden costs – both tangible and intangible. Our primary objective should always be clear: all employment strategies must enhance job quality and bolster the long-term vitality of the organization, while prioritizing the well-being of its workforce.

In this changing work context, the indispensable role of effective management and leadership becomes evident. Balancing the appeal of flexibility with the imperative to maintain job quality and employee well-being is a managerial and leadership responsibility.

Management: The Engine of Engagement

In an ever-evolving work dynamic, the role of management stands out as the linchpin. They navigate the intricate balance between harnessing flexibility and technological empowerment while upholding the psychological contract with employees. The influence of management permeates from team or division levels to the upper echelons of organizational hierarchy, commonly referred to as 'leadership'. However, this term, 'leadership', has often been overused to the point of dilution, masking its true significance as the apex of a continuum.

There's a subtle yet important difference between 'management' and 'leadership', a distinction often overlooked due to their interchangeable use or misunderstood contexts. Although both are pivotal, they operate on different levels, but along a continuum, each with a distinct focus and intensity.

It is useful to envision management and leadership as lying along a spectrum. At one end, there's the granular, day-to-day oversight of frontline supervisors (where 'doing things right' is the primary focus), and at the other, the broader, strategic vision embodied by CEOs (where 'doing the right thing' becomes the key concern). Both influence engagement, yet their mechanisms and scope differ.

On the operational side, effective management ensures alignment between daily tasks and the organization's larger goals. A crucial aspect of this is the quality of relationships employees have with their immediate supervisors, which plays a significant role in engagement levels. There's a well-regarded adage: "people don't leave companies, they leave bad managers." This isn't merely anecdotal; studies, like those from Gallup, reinforce the idea that the relationship between a manager and an employee is central to job satisfaction and retention.

Conversely, leadership operates beyond the immediacy of daily tasks, shaping the organization's strategy and vision. Think of leadership as setting the organizational compass, clarifying the "why" of operations. Simon Sinek's *Start With Why* emphasizes that organizations that have clarity around that have a competitive edge. Leaders need to understand that employees are motivated not just by what they do, but fundamentally, by why they do it.

Daniel Goleman explored leadership styles through a different prism in *Leadership That Gets Results*. He identified six styles and suggested that effective leaders adeptly switch between these, depending on the situation, promoting adaptability and resilience in the process.

As we transition from management to leadership, discussions evolve from immediate concerns to future aspirations. However, within every diligent manager lies potential leadership qualities. The distinction is often one of focus: immediate tasks versus the expansive vision of leadership.

In essence, both management and leadership are pivotal. Effective managers foster engagement by clearly defining expectations, providing consistent feedback, and nurturing a supportive environment. Conversely, the leadership tier, including the C-suite and board, sets the overarching direction, guiding organizational culture, and establishing a blueprint for the future.

Their decisions mold not just the present operational environment but the broader ethos, setting the tone for "how we do things here."

It stands to reason that in the throes of the digital era, businesses must prioritize adapting and evolving, adhering to principles of good management: following practices that foster trust and fuel motivation and engagement. Toward this end, increasingly sophisticated AI tools can help achieve strategic goals while pursuing operational excellence. This hinges on having robust processes combined with effective performance management – which in turn results in key performance outcomes such as operational excellence (see Figure 13).

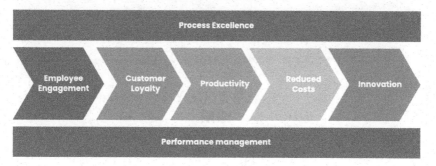

Operational Excellence hinges on process excellence combined with performance management.

FIGURE 13: OPERATIONAL EXCELLENCE

Indeed, the convergence of automation, AI, and other digital advancements challenges traditional workplace norms, making innovation all the more important while remembering that work quality remains a vital concern. But before we explore the topic of innovation in our next chapter, let's look at two case studies that exemplify forward-looking workforce engagement strategies.

CASE STUDY 1:
IBM

IBM stands as a prime example of a responsive organization, particularly as it systematically supports and engages its employees. With their innovative platform, "ACE" (Advice, Coaching, and Education), IBM has moved beyond traditional, static annual surveys. ACE leverages AI to analyze real-time feedback, ensuring employee voices are not only heard but actively influence decision-making processes.

In a scenario where a project bottleneck is reported, ACE promptly identifies and flags such concerns for immediate managerial attention. This responsiveness is indicative of IBM's commitment to ensuring a dynamic and engaging work environment.

Furthering their innovative approach, IBM introduced the IBM Consulting Advantage platform. This initiative represents a significant evolution in workplace technology, offering role-specific AI assistants to support and enhance employee performance. This platform, underpinned by IBM Watson's AI capabilities, provides an intuitive interface for accessing diverse tools and insights, thereby enriching the work experience.

The platform reflects IBM's understanding that modern workforces extend beyond traditional boundaries. Hence, they also launched the Supplier Connection portal for freelancers and contractors, streamlining onboarding and assignment tracking to promote clarity and collaboration.

The company's inclusive approach extends to celebrating achievements across its workforce - recognition programs acknowledge contributions, reinforcing the notion that every role, regardless of its nature, is integral to the organization's success.

Highlight: The case of IBM, with its ACE and IBM Consulting Advantage platforms, showcases how technology can be adeptly used to boost employee engagement, motivation, while enhancing productivity. They exemplify a forward-thinking approach to employee empowerment, setting a standard for harnessing technology to create a more dynamic, innovative, and involved workforce.

CASE STUDY 2:
ZAPPOS

Founded in 1999 by Nick Swinmurn, Zappos started as an online shoe retailer. The company quickly gained attention not just for its vast selection of shoes but also for its unique approach to company culture and customer service. Acquired by Amazon in 2009, Zappos has maintained its distinct identity, emphasizing employee happiness and exceptional customer experiences, all based on a set of 10 core values.

1. Deliver WOW Through Service

2. Embrace and Drive Change

3. Create Fun and A Little Weirdness

4. Be Adventurous, Creative, and Open-Minded

5. Pursue Growth and Learning

6. Build Open and Honest Relationships With Communication

7. Build a Positive Team and Family Spirit

8. Do More With Less

9. Be Passionate and Determined

10. Be Humble

Zappos expects its employees to reflect its 10 core values in everything they do, how they interact with each other, and how they interact with customers, vendors, and business partners. These core values form the framework for all of the company's decisions and are a natural part of employees' everyday language and way of thinking.

The company aims to create a culture that is centered around employee happiness. This is purported to lead to higher engagement, profitability, and low turnover. Zappos also has a strong customer-centric culture, as expressed in its purpose and core values. The leadership believes that it is possible to simultaneously deliver happiness to customers, employees, vendors, shareholders, and the community in a long-term sustainable way.

But the company seems to walk the talk. It has consciously and systematically tried to realize this alignment. In 2013, its leadership adopted "Holacracy," a system that replaces the traditional corporate hierarchy with a more decentralized structure. In this model, there are no job titles or managers. Instead, employees take on various roles based on the tasks at hand, promoting flexibility, autonomy, and rapid adaptation to change.

In the course of its evolution and growth, the company has become legendary for its customer service. It offers free shipping, a 365-day return policy, and a customer service team that goes above and beyond.

Stories abound of representatives chatting with customers for hours, sending flowers, or even helping with non-Zappos related queries. This dedication to "Deliver WOW Through Service" has earned Zappos a fiercely loyal customer base.

Importantly, the company sees the connection between engaged employees and loyal customers. Every new hire, regardless of position, undergoes a four-week training program that covers company values, customer service, and even includes a stint answering customer calls. At the end of the training, the trainees get a cash incentive to quit, a test of their commitment to the company's values and mission. This unique approach ensures that only those truly aligned with the Zappos culture remain.

Highlight: Zappos' emphasis on culture and customer service has made it a case study in business schools and a benchmark for companies worldwide. Its success demonstrates that prioritizing employee happiness and customer satisfaction can lead to strong business outcomes. What is more, it offers a compelling example of how unconventional approaches to corporate culture and customer service can differentiate a company in a competitive market.

CHAPTER 9:
INNOVATION AND ADAPTATION

In the ever-evolving world of business, two forces consistently stand out as harbingers of success: innovation and adaptability. These are the lifeblood powering empires, sparking revolutions, and birthing industry giants. The dance between the new and known, between groundbreaking invention and nimble adaptability, often determines organizations' survival and enduring success.

Historically, seminal thinkers like Schumpeter and Christensen have deeply examined innovation, dissecting its nature, processes, and impacts. Yet as influential as innovation is, adaptability is its silent partner, ensuring businesses can not only introduce new ideas but pivot swiftly to accommodate them in a world of relentless change.

Drawing parallels from nature, innovation is the rain bringing forth new life, while adaptability is the root system allowing a plant to absorb nourishing showers and thrive. Together they become formidable, catalyzing growth, resilience, and longevity. This chapter examines the intricate interplay of innovation and adaptability, exploring how they harmoniously balance continuity and change as the Yin and Yang of modern business.

Defining Innovation: Seminal Thinkers & Concepts

In the world of business, one term consistently emerges as a beacon of progress: innovation. While many perceive innovation as merely introducing something new, its true essence lies in pushing boundaries and relentlessly pursuing improvement.

The term has been the subject of considerable scholarly debate for decades. As early as 1942, Schumpeter recognized innovation as the driving force behind economic transformation. He coined the phrase 'creative destruction' to emphasize that for new entities to flourish, old structures must make way.

Building upon Schumpeter's ideas, Peter Drucker challenged the prevailing view of innovation as a sporadic, spontaneous occurrence. Instead, he asserted that innovation is a discipline—something that can be learned, practiced, and perfected.

Clayton Christensen extended the discussion by introducing the concept of 'disruptive innovation,' a particularly transformative form of change. New entrants challenged established giants by targeting underserved segments, offering streamlined solutions, or adopting entirely new business models. Naturally, this captured popular imagination when viewed against other less transformative or radical developments.

Indeed, innovation has many facets—incremental tweaks and improvements contrast with radical overhauls of entire systems. As Christensen argued, disruptive innovation begins subtly but grows to be revolutionary by helping rearrange existing components into something profoundly different.

Innovation and Adaptability

The pace of global change is accelerating at an unprecedented rate. From emerging technologies to shifting dynamics, transformation is pervasive.

This rapid evolution demands that businesses and individuals embrace both innovation and adaptability to manage the complexities of the future of work.

Innovation is the cornerstone of progress, enabling the envisioning of better solutions to current and emerging challenges. As markets saturate and competition intensifies, the distinction between leaders and followers becomes evident. Leaders not only create new products but also cultivate innovative thinking rooted in fresh perspectives. They view challenges as opportunities to devise smarter ways of operating, adding value along the way.

However, innovation alone may not suffice. As Darwin astutely observed in his treatise on evolution, it is the most adaptable, not the strongest or most intelligent, that survive. This underscores the paramount importance of adaptability. Thriving businesses and individuals recognize change early, grasp its implications, and adapt swiftly. Adaptability complements innovation, acting as a crucial counterpoint. While innovation disrupts the status quo, adaptability ensures resilience when disruption occurs and a new order emerges.

The synergy between innovation and adaptability is paramount in the future of work. With AI, machine learning, and automation transforming jobs and business models, workers need adaptable mindsets and skills. It therefore follows that it pays to foster a culture of continuous learning where innovative thinking is the norm.

In essence, the future of work is not about predicting the next technological wave; it's about cultivating an ethos where innovation thrives and adaptability is ingrained. It's about gearing up for change with the creativity to innovate and the flexibility to adapt. Only then can businesses and individuals excel in the ever-evolving digital age.

AI Enabled Creativity: Authentic or Derivative?

I would argue that the notion of originality, in its essence, is rather problematic. Our creations, invariably, are built upon the ideas of others, a reality that pertains to both human and AI-driven creativity. While there may be a fine distinction in the sources of inspiration and the processes of creation, such distinctions often become less significant when the outcomes are indistinguishable.

Human creativity, rich in experiences, emotions, and choices, contrasts with AI's foundations in programming and data. Yet when their results are closely aligned, the nuances of the creative process may become secondary to the end result – a controversial view, I know, but one we need to debate.

In the realm of creative arts and design, the advent of AI marks a significant paradigm shift, redefining our traditional notions of creativity across various domains. This shift is characterized not merely by AI's capability in data analysis, but more profoundly, by its potential to synergize with human creativity, thus forging a new landscape of innovation and expression.

Architecture and AI: Redefining Spatial Design

In architecture, AI is not merely a tool for data analysis but a collaborator in design. It brings a new dimension to architectural creativity by processing vast datasets on urban planning, environmental sustainability, and historical design trends. This integration results in designs that are not only aesthetically revolutionary but also deeply responsive to modern urban challenges and environmental considerations. AI in architecture is thus fostering a new design language, one that interweaves the precision of data with the intuition of human creativity.

Poetry and AI: Expanding the Boundaries of Expression

The interplay of AI and poetry is a fascinating exploration of how technology can enhance human expression. While the essence of poetry lies in human experience and emotion, AI introduces novel linguistic structures and thematic possibilities. This collaboration does not dilute the poet's voice; instead, it enriches it, offering poets a broader canvas for exploration and expression. AI in poetry represents a symbiosis where technology amplifies human creativity, leading to new forms and depths of poetic expression.

Literature and AI: Crafting New Narratives

In the domain of literature, AI emerges as a partner in storytelling. It assists authors with narrative analysis, character development, and plot generation. Far from replacing the writer's imagination, AI enriches it, allowing for narratives that blend timeless human experiences with contemporary perspectives. This collaboration opens new horizons in storytelling, where the fusion of AI insights and human creativity results in rich, multifaceted narratives.

AI and Originality: Reimagining Creation

The integration of AI in creative domains brings forth a nuanced debate on originality. AI-generated art and literature, which often remix existing works, challenge traditional concepts of originality. Are these AI creations truly novel, or are they advanced iterations of pre-existing ideas? The answer lies in acknowledging the complementary roles of human and AI creativity. As AI technology evolves, it is redefining our perception of originality, suggesting a dynamic interplay between human creativity and technological innovation.

Originality in the AI Era: A Philosophical Perspective

The concept of originality in the AI era transcends simple binaries. Originality is not solely about novel creation but is a continuum that includes reinterpretation and recombination of existing ideas. This holds true for both human and AI-driven creativity. AI's ability to process extensive data and generate unique insights, when combined with human intuition and experience, paves the way for innovations that push the boundaries of what is considered 'original.'

Therefore, it becomes clear that AI-enabled creativity in architecture, literature, and poetry represents a fusion of human artistic expression and technological innovation. It challenges us to rethink our understanding of creativity and originality, opening doors to uncharted territories of artistic and literary expression. As we embrace this fusion, we enter a new era of creativity, one that is richly layered and endlessly evolving.

AI in Business Model Innovation

The role of AI in business model innovation parallels its transformative impact in creative domains. Beyond just enhancing product development, AI reshapes the entire landscape of customer experiences and business strategies. It opens doors to novel revenue streams, innovative partnership models, and untapped market niches.

AI-driven data analysis, predictive modeling, and generative techniques are at the forefront of redefining products, services, customer interactions, and digital platforms. These tools offer businesses a powerful means to reinvent their business models, revealing opportunities that were previously obscured. But as companies navigate this terrain, they must carefully infuse their innovations with a commitment to social responsibility and ethical integrity. This would ensure broad and equitable access to the benefits of AI - leveraging it not just for profit but as a catalyst for inclusive and responsible growth.

Implications for Business

The reevaluation of what constitutes originality in the AI era indicates a strategic shift for businesses. It's no longer just about birthing entirely new ideas; instead, there's immense value in creatively adapting and reimagining existing concepts, with AI acting as a collaborative partner. This evolution redefines originality as a collaborative innovation process, where human creativity synergizes with AI's analytical prowess.

In this context, businesses should broaden their innovation lens. It's essential to recognize that true innovation often arises not merely from novel ideas but from the creative adaptation or extension of existing ones. Here, AI emerges as a pivotal collaborator, providing alternative and even fresh perspectives and augmenting human thought processes. The focus shifts from an obsession with 'pure' originality and creativity to the practical outcomes and impacts of innovation. After all, the pursuit of innovation is less about the singularity of an idea's origin and more about its transformative potential and application.

This paradigm shift requires a new approach to innovation strategies. It's about embracing a model where originality is seen as a collective endeavor - a blend of human insight, AI analysis, and shared vision. For business leaders, this means steering their organizations towards an integrated approach to innovation. This approach should be ethical, socially conscious, and reflective of the collaborative potential between human ingenuity and AI capabilities.

Ultimately, this shift represents a significant opportunity for businesses to harness AI not just as a tool for efficiency but as a catalyst for meaningful and impactful innovation. By fostering this collaborative interplay, businesses can unlock new dimensions of creativity and drive forward-thinking strategies in an increasingly complex and interconnected world.

AI-Enhanced Systemic Innovation

It is worth reiterating here that AI is not just a tool; it's a transformative force redefining how industries operate and evolve. Merging human intuition with sophisticated data analysis, AI is reshaping ideation, design, sustainability, and the democratization of innovation. Let's further explore how AI is revolutionizing these key processes.

Data-Driven Creativity in Ideation

AI's integration into ideation marks a significant shift, moving from a sole dependence on human intuition to a powerful synergy of creativity and data analysis. In sectors like healthcare, AI's sophisticated data analysis tools are pivotal in uncovering complex disease patterns, thereby fast-tracking the development of innovative treatments. In consumer-centric industries such as fashion and electronics, AI's predictive analytics afford businesses the ability to anticipate market trends and consumer preferences with unprecedented accuracy.

In the fashion sector, AI is revolutionizing trend prediction and market analysis, reshaping how brands cater to consumer tastes. A notable example is Heuritech, a leading AI tool in fashion analytics. By parsing through millions of images on social media, the company can pinpoint emerging fashion trends as they unfold. Their analysis extends beyond basic elements like color or style, exploring the nuances of patterns, textures, and even the emotions associated with various fashion elements.

The management implications of this are profound. It leads to a significant diminution in the unpredictability traditionally associated with product development, resulting in collections that are more attuned to trending preferences. This foresight helps mitigate overproduction but also heightens the relevance of their brands in the market – helping align production more closely with actual market demand.

Revolutionizing Design with Rapid Prototyping

In sectors such as automotive and aerospace engineering, AI is revolutionizing design processes through rapid prototyping. Generative design AI tools automatically generate numerous design alternatives, optimizing for performance, safety, and cost-efficiency, thereby enabling faster, more creative problem-solving.

In the automotive industry, the adoption of Autodesk's generative design software illustrates the revolutionary impact of AI in design and manufacturing. This technology enables designers to input design goals along with parameters such as materials, manufacturing methods, and cost constraints. The AI then explores all possible permutations of a solution, quickly generating design alternatives. This process was vividly demonstrated in General Motors' collaboration with Autodesk, where they developed a new, lightweight seat bracket. The AI-generated design was not only more robust but also significantly lighter than the traditional design, consisting of a single part instead of eight. This innovation translates to a reduction in material waste, manufacturing time, and overall vehicle weight, contributing to greater fuel efficiency and reduced carbon emissions.

Promoting Sustainability with AI

AI is also a key driver in sustainable innovation. It aids industries in optimizing resource usage and minimizing environmental impact. From enhancing renewable energy systems to revolutionizing precision agriculture, AI is pivotal in promoting ecological sustainability.

In the realm of agriculture, AI-driven precision farming is revolutionizing how resources are utilized. Companies like John Deere are at the forefront of this transformation. Using AI and machine learning, their systems analyze data from various sources, including satellite imagery, weather forecasts, and soil sensors. This data enables farmers to make informed decisions about planting, irrigation, and harvesting. AI algorithms can predict the optimal planting density, determine the precise amount of water and nutrients needed, and even identify pest threats. This precision in farming not only boosts crop yields but also significantly reduces water usage, fertilizer costs, and environmental impact. It's a prime example of how AI can contribute to sustainable practices while also enhancing productivity and profitability in agriculture.

Democratizing Innovation through AI

AI is democratizing the innovation process by making advanced tools accessible to smaller businesses and startups. This levels the playing field, allowing diverse voices to contribute to the innovation landscape. Open-source AI platforms and collaborative initiatives are essential in creating a more inclusive ecosystem.

The democratization of innovation through AI is exemplified by platforms like TensorFlow and IBM Watson. These open-source frameworks provide small businesses and startups access to powerful AI tools that were once the exclusive domain of tech giants. For instance, a small e-commerce startup can now use AI to personalize shopping experiences, analyze customer data, and optimize supply chains with the same sophistication as larger companies. TensorFlow's open-source libraries enable these startups to build and train machine learning models tailored to their specific needs, leveling the playing field in technological innovation. This democratization extends innovation opportunities to a broader spectrum of the economy, stimulating growth, creativity, and competitiveness across various sectors.

As we consider these transformative roles of AI, let's examine two case studies – Toyota and Wolfram Alpha – that exemplify innovative approaches blending traditional methods with AI, demonstrating how computational intelligence synergizes with human creativity to forge new paths in innovation.

CASE STUDY 1:
TOYOTA

Toyota's response to the oil crisis of the 1970s is a classic example of turning adversity into opportunity. Amidst rising oil prices and a shift in consumer preferences towards fuel-efficient vehicles, Toyota was already a step ahead. Their foresight in developing fuel-efficient cars since the 1960s, culminating in the launch of the Corolla in 1973, positioned them perfectly to capture the market. The Corolla's success, driven by its fuel efficiency, durability, and affordability, is a testament to Toyota's innovative spirit and deep understanding of consumer needs.

At the core of Toyota's success is its pioneering Toyota Production System, which has become a global standard in Lean Manufacturing. However, Toyota's innovation philosophy extends beyond manufacturing efficiencies. It's a balanced approach that combines the excitement of new discoveries with the reliability of time-tested practices. This philosophy is evident in Toyota's commitment to continuous improvement and respect for proven methodologies, ensuring that each innovation is both groundbreaking and rooted in practicality.

Genchi Genbutsu and Monozukuri

Two key principles underpin Toyota's innovative approach: *Genchi Genbutsu* and *Monozukuri*. *Genchi Genbutsu*, which translates to "go and see for yourself," is about understanding problems firsthand and making decisions based on deep, personal insight. This principle encourages a culture of direct engagement and problem-solving at the source, leading to more effective and sustainable solutions.

Monozukuri, on the other hand, is about the art of making things. It's a philosophy that values the process of creation as much as the final product. This approach is deeply ingrained in Toyota's DNA, driving a passion for craftsmanship and a relentless pursuit of perfection in every aspect of their work.

Toyota's product line, including the trailblazing Prius and ventures into electric and hydrogen fuel cell vehicles, alongside its ongoing refinement of combustion engines, showcases a company adept at merging tradition with future-focused innovation. This balanced approach ensures that Toyota remains at the forefront of the automotive industry, continually pushing the boundaries of what's possible while staying true to its foundational principles.

Embracing the Digital Age

In the rapidly evolving digital landscape, Toyota is not just a passive observer but an active participant. The company's significant investments in AI, robotics, and autonomous driving signal a commitment to leading the charge in technological innovation. The establishment of entities like the Toyota Research Institute and Toyota Connected is a clear indication that Toyota is poised to shape the future of mobility while staying grounded in its core values.

Highlight: Toyota's journey is a masterclass in balancing innovation with tradition. It serves as a powerful lesson for businesses in all sectors, demonstrating that true innovation is not about discarding the past but about harmoniously integrating proven fundamentals with forward-thinking enhancements.

CASE STUDY 2:
WOLFRAM ALPHA

Our second case study, Wolfram Alpha, presents a stark contrast to Toyota's approach, showcasing the cutting-edge application of AI in the realm of computational knowledge and information processing.

Launched in 2009 by scientist-entrepreneur Stephen Wolfram, Wolfram Alpha is not your typical search engine. It stands apart in its ability to compute answers to a wide range of queries directly from structured data. This unique positioning allows it to provide computational responses across various domains, from mathematics and science to cultural references, making it a versatile tool in numerous fields.

The Power of Symbolic AI

At the heart of Wolfram Alpha's capabilities is its use of symbolic AI, a form of AI that emulates human cognition by representing knowledge through structured symbols and rules. This approach allows the company to process and analyze information in a way that mimics human logical reasoning, leading to precise and contextually relevant answers.

Wolfram Alpha and ChatGPT

The collaboration between Wolfram Alpha and ChatGPT marks a significant milestone in AI development. While ChatGPT excels in generating human-like text based on statistical patterns, it often lacks factual accuracy. Wolfram Alpha fills this gap with its symbolic AI foundation, ensuring computational and factual soundness.

Wolfram Alpha Pro's business model caters to professionals and academics with advanced computational and analytical tools, now enhanced by ChatGPT's natural language capabilities. API Integration opens up new possibilities for developers to leverage the combined strengths of Wolfram Alpha's computational accuracy and ChatGPT's linguistic fluency. An API, or Application Programming Interface, is a set of defined rules that enable different applications to communicate with each other. It acts as an intermediary layer that processes data transfers between systems, letting companies open their application data and functionality to external third-party developers, business partners, and internal departments within their companies.

This integration allows developers to create applications that can perform complex computations and provide natural language explanations. The definitions and protocols within an API help businesses connect the many different applications they use in day-to-day operations, which saves employees time and breaks down silos that hinder collaboration and innovation.

For developers, API documentation provides the interface for communication between applications, simplifying application integration. Educational initiatives also benefit from this partnership, offering students and educators complex computational outputs in an accessible format, bridging the gap between intricate calculations and comprehension. Commercial collaborations explore new frontiers, combining Wolfram Alpha's rigorous computation with natural language interaction to enhance user engagement across various industries.

Highlight: The collaboration between Wolfram Alpha and ChatGPT represents a groundbreaking milestone in the evolution of artificial intelligence. By seamlessly integrating computational prowess and accuracy with natural language processing capabilities, this partnership has revolutionized the way we interact with and utilize AI.

CHAPTER 10:
EVOLVING ORGANIZATIONAL ARCHITECTURES

In the ever-evolving domain of work, shaped by rapid technological advancements and dynamic market shifts, the importance of organizational design has never been more pivotal. This concept encompasses the methodologies and models used by organizations to structure and manage their workforce, processes, and resources to achieve their objectives. Within this broad and multifaceted interplay of actions, organizational architectures play a crucial role.

Organizational design involves creating a structure that aligns with and supports the organization's strategy and goals. In contrast, organizational architecture refers to the underlying framework or blueprint that shapes structures, processes, and culture. Often termed the "invisible organization," it may not always be overtly visible or explicitly defined, yet it is instrumental in establishing a robust and consistent foundation that underpins long-term organizational success.

It's important to note that structure is just one facet of organizational design. Equally critical are other elements such as management processes, measurement systems, and incentives, all of which contribute to the overall efficacy of the organization.

A foundational model that offers valuable insights into these complexities is McKinsey's "7 S" Framework (see Figure 14). It provides a robust basis for organizational analysis, highlighting both the hard and soft elements that influence an organization's effectiveness.

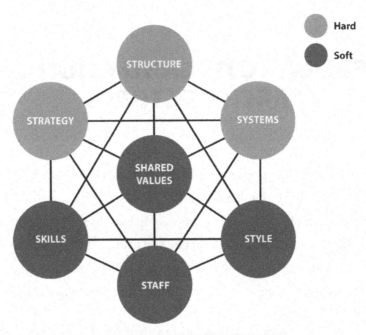

FIGURE 14: MCKINSEY'S "7 S" MODEL

Strategy: The organization's long-term goals and the plan to achieve a competitive market advantage, encompassing decisions about resource allocation, market positioning, and approaches to competition and collaboration.

Structure: The arrangement of the organization, including hierarchy, communication channels, and the distribution of roles and responsibilities.

Systems: The formal and informal procedures that govern daily activities, from workflows and information systems to management processes.

Shared Values: The core principles, beliefs, and philosophies that underpin the organization's culture, acting as a unifying force for behavior and decision-making.

Skills: The capabilities and competencies of the organization's employees, essential for executing strategies and achieving goals.

Style: The leadership approach of top management and the organization's overall operating style, influencing interactions with employees and shaping organizational culture.

Staff: The employees and their general capabilities, focusing on how the organization invests in its workforce through recruitment, training, development, and motivation.

In dissecting McKinsey's 7S Framework, it's crucial to distinguish between its 'hard' and 'soft' elements. The hard elements, comprising Strategy, Structure, and Systems, are often considered easier to identify, define, and manage. They represent the tangible, concrete aspects of an organization that can be directly influenced and altered. In contrast, the soft elements – Shared Values, Skills, Style, and Staff – are less tangible and more influenced by culture. These elements are more challenging to change and require a nuanced approach, as they are deeply rooted in the organization's ethos and employee behaviors.

Understanding these seven dimensions, and the distinction between soft and hard elements, is vital for analyzing an organization's ability to successfully implement its strategy. What is more, a thorough understanding underscores the interconnectedness of these elements, suggesting that changes in one area can significantly impact others. For example, a shift in strategy may necessitate adjustments in structure and systems and could also affect the organization's culture and staff management.

Thus, McKinsey's model serves as an insightful starting point for understanding how organizational architecture integrates into the broader context of organizational design, paving the way for a deeper exploration of an organization's interdependent design elements.

The Evolution of Organizational Design

In the pre-digital era, organizational architectures were predominantly hierarchical, emphasizing clear chains of command and specialized roles. This structure was well-suited to the industrial age, where efficiency and predictability were paramount. But the advent of digital technology and the rise of artificial intelligence (AI) ushered in a new paradigm. The once-reliable hierarchical model became increasingly challenged by the need for more fluid, dynamic, and adaptable organizational forms.

This chapter delves into the evolution of organizational architectures, examining the factors driving this transformation and the emerging practices enabling organizations to thrive in the digital age. We will explore the traditional role of hierarchies, their benefits and limitations, and how the integration of AI and digital technologies is reshaping the very fabric of organizational design.

Our journey will take us through the insights of renowned theorists like Henry Mintzberg and Jay R. Galbraith, whose work provides a foundational understanding of organizational structures, and how these are being reinterpreted and reconfigured in today's fast-paced, technology-driven business environment.

As we explore this organizational challenge, we will uncover the imperative for organizations to evolve beyond traditional models. The future of work demands architectures that are not only responsive to technological advancements but also conducive to fostering innovation, agility, and a deeper engagement with the digital ecosystem.

This chapter examines the evolution of organizational architectures, exploring the factors driving this transformation and the emerging practices that allow organizations to thrive in the digital age. It aims to provide perspective on crafting architectures suited for the future of work.

The Legacy of Hierarchies

Hierarchy is a concept that transcends human institutions, finding its roots in the natural world. It is evident in various species, from the highly organized colonies of ants and bees to the defined social structures of lions and baboons. In nature, hierarchies serve crucial functions: they impose order, enable coordination, and are essential for the survival of these groups.

Similarly, in human organizations, hierarchies play a vital role. They enhance coordination, facilitate efficient resource allocation, and contribute to the survival and success of the organization. Complexity theory suggests an intriguing paradox: complex systems, often bolstered by hierarchical structures, can be more resilient and adaptable than their simpler counterparts. These systems possess the ability to self-organize and respond dynamically to changing conditions, with hierarchies providing the necessary structure and order to enhance their effectiveness.

Consider the example of multinational conglomerates like General Electric, with their global operations spanning diverse business units. The hierarchical structure within such organizations, including the division of labor and established management processes, is fundamental to their efficient decision-making and operational effectiveness. Similarly, military organizations like the army, renowned for their large-scale logistical operations, rely on a hierarchical command system to implement strategies and deploy resources effectively.

Complexity theory underscores that hierarchies are instrumental in enabling complex systems to self-organize and adeptly adapt in response to fluctuating environments. They align activities toward common goals, facilitating agility and reconfiguration, which are crucial in the volatile world we inhabit.

However, hierarchies are not without their limitations. They can lead to a narrow concentration of power, engender cronyism, and create barriers to necessary change. Yet when applied judiciously, hierarchies can act as vital scaffolding for managing intricate organizations and coordinating complex workflows.

The suitability of hierarchical structures is influenced by factors such as an organization's size, industry, culture, and strategic goals. While recent criticisms of hierarchies focus on their potential to perpetuate societal power imbalances and exploitation, this perspective may overlook their nuances. Hierarchies, arguably, are ethically neutral frameworks; their impact is contingent upon how they are structured and utilized. This ongoing debate highlights the complexity and enduring relevance of hierarchical systems in organizing human activity.

Key Structural Lenses

The academic literature on contemporary organizational design, particularly relevant for organizations navigating technological change, is enriched by the contributions of seminal thinkers who laid the groundwork in understanding organizational structures and dynamics.

Jay R. Galbraith's 1973 "Star Model" is foundational in this discourse. It underscores the interdependence of key organizational elements: structure, strategy, technology, people, and rewards. Each point of the star represents a critical aspect of the organization that must be aligned for optimal performance (see Figure 15). His model emphasizes the necessity of a holistic approach in organizational design, a perspective that saw widespread adoption among management scholars.

STRATEGY

STRUCTURE

ORGANIZATION

PEOPLE

BUSINESS PROCESSES

REWARD SYSTEMS

FIGURE 15: GALBRAITH'S STAR MODEL

Henry Mintzberg's research (Mintzberg, 1979) significantly enhanced our comprehension of organizational structuring by identifying five core organizational structures. Each is characterized by distinct features such as centralization, specialization, and formalization levels.

These structures are:

Simple Structure: Often found in small businesses or startups, this structure is characterized by low specialization and formalization with central decision-making, typically under a single leader. It's flexible but can be limited by its reliance on a few key individuals.

Machine Bureaucracy: Common in large, established organizations, this structure is highly formalized and specialized. It operates through standardized procedures and routines, with tasks often performed by lower-level employees, while decision-making is centralized at the top. This structure is efficient for routine tasks but can be inflexible and slow to adapt to change.

Professional Bureaucracy: Found in professional organizations like hospitals or law firms, this structure relies on highly trained professionals who require minimal supervision. Decision-making is decentralized, allowing professionals autonomy in their work, but the organization overall is bound by standard procedures and protocols.

Divisionalized Form: This structure is typical in large corporations with diverse product lines or markets. It consists of semi-autonomous units or divisions, each with its own machine bureaucracy. While each division operates independently, the central headquarters maintains control over financial and strategic decisions. This form allows for specialization in different markets or product areas but can lead to duplication of efforts across divisions.

Adhocracy: Suited to dynamic, innovative industries like technology or media, adhocracy emphasizes flexibility and adaptability. It features a low level of formalization, decentralized decision-making, and a reliance on expert teams that form and disband as needed. This structure fosters creativity and quick responses to changing environments but can suffer from a lack of clear procedures and decision-making authority.

Mintzberg's framework is instrumental in understanding how organizational structures align with an organization's strategy and environment. This becomes increasingly relevant as AI and digital technologies reshape organizational strategies and operational landscapes, demanding structures that can adapt to rapid technological advancements and changing market dynamics.

Building on these foundations, David Nadler and Michael Tushman's 1988 'congruence model' introduced a critical evolution in organizational theory. While Mintzberg focused on structural typologies and Galbraith on the interplay of organizational elements, Nadler and Tushman emphasized the synergy between an organization's structure, strategy, culture, and people for optimal effectiveness. Congruence, in this context, refers to the alignment and compatibility of these elements, ensuring that they work together seamlessly.

This congruence is especially crucial in an AI-driven work environment, where technological integration demands the seamless alignment of these elements. Their model not only highlighted the importance of this alignment for achieving organizational goals but also provided practical tools, such as surveys, interviews, and organizational chart analysis, for diagnosing and rectifying misalignments.

Ensuring Architectural Congruence

At the heart of the Congruence Model is the principle that these elements must not only be individually effective but also consistent with one another. This congruence ensures that the organization functions like a well-oiled machine, with each part complementing and supporting the others.

The first element, tasks, refers to the actual work carried out within the organization. This encompasses everything from daily routines to long-term strategic objectives. The essence of the model lies in understanding how these tasks align with the organization's broader goals. It prompts a deep dive into whether the tasks are structured effectively to meet these goals and how they interact with other elements of the organization.

People, the second element, are the lifeblood of any organization. The Congruence Model underscores the importance of aligning the skills, roles, and values of individuals with the organizational objectives. It's about ensuring that the workforce is not only competent but also motivated and engaged, with their personal goals resonating with the organization's mission.

The third element, structure, pertains to the formal organizational arrangements. This includes the hierarchy, communication channels, departmentalization, and other systemic aspects. The model advocates for a structure that not only supports the efficient completion of tasks but also harmonizes with the people and culture of the organization.

Lastly, culture, often considered the most elusive element, represents the underlying values, beliefs, and norms that permeate an organization. The model places culture at the forefront, recognizing its powerful influence on all other elements. It's about ensuring that the culture supports and is supported by the tasks, people, and structure, creating an environment where each aspect of the organization reinforces the others.

The beauty of the framework lies in its holistic approach. For instance, a change in organizational structure, such as a shift to a more decentralized approach, not only impacts the flow of communication and decision-making (tasks) but also requires a reassessment of the roles and skills of employees (people) and may necessitate a cultural shift to embrace more autonomy and risk-taking.

In applying the congruence principle, organizations often embark on a process of careful analysis and self-reflection - examining each element, assessing its effectiveness, and then looking at the degree of congruence between them. The goal is to identify areas where misalignment occurs and to develop strategies to bring these elements back into alignment.

In essence, the Congruence Model serves as a compass for organizations navigating the complex waters of effectiveness and efficiency – by aligning tasks, people, structure, and culture. This helps ensure that the organization's architectural design is not just robust on paper but also effective in practice.

Complexities & Challenges

As we probe deeper into the intricacies of the Congruence Model, it's imperative to acknowledge the challenges and limitations inherent in its application,
particularly in the context of the rapidly evolving business landscape of today.
The model, while robust in its foundational principles, encounters certain
hurdles when faced with the dynamism and unpredictability of modern
organizational environments.

One of the most significant challenges lies in the model's adaptability to
fast-paced changes. In industries where shifts happen at lightning speed, the
pursuit of congruence, with its emphasis on alignment and stability, might
inadvertently hinder the agility and responsiveness crucial for staying ahead.
This is particularly evident in global organizations, where the complexity
of operating across diverse cultural, regulatory, and business landscapes
can make the achievement of congruence a daunting task. The model, thus,
must be applied with a nuanced understanding of these diverse contexts,
balancing the need for internal alignment with the realities of a globalized
business environment.

Moreover, the quest for congruence could potentially lead to a certain rigidity,
making it challenging for organizations to maintain the flexibility needed to
adapt to market shifts, technological advancements, or evolving consumer
behaviors. This balance – or perhaps, tension – between congruence and flexibility is a delicate dance that requires constant recalibration and reassessment.

But that is not all. With its focus on internal alignment, the quest for congruence might lead organizations to inadvertently overlook external factors. In
a world where external disruptions – be it from competition, market trends,
or technological innovations – are the norm, an overemphasis on internal
congruence can result in a myopic view, potentially limiting an organization's
ability to navigate and respond to these external forces effectively.

Looking towards the future, striving for congruence is poised for an evolutionary leap. As organizations increasingly integrate advanced technologies like AI and machine learning, the model must evolve to encapsulate these new dimensions. This evolution will involve not only understanding how technology impacts the alignment of organizational elements but also how it can be harnessed to enhance decision-making and operational efficiency.

The concept of dynamic congruence is likely to gain prominence – as managers recognize the need for more fluid forms of achieving alignment; where organizations are capable of rapidly rebalancing their elements in response to external changes.

Additionally, the rise of remote and hybrid work models presents new frontiers. The challenge here is to maintain alignment and coherence in increasingly dispersed and digital work environments, a task that requires innovative approaches to communication, collaboration, and culture-building.

Lastly, the future application of structural alignment will likely intertwine closely with sustainability and social responsibility. Organizations will be called upon to align their strategies, structures, and cultures not just with economic objectives but also with broader social and environmental goals.

In essence, the Congruence Model, while a powerful tool in understanding and enhancing organizational effectiveness, must continually evolve and adapt. It needs to embrace the complexities and fluidities of the modern business world, ensuring that it remains relevant and effective through the plethora of challenges that define our times.

Principles Guiding Organizational Transformation

As we explore further the reconfiguration of organizational architectures for the AI era, it's essential to acknowledge the guiding principles that underpin this transformative journey. These principles are pivotal in reshaping enterprises to harness AI's potential fully, ensuring they are agile, data-centric, and innovation-driven.

Data Integration as the Backbone: At the heart of this transformation is establishing a robust data integration system. Centralizing a data repository is critical. It amalgamates customer, operational, and market data from varied sources, forming the bedrock for AI systems to produce precise and actionable insights. This integration goes beyond mere collection; it's about creating a cohesive data ecosystem that fuels all AI-driven initiatives.

Data Governance: The Pillar of Trust and Quality: Effective data governance is the cornerstone of reliable data integration. It encompasses policies and protocols that uphold data quality, security, and ethical usage. A strong governance framework not only safeguards data integrity but also ensures compliance with evolving regulatory landscapes. It balances the need for open data access with stringent privacy and security measures, fostering trust and responsible AI deployment.

AI Infrastructure: Building the Foundation for Innovation: Essential to any AI-powered transformation is the establishment of a comprehensive AI infrastructure. This foundation extends beyond mere technological components to encompass the human element - the talent that innovates and operationalizes AI solutions. Scalability and flexibility are key; the infrastructure must support an array of AI applications, adapting fluidly as technological paradigms shift.

Culture Change: Nurturing a Data-Driven Mindset: The linchpin in this transformative process is the cultivation of a culture change. Transitioning to a data-driven enterprise requires more than technological adoption; it demands an organizational culture that endorses data as a critical decision-making tool. This cultural shift encourages cross-departmental collaboration and empowers employees to leverage AI for innovation and efficiency. It's about embedding a mindset that embraces continuous learning and adaptation in the face of AI-induced changes.

In tandem with these guiding principles, the very architecture of organizations is evolving. This evolution is characterized by a strategic reimagining of decision-making processes, collaborative dynamics, and structural designs to align with the opportunities and challenges of an AI-driven business landscape. The goal is to foster organizations that are not only technologically advanced but also agile, interconnected, and proficient at leveraging AI for strategic advantage. This reconfiguration seeks to create an enterprise architecture that is responsive to rapid market changes, cultivates innovation, and thrives on data intelligence, setting a new standard for organizational excellence in the digital age.

Emerging Organizational Architectures

As the architectural fabric of organizations undergoes significant transformation, a strategic reimagining of decision-making processes, collaborative dynamics, and structural designs becomes imperative. This transformation aims to create organizations that are more responsive, interconnected, and adept at navigating the complexities of an AI-driven era.

Traditionally, organizational hierarchies have been linear, characterized by clear, top-down authority. However, rethinking organizational architectures requires a nuanced understanding of non-linear, or intransitive, hierarchies. While most social systems, including human organizations, traditionally conform to a linear hierarchy, research suggests that alternative structures, such as the inverse pyramid or diamond shape, are increasingly relevant in certain contexts (Wellman et al., 2020). These alternative forms offer a more flexible approach to hierarchical design, accommodating varying numbers of components at each level and allowing for a dynamic distribution of authority and responsibility.

The study of emergent hierarchies in animal social structures, as explored by Hobson and DeDeo (2015), provides valuable insights into the complexity of organizational systems. In animal societies, hierarchies often emerge organically from the interactions of individual members, rather than being imposed from above. This emergent nature of animal hierarchies can shed light on how human organizations might similarly develop and adapt their structures. In these systems, hierarchy is not a rigid ladder of command, but a fluid and responsive network, shaped by the needs, behaviors, and interactions of its members.

Understanding the mechanisms behind animal social hierarchies can illuminate the potential for human organizations to develop adaptive and responsive structures, capable of evolving in response to internal and external changes. Just as animal groups reorganize their social structures in response to environmental challenges and opportunities, we can learn to adapt our hierarchical models to better meet the demands of a rapidly changing social environment. This perspective encourages a view of organizational hierarchies as living systems, capable of growth, adaptation, and resilience, much like their counterparts in the natural world.

Therefore, flexibility in organizational design is not just about the distribution of authority; it reflects a deeper understanding of how order, whether formal or emergent, establishes norms and expectations that guide actions within an organization. Such order is intrinsically tied to the ranking of components within a hierarchy, influencing everything from decision-making processes to collaborative dynamics.

In this context, hierarchy necessitates a balance between order and adaptability. The order can be formal, akin to the reporting structure of a business, or informal and emergent, similar to the dominance hierarchies that naturally arise in animal groups. This understanding of hierarchical structures underscores the need for organizational systems that are not only structured but also flexible and responsive to the dynamic demands of a modern, interconnected business environment.

Central to this transformation is the shift towards decentralized decision-making. Empowering individuals at all levels with real-time data and AI-driven insights fosters agility and responsiveness, essential in today's fast-paced business environment. This move away from traditional top-down hierarchies is complemented by the rise of cross-functional collaboration. Modern organizational structures are breaking down departmental silos, fostering holistic problem-solving and innovation that extend beyond internal operations to include external stakeholders.

Networked structures are becoming a defining feature of contemporary organizational design. In this interconnected setup, organizations are part of a broader ecosystem that includes partners, suppliers, and customers. This model balances the clarity of traditional hierarchies with the fluidity of more open, decentralized models, adapting swiftly to market shifts, consumer demands, and global trends.

Integrating AI into organizational structures is reshaping resource allocation and task automation, enhancing human talent for complex and creative endeavors. AI's predictive capabilities enable proactive and strategic decision-making. However, this integration presents challenges, including the need for a robust data strategy that ensures ethical and responsible AI use.

Navigating these changes underscores the need for a new architectural approach in today's complex business environment. This approach involves rethinking organizational structures and operations, creating adaptable, resilient systems where decision-making is decentralized yet strategically coherent, and innovation is integral to the organizational ethos.

In this dynamic landscape, leaders evolve from traditional managers to architects of fluid, responsive systems. They must navigate the intricacies of AI integration and harness its potential to drive organizational success, shaping structures that are efficient as well as ethically and socially attuned.

Bridging Gaps: Boundary Spanning

Leaders in this new era are not just managers of complexity but architects of change towards more fluid and networked structures. They are tasked with creating environments where control and innovation coexist and reinforce each other. This evolution signifies a shift towards systems that are resilient and adaptable, capable of responding swiftly to changes and seizing new opportunities.

To bridge gaps that arise amidst complexity and rapid change, boundary spanning has a vital function in today's large organizations. It serves as a bridge, linking diverse stakeholders and functions within an organization or even across different organizations, fostering collaboration and knowledge sharing.

Scholars such as Van de Ven (2007) have highlighted the instrumental role of boundary spanners as both informational gatekeepers and agents of transformative change. These individuals or teams can work across different departments, specialties, or organizations, facilitating communication and collaboration that might otherwise be hindered by silos. For example, companies like 3M and Apple have successfully utilized boundary spanners to drive innovation by encouraging the flow of ideas and insights across different parts of the organization.

These boundary spanners often possess unique skills in networking, negotiation, and cross-cultural communication, enabling them to interact with diverse groups and align them towards common goals. The effectiveness of boundary spanning, however, is contingent on several factors, including the skills of the boundary spanners, the supportiveness of the organizational culture, and the structural mechanisms in place to facilitate such interactions.

As organizations grow and become more complex, integrating the principles of boundary spanning into the fabric of organizational design becomes increasingly crucial. It helps prevent fragmentation and ensures that organizations can leverage the full spectrum of their resources and capabilities.

As we approach the end of this chapter, we turn our attention to two distinct case studies that illuminate the evolving landscape of organizational architectures. These studies not only highlight the transformative impact of AI on business structures but also demonstrate the varied approaches companies can take. We will first examine Alphabet (Google), a tech giant that restructured its operations to encourage innovation and agility. Following that, we will explore Haier, a company that underwent a radical transformation from a traditional hierarchy to a network of micro-enterprises.

CASE STUDY 1:
GOOGLE (ALPHABET)

In 2015, Alphabet Inc. emerged as a bold response to the burgeoning complexities and opportunities within Google. This restructuring was not merely administrative but represented a philosophical shift towards a conglomerate model where independence and innovation were paramount. Alphabet became a holding company for Google and its diverse ventures, such as Waymo's self-driving technology, Verily's health sciences, and DeepMind's AI research.

Detailed Structure and Impact:

Alphabet's structure allowed each 'Bet' to pursue its unique goals, fostering a startup-like agility within the umbrella of a corporate giant. This independence was crucial for attracting top talent and pursuing ambitious projects without the constraints of Google's broader business model. For example, Waymo could focus on long-term goals in autonomous vehicle technology, a field that demands considerable investment and a different risk profile compared to Google's core businesses.

Challenges and Responses:

However, this model also brought forth significant challenges. The autonomy of each 'Bet' sometimes led to strategic dissonance with Alphabet's overall vision. For instance, tensions within Google Cloud around strategic direction versus the broader corporate goals led to leadership changes, reflecting the complexities of balancing independence with strategic cohesion. Alphabet had to continuously refine its approach to ensure effective collaboration and resource allocation across its diverse portfolio, all while maintaining a unified strategic direction.

Highlights: Alphabet's transition to a decentralized model underlines the necessity of organizational agility in the rapidly evolving tech industry. It showcases how large corporations can foster a culture of innovation and risk-taking, akin to startups, while navigating the challenges of strategic alignment and operational coherence. Alphabet stands as a pioneering example of how a tech giant can adapt to the demands of advancing technology, particularly in AI, by embracing a flexible and decentralized organizational structure.

CASE STUDY 2:
HAIER

Haier's transformation journey is a compelling narrative of a traditional company's evolution into a pioneering decentralized organization. Initially a typical hierarchical conglomerate, Haier confronted the limitations of this structure in the early 2000s, particularly its impact on innovation and responsiveness.

Transformation into Micro-Enterprises:

Under CEO Zhang Ruimin's leadership, Haier dismantled its conventional hierarchy, replacing it with a radical model of micro-enterprises. Each unit operated like an independent startup, with the freedom to innovate and respond to market needs rapidly. This approach was revolutionary in that it distributed decision-making power to frontline employees, who were closer to market dynamics and customer needs. For instance, one micro-enterprise might focus exclusively on a niche market segment, developing tailored products much faster than a traditional, centralized R&D department could.

Technological Integration and Cultural Shift:
To facilitate this complex structure, Haier invested
heavily in sophisticated IT systems, enabling seamless
communication and data sharing across micro-enterprises. Additionally, Haier's internal market system for
talent, resources, and ideas encouraged a dynamic
and competitive environment, fostering collaboration and innovation. Culturally, this shift required a
significant change in mindset, from a top-down command model to a more collaborative and entrepreneurial approach. Leadership roles transformed from
being directive to supportive, focusing on empowering employees and facilitating resource access.

Highlights: Haier's journey from a hierarchical conglomerate to a network of entrepreneurial micro-enterprises demonstrates the transformative power
of decentralization in fostering innovation, agility,
and market responsiveness. This case study is a vivid
illustration of how flattening organizational structures can unleash creativity and rapid response to
market changes, aligning employee initiatives with
overarching corporate goals. Haier's model serves
as an inspiring blueprint for companies seeking to
reinvent themselves in an era of rapid technological
and market evolution.

CHAPTER 11:
COMPLEXITY & ADAPTIVE SYSTEMS

The tectonic shifts in the nature of work, fueled by technological, demographic, and social megatrends explored in Chapter 4, have significantly increased complexity for modern organizations. Exponential advances in AI and automation, as discussed in Chapter 5, further contribute to this complexity. The dismantling of traditional organizational structures and the rise of dynamic, skills-based work arrangements, covered in Chapters 6-9, inject additional fluidity and uncertainty into the business environment. Additionally, as highlighted in our previous chapter, the rapid pace of disruption and innovation places intense competitive pressures on firms, compelling them to operate with increased agility and adaptability.

In this intricate and interconnected environment, linear models of work and rigid corporate structures are increasingly inadequate. Business leaders must now embrace systems thinking and complexity theory, offering more suitable mental models to navigate today's complex adaptive landscapes.

The Nature of Complexity

Complexity in the modern work environment arises from the intricate interplay between diverse factors influencing work's evolution. Technology's impact extends beyond isolated operations, permeating organizational culture and management strategy. Modern organizations face a myriad of complex challenges, such as managing global supply chains and fostering innovation through cross-functional, remote collaborations.

Traditional reductionist approaches, which seek clear cause-effect relationships, struggle to address such multidimensional challenges. In a complex system, the dynamic interaction of numerous variables obscures predictability and makes isolating individual factors challenging. This interconnectedness, while fostering innovation, also introduces novel risks, demanding adaptive frameworks to navigate the unpredictability inherent in complex, networked environments.

Entropy and Organizational Resilience

You may recall your physics lessons on the subject of entropy and the second law of thermodynamics. This law states that entropy, as a measure of disorder or randomness in a system, will always increase over time, meaning that the universe is constantly moving towards disorder. This principle is easily understood when considering the inevitable tendency of ordered systems to fall into disarray, decay, wear down, or deteriorate over time. It takes an input of energy from outside the system and real work to reverse such thermodynamic processes and restore the system to a functional state.

As a physical law, the second law of thermodynamics has profound philosophical and practical implications for understanding the natural world. But it can also serve as a potent metaphor to illuminate the state in which human organizations and institutions find themselves, faced with a socioeconomic context in a constant state of flux. The natural tendency of institutions in such circumstances would be to accumulate 'entropy' – becoming more dysfunctional as their environment changes and previously robust models of operation are disrupted by new technology or superior competition.

Faced with these challenges, the second law tells us that attempting to remain static in the face of such forces is to embrace stagnation and irrelevance. Through proactive efforts and strategic dynamism, organizations can adapt to external pressures and avoid becoming obsolete. Such actions are an expected and necessary aspect of operating in a dynamic and evolving environment, just as nature is subject to the second law.

In addition, the analogy helps us understand which kinds of systems might be more resistant to 'entropic forces', and can guide us in creating organizations better able to weather the storm. Physical systems that rely on rigidity and strict ordering of their component parts, such as solid bodies, are most vulnerable to the slow decay mandated by thermodynamics. It takes comparatively little external pressure to greatly increase their entropy and trigger a collapse. On the other hand, more flexible systems, such as gases or liquids, can undergo great disruption of form without an increase in entropy. Flexibility and adaptiveness are thus not simply bonuses, but are, in the long run, absolutely vital to the survival of any system, when viewed in light of the inevitability of entropic pressure.

It's of course crucial to recognize the limitations of using entropy as a metaphor in the context of human social systems. In any physical system, reducing disorder involves transferring entropy to a neighboring system, resulting in a net increase in entropy overall. However, if an institution responds to change by adapting in ways that harm a number of external stakeholders — essentially externalizing the costs of adaptation — it acts in a societally undesirable manner.

Unlike mindless processes governed by the laws of thermodynamics, our organizations are formed and operated by intelligent agents that engage in deliberate action. To survive and prosper, they must confront the challenges of a changing environment in an ethical and socially conscious way.

Relating entropy to AI-driven organizational change can be a useful metaphorical lens, yet it has its limits, as do all metaphors. While the rapid growth in AI capabilities seems boundless, it inevitably faces (at least in the short term) some practical constraints like data availability, algorithmic efficiency, and computing power limitations. These barriers, unlike the immutable second law, represent the natural boundaries encountered by any technological system.

To overcome these constraints, organizations must prioritize innovation by developing more efficient algorithms and pioneering new methods for data collection and processing – thus enabling them to adapt and prosper over time. Remember, while metaphors can guide and enrich our understanding, they should not be stretched beyond their intended scope.

Complexity Drivers and Adaptability

The introduction of new technologies is a key driver of complexity, necessitating organizational adaptability. Yet technology alone does not encapsulate the entirety of rising complexity. Forces such as globalization, shifting consumer behaviors, and regulatory challenges weave a web of continuously evolving dynamics. Thriving in this environment requires organizations to foster adaptability in their systems, operations, and workforce.

Some companies have risen to the challenge. Indian conglomerate Tata Group operates over 100 companies across industries like steel, automobiles, and consulting. To enable collaboration and adaptation across its diverse businesses, Tata pioneered an internal Business Excellence Model to systematically share best practices. This aids companies under the Tata umbrella in quickly adopting proven solutions for improving processes and products.

Another sector grappling with rising complexity is healthcare. Narayana Health, one of India's largest hospital chains, understood that effectively serving patients required adapting care delivery models. They developed robust telemedicine and virtual care capabilities to increase accessibility and affordability. During the pandemic, these systems allowed Narayana to rapidly transition to virtual consultations and monitoring. This demonstrated the merits of an adaptive approach in the healthcare sector.

These cases highlight the importance of adaptability across various sectors in managing complexity. Both Tata and Narayana Health have transitioned from rigid structures to agile, adaptive frameworks.

Insights from Neuroscience

Our understanding of complexity gains depth from breakthroughs in neuroscience research. For example, leading neuroscientist Karl Friston's 'free energy principle' posits that the brain functions as a 'prediction machine,' consistently refining its internal model of the world to minimize surprise and uncertainty (Friston, 2017). This concept resonates with the idea of complex adaptive systems, wherein agents continuously interact with and adapt to their environment to reduce uncertainty. It also parallels the functioning of emerging AI systems, which train neural networks through prediction-error minimization, albeit the brain's mechanisms are far more sophisticated.

Indeed, traditional organizational theories, primarily based on mechanical models, are inadequate for grasping the subtleties of modern business dynamics. In contrast, systems thinking and complexity theory, drawing inspiration from natural processes like the brain's hugely intricate mechanisms for managing complexity, provide more nuanced and effective frameworks for navigating environments marked by uncertainty and rapid change.

Systems Theory and Complex Adaptive Systems

Complexity theory and chaos theory, originating in the natural sciences, shed light on the behavior of contemporary organizations. These theories underscore the unpredictable yet patterned nature of complex systems, where minor alterations can precipitate significant outcomes. In this view, organizations are intricate ecosystems, where departments, teams, technologies, and external factors continuously interact, influencing the organization's direction.

The Boston Consulting Group's 2023 report, 'A New Architecture to Manage Data Costs and Complexity,' delves into the escalating complexity in business, particularly concerning data management. It reveals a critical challenge faced by organizations: managing the exponential growth in data volumes and the rapid innovation in data technologies. The report projects a compound annual growth rate of 21% in data volumes from 2021 to 2024, resulting in an estimated 149 Zettabytes by 2024. This burgeoning volume and velocity of data represent a 'perfect storm' of complexity, impacting both analytics and AI initiatives.

Furthermore, the report highlights two emerging trends in the data landscape. Firstly, the rise of "citizen data scientists," facilitated by open, accessible architectures, empowers more individuals to engage in self-service analytics and explore specialized data use cases. Secondly, advancements in data technologies are transforming data economics. The ability to apply computing across various storage formats and locations is granting architectural freedom and reducing costs.

In response to these insights, this chapter emphasizes the importance of adaptive systems in the workplace. These systems, designed to be flexible and resilient, seek to harness the positive aspects of complexity while mitigating its challenges. Organizations are encouraged to draw inspiration from nature's adaptability, as seen in species like the Arctic fox and the chameleon, which demonstrate agility in the face of environmental shifts. Emulating these natural examples, organizations can adopt a services-oriented architecture that enhances flexibility and accessibility, empowering both business and technical users to thrive amidst these complex data landscapes.

In physics, a phase transition, driven by thermodynamic forces, seeks to maximize a system's entropy, marking a shift to a more optimal state. Similarly, in a social context, a transition from rigid structures to more flexible, decentralized ones can unleash efficiency and dynamism. These organizational 'phase transitions' are often precipitated by new technologies or changing market conditions, leading to significant structural and cultural shifts. Such transitions offer organizations opportunities to renew themselves, adapt, and enhance their resilience.

My own interest in the systems perspective was first sparked by a lecture I attended decades ago by MIT Professor Peter Senge, the acclaimed author of 'The Fifth Discipline: The Art and Practice of the Learning Organization.'

In his lecture, Dr. Senge employed the metaphor of a tree to elucidate the process of knowledge creation within an organization. He likened the underlying theories that sustain an organization to the roots of a tree and compared the branches to the methods and tools that translate these theories into practical outcomes. He also drew a parallel between the process of photosynthesis and the dissemination of theories throughout an organization, ultimately leading to the 'fruit' of applied knowledge. The insights gained from this lecture continue to shape my understanding of successful organizational functioning.

As we explore complex adaptive systems, we recognize organizations as networks of interconnected agents, each contributing to emergent properties that surpass the sum of individual parts. Netflix's success in the entertainment industry, for example, isn't just due to a single decision or feature but is the cumulative effect of numerous decisions and interactions, both internal and external.

Applying the concept of 'emergence' to organizations requires a nuanced approach, recognizing the complex interplay of motivations, strategies, and unintended consequences. Managing complexity in this context goes beyond simple cause-and-effect; it involves understanding the intricate interactions leading to emergent outcomes.

From a management science perspective, what is needed are practical strategies for managing complex adaptive systems, deriving insight from cases of organizations that have successfully navigated these challenges. Indeed, we need to consider ways to leverage complexity as an opportunity: how understanding and harnessing it can be a considerable strategic advantage.

Balancing Complexity and Adaptability

Modern business management necessitates a nuanced balance between embracing complexity and seeking predictability. Having previously examined the intricate nature of organizations and their multifaceted components, we now shift our focus to the critical role of adaptability in this dynamic landscape.

In an era characterized by profound interconnectedness, rapid technological advancements, and fluid organizational boundaries, adaptability is imperative. A prime example of this is Netflix's transformation from a DVD rental service to a leading streaming platform and content creator. This evolution illustrates adaptability not just in technology, but also in business strategy and understanding market dynamics.

Adaptability, however, transcends technological evolution. Our professional landscapes and the networks we engage in have undergone significant transformation, evolving into expansive, collaborative networks that defy traditional organizational and industry boundaries.

Take Apple's comprehensive ecosystem as an instance. This ecosystem, comprising hardware, software, and services, represents a strategic approach to multidimensional adaptability. Apple's evolution from primarily a personal computer company to offering a diverse array of interconnected devices and services—encompassing smartphones, tablets, wearables, and content streaming—demonstrates keen responsiveness to consumer behaviors and market trends.

More than diversifying products, Apple's adaptability lies in creating a cohesive, evolving user experience that anticipates and aligns with customer needs and technological shifts. Apple's success is rooted in its ability to continually innovate and adapt its business model, ensuring each component of its ecosystem synergizes, setting a standard in harmonizing complexity with adaptability.

But how do we define 'adaptability' in an organizational context, and what role does it play in navigating complexity while striving for predictability?

Adaptability in an organization manifests as agility, resilience, and a relentless drive for innovation. Amazon's expansion into various sectors, from cloud computing to smart home devices, underscores this adaptability. Alexa, Amazon's voice assistant, is a testament to this, evolving continuously to enhance its capabilities through constant learning and adaptation.

However, adaptability doesn't arise spontaneously or in isolation, as highlighted in our discussions. It emerges from complex interactions among diverse stakeholders, especially in rapidly changing environments. The key to effectively managing these interactions lies in the strength of cohesive teams and collaborative networks, which are fundamental in modern workspaces.

Considering the pivotal role of teams, the structure and development of these teams become crucial. Google's focus on team-based collaboration and innovation is a stellar example. These high-performing teams, essential to adaptive systems, excel in collaboration, communication, and continuous learning, equipping them to navigate the intricate layers of complexity proficiently.

In the following section, we probe deeper into fostering adaptive systems within organizations. Navigating our highly interconnected world requires a sophisticated understanding of complexity, coupled with a pursuit of predictability. Achieving this balance, though challenging, is crucial for the sustained success of any organization.

The Anatomy of Adaptive Organizations

As previously argued, the traditional perspective of organizations as predictable, mechanistic systems has become increasingly outdated amid rapid change and the resulting fluidity. The paradigms that formerly anchored organizational structures, with their focus on efficiency and compliance, now find it challenging to keep up in a world marked by globalization, digital transformation, and rapid technological advancement. Emerging in response is a new archetype of organization, one that is adaptable, agile, and human-centric, recognizing the importance of innovation and ingenuity. Companies such as Automattic, Basecamp, and Spotify are emblematic of this evolutionary shift.

In the current fluid and fast-paced business climate, the ability to adapt and pivot rapidly distinguishes leading organizations. But what precisely characterizes these adaptive entities? Let's delve into the defining features that set them apart.

Empowerment from the Ground Up

Adaptive organizations differ in that authority isn't confined to the upper echelons. Here, decision-making power is diffused across the organization, empowering individuals at every level. This decentralization boosts agility and fosters a sense of ownership and responsibility among staff. However, it's crucial to maintain a degree of structured oversight through a distributed hierarchy to prevent chaos.

Team Autonomy & Distributed Hierarchies

Empowering teams with the autonomy to operate independently cultivates an environment ripe for creativity and innovation. This level of freedom often leads to groundbreaking ideas that might be suppressed in more rigid settings.

The concept of "flat hierarchy" is commonly mentioned, but it's more accurate to describe these organizations as having distributed hierarchies. This model facilitates faster communication and decision-making while maintaining necessary organizational structure.

Navigating Hierarchical Complexity

In fostering adaptive organizations, it's vital to understand and manage the complexities of hierarchical structures. The traditional pyramid-shaped hierarchy is evolving into dynamic, flexible models. Such alternative structures, like the inverse pyramid, have significant implications on team dynamics and performance, especially in environments with a variety of tasks. This concept is further explored in our chapter on organizational architectures, where we discuss the strategic use of different hierarchical models to boost adaptability and responsiveness.

Learning, Feedback Loops and Agility

Commitment to continuous learning and flexibility is a hallmark of adaptive organizations. They implement strong feedback mechanisms, integrating learnings from both successes and failures into their operational ethos.

Open communication fosters trust and collaboration. By sharing information openly, these organizations break down silos and promote collective problem-solving. They offer flexibility to adapt to the changing dynamics of work, ensuring they meet diverse needs and lifestyles. Digital enablement is a key component, enhancing human capabilities and optimizing processes.

Iteration: Small Steps, Big Changes

Embracing an iterative approach, adaptive organizations make gradual, continuous improvements based on feedback and results. Initiatives like Netflix's 'Netflix University' exemplify their commitment to ongoing learning and staying at the innovation forefront. They maintain fluidity in their structures, with approaches like Haier's 'micro-enterprise' model highlighting the importance of organizational design flexibility.

Utilizing digital tools and platforms, such as Adobe's cloud-based model, these organizations enhance their agility and responsiveness. They foster a culture that values and rewards innovation, ensuring a steady flow of new ideas. Leading these organizations are resilient leaders, adept at steering their teams through challenging times and keeping the organization on track.

Building adaptive organizations is, therefore, a continuous process, requiring ongoing adjustments to align with the ever-evolving external environment. With the principles outlined above, organizations are better equipped to navigate the complex landscape of today's business world, positioning themselves as relevant, resilient, and future-ready.

To illustrate these concepts with a real-world instance, let's examine the case of Walmart, which exhibits many of the adaptive organization characteristics we have just discussed.

CASE STUDY 1:
WALMART

For an illustrative example of an adaptive system, we look no further than Walmart, a multinational retail titan. Despite facing numerous challenges such as the digital revolution, evolving consumer behaviors, fierce competition, and global economic shifts, Walmart has not only survived but thrived. The key to their success? Their ability to adapt and adjust in response to these external forces, reflecting the robustness of an adaptive, agile system.

Central to the company's strategic adaptation was harnessing technology and data analytics to refine its operations and supply chain management. At the heart of this transformation was their advanced logistics system. This system tracks every item in its inventory, and with data analytics, it can predict customer demand trends. Real-time inventory management streamlined efficiency and made Walmart's supply chain highly responsive to customer needs.

Further, the company's leadership revolutionized in-store operations by equipping associates with handheld devices that access the company's centralized database in real-time. This not only improved customer service but also increased employee productivity and job satisfaction, reinforcing Walmart's adaptive and agile system.

Walmart's focus on people and fostering collaboration is another vital facet of its adaptive strategy. Emphasizing intrinsic motivation, the company provided employees with autonomy and helped them find meaning in their work. By fostering a collaborative culture, they built a sense of community and shared purpose, enabling effective responses to changing market dynamics.

The company's commitment to continuous learning and skill development, evident in initiatives like the Walmart Academy, further augmented the adaptability of their workforce. They understood that for the company to stay ahead, their employees needed to constantly learn and improve.

Finally, Walmart recognized the benefits of a diverse workforce. By implementing initiatives aimed at attracting and retaining a broad range of talents, they fostered innovation and adaptability. This included targeted recruitment programs and employee resource groups to support the career development and engagement of diverse employees.

Our case study offers valuable insights into how organizations can build and nurture adaptive systems to flourish in a complex and rapidly evolving environment. It shows us that the goal isn't to sidestep complexity but to understand it, embrace it, and leverage it.

In addition to human organizations, we can look to nature itself for insights on complex adaptive systems. The human immune system provides a compelling biological example, displaying the key properties of decentralized coordination, emergent intelligence, and adaptive resilience

CASE STUDY 2:
THE HUMAN IMMUNE SYSTEM

The human immune system stands as a testament to nature's brilliance, embodying the principles of complex adaptive systems. Rather than just a defense mechanism, it is a dynamic, evolving network that exhibits adaptability, resilience, and intelligence.

For example, neutrophils immediately migrate to sites of infection and ingest invading bacteria through phagocytosis. Macrophages detect pathogens and produce chemokines to recruit more neutrophils to the site. Different types of lymphocytes, including T cells (T lymphocytes) and B cells (B lymphocytes), adapt to recognize specific pathogens and activate long-lasting immunity.

The coordination of these varied responses minimizes collateral damage and maximizes efficiency.

Components and Coordination: The immune system consists of a symphony of cells, tissues, and organs, each playing a distinct role. Key components include white blood cells such as T cells and B cells, the thymus, bone marrow, and the lymphatic system. These parts communicate, collaborate, and coordinate responses to perceived threats.

Learning and Memory: One remarkable capability of the immune system is its immunological memory. When it first encounters a pathogen, it not only defends against it but also retains information about it. This memory, mediated largely by memory cells, enables a faster and more robust response if the same pathogen attacks again in the future.

Self-Organization and Emergence: The immune system's responses emerge from complex interactions between its components rather than a centralized command. For example, when a wound occurs, platelets spontaneously rush to clot the wound, leukocytes identify and target invading microbes, and healing processes activate - all in a self-organized manner.

Challenges and Future Directions

While remarkably agile, the immune system must overcome novel threats and maintain equilibrium. Globalization and environmental changes introduce new pathogens that the system has never encountered before, like emerging flu strains or viruses. Yet its inherent adaptability often allows it to recognize and combat even these unfamiliar invaders, albeit after an initial adjustment period.

In autoimmune diseases such as multiple sclerosis and type 1 diabetes, the immune system falters, incorrectly identifying healthy cells as foreign threats and attacking itself. This self-targeting damages organs and tissues in complex and sometimes unpredictable ways. For instance, in multiple sclerosis, the myelin sheath protecting nerve fibers becomes the target of aberrant immune activity, leading to neurological impacts.

Research continues to seek ways to accurately diagnose, predict progression, and hopefully cure autoimmune disorders. Promising areas include studying genetic factors, environmental triggers, the microbiome's role, and potential therapies that can precisely calibrate the immune response.

Highlight: The human immune system, with its intricacy and adaptability, offers important lessons about complex adaptive networks. The difficulties it encounters reveal the delicate equilibrium these systems must maintain. Meanwhile, its capabilities showcase the tremendous potential of decentralized, self-organizing systems. As we study complexity in other domains, the immune system remains an excellent model of nature's ingenuity, providing insights that can guide future research.

CHAPTER 12:
THE SUSTAINABILITY IMPERATIVE

In the modern business environment, sustainability has emerged as a dominant and increasingly significant theme. Amidst the challenges of the digital age, a societal shift towards sustainability is reshaping both organizational and societal priorities in response to environmental degradation and climate change.

As we transition from an age of relentless growth to an era of responsible progress, we encounter significant challenges and complex trade-offs. It's becoming increasingly evident that sacrificing environmental and societal welfare for narrow economic progress is no longer viable. Instead, there's a pressing need to integrate these aspects, forging a sustainable future for us and our progeny.

The 'Moloch' Metaphor

Historically, business practices have been driven by growth and profit, primarily to benefit shareholders. However, this perspective can be myopic. The logic of capitalism, while difficult to reshape, especially from the vantage point of a manager in an organization, necessitates a more comprehensive approach to decision-making and trade-offs.

Allen Ginsberg, in his 1956 poem "Howl," portrays Moloch as a monstrous entity devouring everything in its path, a metaphor for the destructive nature of unchecked growth. Moloch, symbolizing the ruthlessness of industrial society, consumes the youth for the enrichment of the present generation, epitomizing the disregard for future consequences in the pursuit of immediate gain.

Ginsberg's allegory warns of the perils of uncontrolled capitalism, where market forces dictate resource allocation. It's a poignant reminder that the pursuit of profit must not override human life and environmental sustainability.

Recent decades have underscored the necessity of balancing economic growth with environmental protection to secure a sustainable future. This evolving mindset recognizes the dangers of toxic incentives leading to "multipolar traps."

Understanding Multipolar Traps

A multipolar trap arises when competitive pressures in one area compel others to either engage in similar practices or face obsolescence. These dynamics, often seen as zero-sum or negative-sum games, can drive entities into a detrimental race to the bottom, prioritizing survival over collective advancement.

Avoiding these traps requires aligning incentives toward mutual benefits and a realignment of collective priorities. Moving away from a sole focus on individual profit to emphasize collective well-being is crucial. It also involves creating new institutions and frameworks capable of navigating the complexities of a multipolar world.

Advocating for Sustainable Thinking

Sustainable thinking proponents like Liv Boeree and Daniel Schmachtenberger advocate for a shift from narrow profit objectives. Their perspectives reinforce the call for a future that moves beyond multipolar traps to collaborative, positive-sum games. In such a scenario, the collective good, including the welfare of future generations, is prioritized over individual gains.

This chapter argues for a paradigm shift in how businesses operate and make decisions. Embracing sustainable practices isn't just about ecological responsibility; it's a strategic necessity that encompasses economic, social, and environmental dimensions. As we delve deeper into the intricacies of sustainable business models, we will explore how organizations can transition to these models while maintaining viability and competitiveness.

Transitions to Sustainable Practices

As we delve into the pursuit of sustainability, it becomes clear that it demands both philosophical shifts and concrete actions from organizations. To understand how this manifests in practice, let's look at how leading companies are embedding sustainability into their organizational frameworks.

Supply Chain: Consider IKEA's initiative to use only renewable, recyclable, or recycled materials by 2030. This ambitious goal necessitates a complete overhaul of their sourcing and production processes, reflecting a deep commitment to sustainable practices that extend throughout the supply chain.

Operations: Microsoft has taken a proactive approach by implementing an internal carbon tax. This initiative aims to reduce emissions not just within the company but also across its extensive supply chain. Such measures illustrate how operational changes can have far-reaching impacts on sustainability.

Marketing: Marketing plays a pivotal role in communicating a company's sustainability commitments. For instance, Patagonia's advocacy initiatives are not just marketing campaigns; they are integral to the brand's identity and mission. These campaigns align with the purpose of promoting environmental stewardship, reflecting a commitment that goes beyond traditional corporate social responsibility.

Transparency and Reporting: Unilever's approach to transparency is also noteworthy. By openly reporting on both the progress and challenges of its sustainability initiatives, Unilever sets a standard for corporate accountability. Their annual sustainability reports provide stakeholders with a clear view of the company's efforts and setbacks, fostering trust and credibility.

These examples demonstrate that embedding sustainability goes beyond ethical sourcing and greener operations. It involves aligning branding with the organization's core values and purpose, which, in these cases, is deeply intertwined with sustainable practices. This shift aims to reconcile profit with broader societal and environmental responsibilities, signifying a departure from unbridled growth to responsible progression. It's about adopting a new paradigm where sustainable development becomes integral to business strategy, shaping a future where economic success and environmental stewardship are not mutually exclusive but mutually reinforcing.

Technology and Organizational Sustainability

Technology holds tremendous potential to enable organizations to adopt sustainability practices. But technology alone is not sufficient; we must ensure new corporate governance models align with ecological and social well-being.

Sustainability represents a commitment to the future and balanced resource use even in metropolises. As work evolves aided by technology, it must be rooted in this commitment. For example, remote work enabled by digital

THE FUTURE OF WORK: MANAGING IN THE AGE OF AI

tools is not just a trend but a means to reduce environmental footprints while giving workers more flexibility.

Emerging technologies also allow new approaches to ingrain sustainability:

- AI and automation can optimize supply chains to eliminate waste, as Amazon has done in its fulfillment centers.

- Blockchain enables traceability for ethical sourcing and transparency across supply chains.

- Digital platforms facilitate open models like crowdsourcing to collaboratively innovate for sustainability solutions.

In essence, technology can enhance organizations' sustainability efforts, but cannot be a cure-all. With mindfulness, technology and sustainability can work in synergy, improving ecosystems and society, provided that there is a genuine shift in corporate mindsets and priorities. Not just lip service and slogans!

At the end of the day, a critical question arises: how can we ensure that these technological advancements, especially in the world of work, align with our environment's delicate balance and societal needs while maintaining economic competitiveness? Is a modest recalibration enough?

Sustainability is not just a buzzword; it is a commitment to the future. It represents a balance between environmental care, societal prosperity, and equitable resource distribution. As work paradigms evolve, they must be rooted in this commitment. The rise of remote work is an example of a conscious step towards ecological responsibility, reducing carbon footprints and conserving resources.

Societal Value Shift and Business

The growing emphasis on sustainability is transforming the essence of organizations and the nature of entrepreneurship. As societal values evolve to prioritize social and sustainable objectives, the business world must adapt in kind. This evolution affects how opportunities are identified and pursued, the dynamics of competition and collaboration, and the sharing of knowledge on sustainable practices.

Entrepreneurship, traditionally a catalyst for economic growth, is now pivotal in driving this societal value shift. While 'Environmental, Social, and Governance' (ESG) priorities gain traction, challenges arise from the broad scope of objectives encompassed by ESG. Measuring sustainability, inherently multi-dimensional, calls for a balanced set of metrics that integrate economic, social, and environmental outcomes.

Historically, market-driven institutions have prioritized economic growth for shareholder value. Now, there's an increasing demand for governments to balance economic objectives with social and ecological goals, thereby intensifying state involvement in entrepreneurial and corporate activities. This shift has significant implications for the workplace, compelling organizations to align with these evolving priorities while maintaining business viability and innovation.

Sustainability and the future of work are intertwined narratives of human evolution. As we progress, we are tasked with a dual mandate: fostering economic development while safeguarding our planet and future generations' wellbeing.

Through exploring the interplay of trends and innovations, the symbiotic relationships among these elements become evident. This complex interplay invites further exploration, offering insights into the evolving landscape of work.

Organization-Level Actions

Sustainability must transition from a peripheral agenda item to a core element of business strategy, reflecting organizations' broader responsibilities to society and the environment. This requires a fundamental shift in mindset, urging leaders to balance profit motives with environmental and social welfare.

Key imperatives for managers guiding this transition include:

Walk the Talk: Executives and managers must embody sustainability in their actions. This involves prioritizing ESG goals, inspiring the workforce through communicated values, and being accountable for sustainable progress.

Strategic Integration: Sustainability should be interwoven with core business strategy, identifying intersections between ecological and social aims and business objectives to create synergy rather than conflicts.

Innovation: Prioritizing resources and frameworks for sustainability innovation, including R&D focused on circular economy principles, and setting ambitious goals to encourage disruptive thinking.

Technology Readiness: Utilizing technologies like AI, blockchain, and analytics to enhance supply chain efficiency, minimize waste, enable transparency, and monitor sustainability metrics in real-time.

Stakeholder Engagement: Maintaining open dialogue with all stakeholders, regularly seeking their feedback to refine ESG efforts and address concerns.

Performance Integration: Embedding concrete sustainability metrics into organizational dashboards, KPIs, performance reviews, and decision-making processes to establish clear goals and accountability.

Examples of companies successfully navigating this transition include Patagonia, Microsoft, IKEA, and Unilever. Patagonia, known for its environmental commitment, has embedded sustainable practices into its core operations, from material sourcing to carbon neutrality goals.

Microsoft has set an example by leveraging technology to reduce emissions across its operations and supply chain, while IKEA's business model aligns with circular economy principles. Unilever's Sustainable Living Plan exemplifies stakeholder engagement and transparency in sustainability efforts.

These cases illustrate that with committed leadership, strategic alignment, innovation, and stakeholder engagement, companies can lead their industries towards a sustainable future. It requires rethinking traditional business assumptions, success measures, and the role of business in society.

Instilling a Sustainability Mindset

In this transformative era, the role of managers has evolved significantly, now encompassing responsibilities that extend far beyond traditional management paradigms. They are now pivotal advocates for green technology, champions of remote work, and cultivators of sustainability awareness among employees. Understanding the economic nuances of these shifts, from harnessing potential tax incentives for sustainable practices to leveraging the competitive advantage of eco-friendly branding, positions managers to spearhead impactful and lasting sustainable changes.

To seamlessly integrate sustainability into workplace practices, a variety of specific strategies can be employed. These include:

Energy Consumption:

- Transitioning to energy-efficient lighting, such as LED bulbs.
- Upgrading to energy-efficient appliances and office equipment.
- Installing motion sensors for automatic light control in unused spaces.

- Encouraging employees to be mindful of energy usage, like turning off lights.
- Conducting regular energy audits to identify inefficiencies.

Water Consumption:

- Installing water-saving fixtures, such as low-flow toilets and faucets.
- Promptly addressing any leaks to prevent wastage.
- Cultivating water conservation habits within the workforce.
- Exploring water recycling possibilities.

Waste Management:

- Establishing comprehensive recycling programs for various materials.
- Composting food waste.
- Encouraging the use of reusable items to decrease single-use plastics.
- Ensuring proper disposal of hazardous materials.

Transportation:

- Incentivizing public transport, carpooling, or biking.
- Providing electric vehicle charging stations.
- Supporting remote work options to reduce commuting emissions.

Sustainable Vendors:

- Selecting vendors based on their commitment to sustainability, prioritizing those using recycled materials or renewable energy sources.
- Supporting local businesses to minimize transportation emissions.

Education and Engagement:

- Educating employees and the community about sustainable practices.
- Offering training and regular updates on sustainability.
- Organizing events and workshops focused on sustainability.
- Encouraging active participation in green initiatives.

Measuring and Tracking Progress:

- Setting specific sustainability goals and monitoring progress through specialized software.
- Regularly communicating achievements and areas for improvement.
- Celebrating sustainability milestones to maintain momentum and engagement.

As we probe deeper into the significance of sustainability in the modern workplace, it becomes clear that organizations need to be both resilient and adaptable to navigate the challenges of the 21st century. The upcoming chapter will further explore the necessary structures and strategies for reimagining traditional organizational missions in light of evolving societal expectations and environmental as well as ethical considerations.

Before we proceed, let's examine two case studies that illuminate how pioneering organizations are embracing the sustainability imperative, overcoming challenges, and capitalizing on opportunities.

CASE STUDY 1:
RAINFOREST CONNECTION (RFCX)

In the heart of the Amazon rainforest, where lush greenery teems with life, a silent threat looms - illegal logging. This destructive practice, fueled by demand for timber and land for agriculture, is ravaging the rainforest's delicate ecosystem, releasing carbon dioxide and disrupting the delicate balance of life. In fact, deforestation accounts for 15% of greenhouse gas emissions, with illegal logging being a major contributor. Consequently, tackling this huge environmental problem requires real-time monitoring, which is resource intensive.

Enter Rainforest Connection (RFCx), a non-profit organization that has turned old smartphones into ingenious guardians of the rainforest. By repurposing these devices, RFCx has created a network of solar-powered "Guardian" devices that can detect the sounds of chainsaws and other equipment used in illegal logging.

These devices, deployed deep within the rainforest, analyze the sounds using cloud-based AI, sending instant alerts to authorities and local communities. This real-time monitoring has proven to be an effective deterrent against illegal logging, empowering communities to protect their ancestral lands and safeguard the precious rainforest.

Highlight: RFCx's innovative approach, combining the accessibility of discarded smartphones with the power of AI, has revolutionized rainforest monitoring. It has demonstrated how technology can be harnessed for sustainability, not just in terms of environmental impact but also in empowering local communities and fostering a sense of ownership over the rainforest's preservation.

CASE STUDY 2:
TESLA

Tesla, a titan in the realm of automotive innovation, epitomizes sustainability-oriented innovation, challenging conventional norms and spearheading the transition to a cleaner future. Founded with the ambitious mission to expedite the world's shift to sustainable energy, Tesla has been a transformative force in the auto industry, introducing electric vehicles, solar energy products, and energy storage solutions.

The company's ethos traces back to Nikola Tesla, the visionary inventor and engineer. Tesla's seminal contributions, particularly in the development of the electrical transformer – a device crucial for converting direct current (DC) to alternating current (AC) and vice versa – revolutionized the transmission of AC electricity over long distances with minimal energy loss. His inventions, including the induction motor and the Tesla coil, are cornerstones of modern electrical systems and were instrumental in society's electrification.

While Tesla's innovations were underappreciated during his lifetime, his legacy has continued to inspire. Elon Musk, Tesla's co-founder and CEO, is deeply influenced by Tesla's vision and commitment to sustainable energy. Musk envisaged electric vehicles as pivotal in transforming transportation and safeguarding the environment, propelling him to actualize Tesla's vision in the contemporary world.

Under Musk's leadership, Tesla has emerged as a disruptor in the automotive sector, challenging traditional incumbents and catalyzing innovation. Tesla's electric vehicles, including the Roadster, Model S, and Model 3, have redefined performance, technology, and design standards, dispelling the notion of EVs as mere niche products.

Beyond vehicles, Tesla's advancements in sustainable energy solutions are notable. Its solar panels and energy storage systems empower users to harness and store renewable energy, diminishing fossil fuel dependency. The company's vertically integrated model, spanning manufacturing to sales and service, optimizes both efficiency and affordability, making sustainable technology more accessible.

Tesla's influence transcends its product line. It has instigated a cultural shift towards electric mobility and sustainable energy, motivating other manufacturers and industries to adopt innovation and environmental stewardship. The unwavering commitment of Tesla's leadership to sustainability, coupled with their ability to turn vision into tangible reality, positions Tesla as an exemplar globally.

Highlight: Tesla's journey is a testament to the potency of innovation and the quest for a cleaner future. Although Nikola Tesla's pioneering work wasn't centered on sustainability in the modern sense, his groundbreaking approach to energy distribution and electrification aligns symbolically with Tesla Motors' objectives. Both Tesla the individual and Tesla the company exemplify the spirit of transcending conventional technologies to create new systems – a fitting parallel for the contemporary challenges of the sustainability era. Tesla, alongside Musk, illustrates that technology can be a formidable agent of positive change, reshaping industries and forging pathways for a sustainable, environmentally conscious future.

CHAPTER 13:

ETHICAL, DATA SECURITY AND GOVERNANCE FRONTIERS

In an era where sustainability transcends mere environmental conservation, its essence deeply intertwines with the realm of ethics. This fusion represents a commitment to making choices that not only protect our planet but also ensure that our actions today do not impair the well-being and opportunities of both current and future generations. As we venture into the realms of artificial intelligence (AI), particularly with the advent of Generative AI and Large Language Models (LLMs), this commitment challenges us to evaluate not only the ecological impacts of our actions but also their broader ethical and governance implications.

In the dynamic landscape of modern business management, the conversation around ethics, data security and governance is increasingly complex and multifaceted. Ethical considerations and fair practices, long-standing pillars of good business, now intersect with a relatively new yet critical dimension: data security and confidentiality. This chapter delves into these intertwined aspects, focusing particularly on the implications of the latest generative AI models for organizational management.

Today's organizational leaders find themselves navigating a dual challenge: making ethical decisions in a landscape complicated by AI and safeguarding sensitive information when data breaches and privacy violations are alarmingly common. The integration of AI into business processes has amplified these concerns. AI's capability to process vast amounts of data offers unprecedented insights but also poses significant risks. These risks include threats to data security, potential breaches of confidentiality, and the emergence of biased decisions that may lack the nuance or ethical considerations of human judgement.

Consider the example of a financial services firm employing AI for customer data analysis. While AI can process vast amounts of data with remarkable speed, bringing efficiency gains, the firm must carefully consider the potential risks. These risks go beyond the exposure of client financial information. There's also the concern that AI, in its current state, might not fully capture the subtleties that human experience and judgment bring to complex financial decisions. AI might overlook critical contextual factors or undervalue the non-quantifiable elements that seasoned financial experts consider. This gap between AI's capabilities and the nuanced decision-making that seasoned professionals provide is a crucial area of focus.

In such scenarios, the integration of AI into business processes demands a balanced approach. It's not just about harnessing AI's power for efficiency but also about complementing it with human insight and judgment. This balance is essential to ensure that decisions are not only data-driven but also ethically sound and aligned with the broader context and subtleties of human experience.

The trajectory of LLM adoption mirrors these challenges. Initially, these models found use in individual experimentation and exploration, with limited enterprise adoption as companies grappled with integrating them into existing workflows. Regulatory oversight, crucial in this context, began to be debated, but its development lagged behind the rapid technological advancements.

This lag in regulatory oversight underscores the urgent need for a proactive approach to AI governance. Governments, industry leaders, and AI platform developers must collaborate to bridge the gap between rapid technological innovation and the establishment of comprehensive regulatory frameworks. This collaboration is essential for fostering open dialogue, promoting transparency, and ensuring that ethical considerations and data security safeguards are integral to the development and deployment of AI technologies.

Such a shift necessitates a proactive approach to AI governance, where data security and confidentiality are not afterthoughts but foundational elements in the design and deployment of AI technologies. Organizations need to establish stringent protocols for data handling, access control, and incident response. For instance, the adoption of advanced encryption technologies and regular security audits can significantly mitigate the risk of data breaches.

Moreover, maintaining transparency and accountability is key to preserving stakeholder trust. This involves adhering to legal requirements and going beyond mere compliance to establish clear policies on data usage and privacy. For example, a healthcare provider using AI for patient diagnosis should implement explicit consent protocols and transparent data usage policies to maintain patient trust and confidentiality.

As AI becomes increasingly embedded in business operations, managers must navigate an environment where data security, confidentiality, and the ethical use of AI are deeply intertwined. This chapter aims to provide insights and strategies for effectively managing these challenges, ensuring that the integration of AI into business processes not only enhances operational efficiency but also upholds the highest standards of ethics and governance (see Figure 16).

LEVELS OF AI ADOPTION

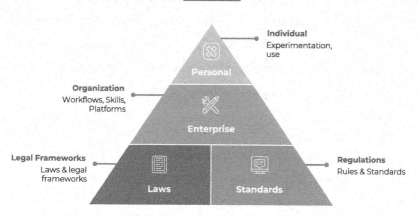

Individual
Experimentation, use

Organization
Workflows, Skills, Platforms

Legal Frameworks
Laws & legal frameworks

Regulations
Rules & Standards

Personal

Enterprise

Laws

Standards

FIGURE 16: LEVELS OF AI ADOPTION

At the individual level, AI ethics and governance touch on the direct impact of AI technologies on employees, customers, and other stakeholders. It involves considerations like personal data privacy, user consent, and the fairness of AI-driven decisions affecting individuals. For instance, consider the case of a major retail company that experienced a data breach due to vulnerabilities in its AI-powered customer recommendation system. The breach led to the unauthorized access of thousands of customers' personal data, including names, addresses, and purchase histories.

The breach resulted in a significant erosion of trust among the company's customer base and sparked widespread concern over the adequacy of data protection measures in AI systems more broadly. Such examples underscore the importance of robust data privacy protocols and highlight the potential consequences of their absence in AI applications.

At the organizational level, the focus shifts to how companies implement AI in alignment with their core values and ethical standards. This includes managing risks like algorithmic bias, ensuring transparency in AI operations, and safeguarding sensitive data, all while striving for efficiency and innovation.

A pertinent example is a leading financial institution that implemented an AI system for credit scoring. The AI model was initially praised for its efficiency but soon raised concerns due to inherent biases against certain demographic groups. This issue came to light when it was revealed that applicants from specific neighborhoods were disproportionately receiving lower credit scores, leading to accusations of digital redlining.

This incident prompted the financial institution to reevaluate its AI deployment strategy. It undertook a comprehensive review of its AI model, incorporating feedback from diverse stakeholder groups to identify and mitigate biases. The company also enhanced its transparency by publicly sharing its approach to AI-driven credit scoring, including the measures taken to ensure fairness. Furthermore, it established a dedicated ethics committee to oversee AI operations, ensuring ongoing alignment with ethical standards and core values.

This example demonstrates the multifaceted challenges organizations face when integrating AI into their operations. It highlights the importance of continuous monitoring and auditing of AI systems for biases, the need for transparency in AI decision-making processes, and the critical role of stakeholder engagement in upholding ethical standards. For organizations, it's not just about leveraging AI for business efficiency; it's equally about ensuring that these technologies are used in a manner that is fair, transparent, and aligned with the organization's ethical commitments.

The societal level encompasses the broader implications of AI on communities and societies at large. Here, the discussion centers not only on the immediate impacts of AI but also on the overarching frameworks that govern its development and deployment. This includes a critical examination of how regulation should be shaped, particularly the distinction between regulating AI products and the R&D processes behind them – a topic we shall further explore below. Such regulation is pivotal in addressing the challenges posed by AI, from ensuring safety and compliance to fostering ethical innovation. Later in the chapter, we explore how effective regulation at the societal level can balance the need for technological advancement with ethical and social responsibilities.

The discussion also extends to issues like the digital divide, the societal impacts of automation, and the role of AI in shaping public policy and social norms. The concentration of AI development in the hands of a few large private actors, as noted in Stanford University's Institute for Human-Centered Artificial Intelligence report issued in 2023, poses a significant challenge for governance and ethical oversight – not just adoption.

This concentration underscores the need for robust regulatory frameworks that can adapt to the rapid pace of AI innovation while ensuring that its benefits are distributed equitably across society. In the following sections, we will explore each of these levels in detail, examining the challenges and opportunities that AI presents. We will also discuss practical strategies for managers to implement effective governance within their organizations, ensuring that AI's immense potential is harnessed in a way that is beneficial and equitable for all stakeholders.

Ethical Frameworks in AI Governance

When considering issues related to AI governance within organizations, drawing upon various philosophical and ethical frameworks can enrich our understanding and approach. One such framework is Lawrence Kohlberg's theory of moral development. While originally developed with individual moral reasoning in mind, its principles can be adapted to the context of AI ethics in management.

Kohlberg's model outlines three levels of moral reasoning – preconventional, conventional, and postconventional. Applied to organizations, this framework offers a structured way to assess and enhance our approach to AI ethics.

Preconventional Level: At this stage, an organization's approach to AI ethics is primarily driven by compliance and self-interest. For example, a company might implement basic AI data security measures solely to avoid legal penalties or reputational damage, rather than out of a genuine commitment to user privacy. Decision-making at this level is often guided by a desire to avoid negative consequences rather than a proactive pursuit of ethical AI practices.

Conventional Level: Here, the organization begins aligning its AI practices with broader societal norms and industry standards. This could manifest in adopting widely recognized AI ethical guidelines or frameworks, and making decisions that are influenced by external expectations and the desire to maintain legitimacy. For instance, a company might enhance its AI systems to ensure greater fairness and transparency, not just for compliance, but to meet industry benchmarks and public expectations.

Postconventional Level: At this advanced stage, the organization adopts a principled approach to AI ethics, guided by values of justice and fairness. Decisions are made with a commitment to societal well-being and ethical progress, transcending legal compliance and industry norms. An example could be a company proactively seeking diverse stakeholder input to ensure its AI systems do not perpetuate societal biases and actively contribute to social good.

This perspective encourages organizations to evolve from a compliance-based approach to a more principled and proactive stance in their AI practices. It highlights the importance of moving beyond mere adherence to rules, towards embedding ethical considerations deeply into the fabric of AI decision-making processes.

Of course, this is just one framework among many we can draw on. Other ethical theories, such as utilitarianism, deontology, and virtue ethics, also offer valuable insights. Utilitarianism, for example, encourages actions that maximize overall well-being, which can guide decisions on AI deployment to ensure the greatest benefit. Deontology focuses on the inherent morality of actions, urging managers to consider the ethical nature of AI practices beyond their outcomes. Virtue ethics emphasizes the importance of moral character and virtues like honesty and empathy in decision-making processes.

These diverse ethical perspectives can offer useful lenses through which to view AI-related ethics and governance issues – as we face challenges around ensuring fairness, transparency, and accountability in AI systems. The ethical frameworks we adopt will shape not only how AI technologies are developed and deployed but also how they impact our workforce and society at large.

In the subsequent sections, we will explore these ethical dimensions in greater detail, examining how they manifest at the individual, organizational, and societal levels. This comprehensive approach will provide managers with a nuanced understanding of the ethical landscape in the era of AI, equipping them to make informed, responsible decisions in this rapidly evolving domain.

Great Potential, With Pitfalls

The transformative potential of Artificial Intelligence (AI) is undeniable. Its applications, ranging from healthcare innovations to sustainability efforts, hold the promise of significantly improving human lives and societies. In healthcare, AI's role in early disease detection and personalized treatment plans is groundbreaking. Its contributions to combating climate change through optimizing renewable energy systems and waste reduction are equally noteworthy. In the realm of arts, AI's ability to augment human creativity is opening new frontiers.

However, this remarkable potential comes with its own set of challenges and risks. As AI systems become more prevalent, issues such as algorithmic bias, transparency deficits, and the misuse of personal data emerge, necessitating vigilant governance. Public skepticism about AI's role in privacy and decision-making is growing, as evidenced by numerous surveys. The concentration of AI power in the hands of a few corporations and the widening digital divide are additional concerns that highlight the need for inclusive development of AI systems.

From a managerial standpoint, we must strike a delicate balance between maintaining ethical standards and keeping pace with the relentless competition within the AI sector. As corporations rush to capitalize on the benefits of emerging technologies, sticking firmly to principles of fairness, transparency and accountability can seem at odds with rapid prototyping and deployment. The recent incident involving OpenAI, where the CEO was temporarily ousted amid disagreements over the pace of development, epitomizes this tension.

Managers may face pressures from stakeholders and investors seeking swift returns on AI investments, making considerations around bias testing, auditing protocols and explainability mechanisms appear obstructionist. However, as incidents like Amazon's resume screening tool underscore, neglecting rigorous governance can severely impact public trust and social license to operate.

The dilemma exists in determining governance frameworks robust enough to align with ethical imperatives yet flexible enough to enable responsible innovation within competitive constraints. Striking this balance requires managers to take a principled stand, educating stakeholders on the value of ethical AI adoption and leading by example in prioritizing holistic, socially-conscious development.

Ethical Applications and Strategies

In the dynamic landscape of artificial intelligence, the interplay between technological innovation and ethical considerations is complex and multifaceted. AI's burgeoning potential for enhanced efficiency and deeper insights is accompanied by substantial ethical responsibilities. These responsibilities, incumbent upon both managers and developers, are integral to the advancement of technology. Navigating the ethical terrain of AI involves confronting real-world challenges and necessitates vigilant and informed governance.

In practical terms, strategies like data anonymization and regular audits are pivotal for maintaining ethical standards in AI deployment. This proactive stance in managing AI's ethical risks is essential for organizations to not only comply with regulatory frameworks but also to pioneer in responsible AI utilization. By incorporating these ethical practices, organizations can exploit AI's benefits while upholding ethical integrity and sustaining public trust.

Take the case of AI in the domain of recruitment. Here, AI's efficiency is shadowed by the risk of perpetuating historical biases. For instance, Amazon's AI recruitment tool, which was designed to identify top talent, inadvertently seemed to favor male candidates due to gender biases in its training data. This initial design flaw highlights the imperative for thorough auditing and careful application of AI in such critical organizational processes to ensure that societal biases do not inadvertently seep into them. This commitment to ethical AI practice, of course, should not be confined to recruitment alone. It should extend to other critical areas such as AI-driven performance evaluations, where similar risks of embedded biases can significantly impact fairness and objectivity.

Privacy, Trust, and Responsible Data Practices

The ethical scope of AI also spans privacy and trust. When personal data is involved in AI development, establishing trust necessitates stringent privacy safeguards and transparent data handling policies. Balancing the exploitation of data for AI's benefits with the protection of user privacy is critical. Strategies like anonymizing datasets, incorporating diverse training data, and conducting regular, human-supervised audits are key to mitigating risks and fostering trust. These practices are fundamental to responsible AI adoption.

Explainable AI (XAI)

The trustworthiness of AI systems also depends on their impartiality and explainability. XAI is vital for rendering AI decision-making processes transparent and comprehensible, a necessity for accountability, particularly in critical sectors like healthcare and finance.

For instance, XAI can clarify the decision-making process in medical imaging diagnoses, illustrating how AI detects disease indicators from MRI scan patterns. This ability to decode complex AI decisions, particularly in opaque models like deep learning neural networks, is an ethical cornerstone of XAI.

Consider a neural network as a structured system comprising layers that transform input data into meaningful outcomes (see Figure 17). An image input undergoes initial analysis in the first layer, detecting basic features like edges and colors. Subsequent layers conduct more intricate analyses, identifying complex patterns and textures. The final output, such as the detection of a medical condition, is a culmination of this layered processing. XAI sheds light on each stage of this process, elucidating how the AI systematically transforms raw inputs into final conclusions. Indeed, this transparency and traceability are essential for AI systems to be perceived as trustworthy and accountable.

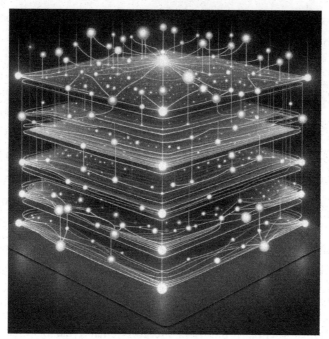

**FIGURE 17: NEURAL NETWORK ARCHITECTURE
(CREATED WITH THE ASSISTANCE OF DALL·E 2)**

As data progresses through the neural network's layers, the analysis becomes more nuanced, allowing the AI to discern intricate features and construct a comprehensive understanding of the input. In the terminal layer, it formulates a decision or prediction, like identifying disease indicators in a medical scan.

Without XAI, this multilayered process can appear enigmatic. XAI plays a critical role in demystifying each step, mapping how raw inputs are methodically processed into final conclusions. This clarity not only aids in detecting and correcting biases but also ensures fairness. When an AI system exhibits bias, XAI can identify the specific data or model components at fault.

Furthermore, XAI enables informed consent in significant applications, like medical diagnosis, by empowering users to understand AI reasoning and make educated decisions about its use. In essence, XAI underpins accountability and trust in AI systems, making it an indispensable element in the ethical framework of AI development and application.

Governance and Organizational Challenges

Probing deeper into the ethical landscape of AI, we confront complex data ethics challenges spanning individual, organizational, and societal realms. Safeguarding privacy and ensuring informed consent are paramount at the individual level. Organizations face dual imperatives: protecting proprietary data including intellectual property and managing consumer data ethically. Societally, AI systems must be inclusively designed, avoiding harm to marginalized groups.

To illustrate, consider the hypothetical example of Sarah, a research integrity editor at a major scholarly publisher. Her role demands balancing confidentiality and fairness while enabling rigorous and ethical scholarship. Emerging technologies like AI offer potential efficiency gains but require cautious implementation reflecting industry uncertainties.

Sarah recognizes the immense potential of AI to enhance the publishing process, yet proceeds cautiously given ethical and data security concerns. She participates in internal discussions on governance protocols for AI adoption with the aim of ensuring robust editorial standards while leveraging efficiency gains.

Focusing on machine learning applications, Sarah's team experiments with using AI for identifying research integrity breaches (such as coerced citations, plagiarism, fabricated data or use of paper mills) but not ultimate acceptance decisions.

Externally, academic editors such as Sarah advocate for industry collaboration on AI best practices. In fact, the editorial community calls for transparency frameworks to build public trust that new technologies adhere to integrity standards as well as data security. This may involve establishing centralized anonymous manuscript databases to train AI models without compromising sensitive unpublished work. It may also involve encrypting datasets, anonymizing personal information, and conducting mandatory bias audits.

Although AI tools enhance efficiency, we must be vigilant about their potential for misuse. Their capabilities can be a double-edged sword. Indeed, generative writing models could enable rapid plagiarism and the production of AI-generated fake research papers, undermining the efforts of research integrity processes. Without proper safeguards, these models could provide fraudsters with tools to circumvent integrity checks

Sarah believes actively addressing this threat is imperative, though complex. Simply restricting AI access could stymy innovation among ethical scholars. Instead, verification systems must coevolve with generative technologies – including robust computational detection methods combined with human oversight may mitigate AI misinformation risks.

Nevertheless, the cat-and-mouse game between AI creators and exploiters is likely to continue. Similar to how email spam filters constantly evolve to counter increasingly cunning tactics, publishing gatekeepers must stay vigilant as manipulators devise more sophisticated attacks. Yet, Sarah remains hopeful that authoritative and skilled scholars will prevail over those seeking shortcuts, ensuring the integrity of publishing as it transforms.

On balance, AI presents significant opportunities alongside certain risks. Machine learning could improve the impartiality and accuracy of editorial decisions, but issues like data privacy and consent are paramount and must not be compromised. Furthermore, the opaque nature of some AI techniques, such as deep learning, prompts serious questions about accountability. These concerns underline the need for transparent and responsible AI use in publishing, ensuring that its benefits are harnessed without undermining ethical or data security standards.

Levels of Data Security & Ethics

It follows from the above discussion that when we probe deeper into the ethical fabric of AI, we confront complex challenges in data ethics that span individual, organizational, and societal dimensions. At the individual level, the sanctity of privacy and the imperative of informed consent are paramount. For organizations, the challenge is twofold: safeguarding proprietary data, including intellectual property and trade secrets, and managing consumer data ethically. On a societal scale, the responsibility intensifies – AI systems must be designed inclusively, ensuring they neither exclude nor disadvantage marginalized groups.

Internal governance bodies that continuously scrutinize AI systems through an ethical lens are vital, particularly as external regulatory oversight struggles to keep pace. The prudent integration of emerging technologies hinges not just on technical expertise but also on a steadfast commitment to ethical progress. Leaders attuned to this balanced vision can pave the way for ethically and equitably nurturing innovation through AI.

Transitioning from the microcosm of organizational challenges to the broader landscape, we recognize the need for comprehensive AI governance. The rapid advancement of AI technology often outpaces the development of governance frameworks within many organizations, posing a dilemma: slow innovation for thorough governance or risk public trust with hasty AI system deployment. While privacy regulations have emerged, broader governance issues like transparency, bias mitigation, and explainability require more focused attention.

In response to these challenges, several global initiatives have taken shape. For example, the United Nations System Chief Executives Board for Coordination endorsed the Principles for the Ethical Use of Artificial Intelligence in September 2022. Developed collaboratively by UNESCO, OICT, and the HLCP Inter-Agency Working Group on Artificial Intelligence, these principles aim to ensure AI aligns with ethical values, human rights, and the UN's Sustainable Development Goals.

At the regional level, the European Union has been proactive with its draft Artificial Intelligence Act (AI Act), targeting the regulation of high-risk AI applications. The AI Act is set to influence AI policies globally. Southeast Asia's ASEAN AI Blueprint 2021-2025 also reflects this trend, emphasizing responsible and beneficial AI development and deployment. These regional efforts highlight the diverse approaches to AI governance, each tailored to their unique cultural and societal contexts.

In the realm of generative AI and large language models, the United States and Canada have emerged as leaders, not just in technological advancements but also in establishing ethical frameworks for AI development. Companies like Google, IBM, and Amazon in the U.S. are at the forefront, creating comprehensive AI ethics boards and principles.

These principles emphasize transparency, fairness, and accountability, crucial in the context of generative AI and large language models. For example, Google's partnership with Stanford University to establish the Human-Centered Artificial Intelligence (HAI) Institute highlights a commitment to AI that aligns with human values and ethical considerations.

Similarly, in Canada, initiatives like the Algorithmic Impact Assessment (AIA) provide structured frameworks for assessing and mitigating risks associated with AI, particularly in the development of new AI technologies like generative models. Canadian organizations are integrating these principles into their operations, focusing on fairness, transparency, and accountability in AI usage.

However, the global AI landscape is not monolithic. While the U.S. and Canada lead in certain aspects of AI development, other regions, notably China, demonstrate strengths in different areas. China's focus has been on the widespread adoption and implementation of AI systems in sectors like manufacturing, surveillance, and smart cities. This approach, characterized by rapid development and deployment, reflects a different set of priorities and strategies in AI development.

This global tapestry of AI development, with its varied regional focuses and strategies, underscores the complexity and diversity of AI's evolution. The U.S. and Canada's leadership in generative AI and large language models, particularly with an emphasis on ethical considerations, represents a significant aspect of AI's global evolution. At the same time, China's rapid adoption and application of AI across various sectors showcases another critical dimension of AI's global impact.

Safeguarding Data Security

As AI systems grow more advanced, data threats escalate correspondingly, necessitating continuously updated defense strategies spanning technology and policy. Emerging attack avenues like adversarial AI and model poisoning can severely compromise system integrity. Without vigilant governance, complex vulnerabilities introduced across the machine learning pipeline - from flawed data preparation to algorithmic instability - could undermine AI dependability.

Robust safeguards mandate multilayered approaches. At the technical layer, promising strategies include differential privacy, federated learning, and just-in-time data access to limit exposure. Beyond technologies, policy foundations promote organizational security awareness and accountability through governance bodies providing oversight, transparency protocols and redress mechanisms.

AI itself aids threat detection and response via vast pattern recognition and rapid automation. However, human discernment remains indispensable in security frameworks, applying wisdom and contextual understanding no algorithm can fully replicate. Only by combining AI's scalable security capabilities with ethics and strategic insight unique to humans can defense systems attain the adaptability, resilience and trustworthiness modern deployments demand.

Regulating Products Vs Regulating R&D

In AI development, two critical but distinct forms of regulation are essential: regulating AI products and regulating AI research and development (R&D). Understanding this distinction is crucial for navigating the ethical dimensions of AI development and use.

Regulating AI Products involves ensuring that AI applications, once deployed, are safe, ethically compliant, and beneficial for society. This mirrors the oversight in the pharmaceutical industry, where drugs must pass safety and efficacy tests before market release. For AI, this means products must undergo thorough evaluations for societal impact, adherence to data privacy norms, and potential for unintended consequences. For instance, an AI-driven diagnostic tool in healthcare must be rigorously vetted for accuracy and reliability before clinical use, ensuring it does not perpetuate biases or infringe on ethical norms.

Regulating AI R&D, in contrast, focuses on guiding the development process of AI solutions. This involves setting ethical and operational guardrails, addressing issues like data sourcing, algorithmic transparency, and bias mitigation right from the developmental stages. This regulation is akin to ethical guidelines in scientific research, balancing innovation with ethical oversight. Overregulation could stifle creativity, while under-regulation risks ethical lapses and public mistrust. The international nature of AI research further complicates this, necessitating global standards and collaborative efforts for harmonious and beneficial AI advancements.

The Debate Around Pausing AI Development

As generative AI platforms began to see widespread adoption, a thought-provoking debate emerged on whether pausing AI development could enable addressing ethical and governance challenges. Figures like Eliezer Yudkowsky, known for dire warnings about uncontrolled artificial general intelligence (AGI), argue that without alignment mechanisms to ensure human values are upheld, an AGI system could potentially optimize functions detrimental to humanity – with extremely dire consequences.

Yudkowsky's provocative assertions regarding the potentially unstoppable power and existential risks of Artificial General Intelligence (AGI) have ignited rigorous debates about the necessity of implementing robust safeguards. Such debates, with their varying opinions on the likelihood and severity of these risks, are crucial in the evolving discourse of AI. Despite differing viewpoints, these discussions underscore the pressing need to address the complex interplay between AI's rapid advancement and the imperative for effective control mechanisms.

This debate was further amplified by the dramatic events at OpenAI, where CEO Sam Altman's initial ouster, prompted by board members advocating for a more cautious approach to AI development, starkly highlighted these tensions. The subsequent reinstatement of Altman, driven by protests from employees and major partners like Microsoft, who were in favor of continuing aggressive progress, illustrates the deep divides among stakeholders. This high-profile incident serves as a potent reminder of the diverse and significant societal implications tied to the trajectory of AI development. It exemplifies the critical need for a balanced and thoughtful approach to AI advancement, one that harmonizes the pursuit of innovation with the ethical and safety concerns that come with such powerful technology.

Those advocating a temporary yet coordinated industry-wide pause suggest it could facilitate vital research into ensuring future AI respects human autonomy, dignity, and sociocultural values. Nevertheless, stalled progress might also impede healthcare, sustainability and other public good applications with immense potential. Enforcing a unilateral pause appears infeasible given the decentralized, international nature of AI research and development.

Responsible continuous advancement with governance guardrails could stimulate innovations addressing current ethical dilemmas while working to align long-term objectives.

The intensely competitive climate also poses barriers to coordination as one player pausing risks ceding advantage to others. Furthermore, global AI development features markedly diverse national strategies. A cautious nation could enable bolder rivals to advance capabilities and influence, thus gaining ground on multiple fronts (political, economic, security). China notably aims to lead AI globally by 2030 using more flexible policies around data and privacy.

This presents a profound policy dilemma between balancing responsible ethics and global competitiveness. While a moratorium seems ethically commendable to some, enduring political and economic realities will almost certainly foil implementation. International cooperation establishing shared norms and best practices could enable more coordinated governance and standards across borders. Alongside robust regulation, such collaboration offers a viable path so that AI progress aligns broadly with ethical priorities.

Now, let's examine two case studies that help illustrate forward-looking AI practices around the topic of ethics and governance. The efforts of companies like Anthropic and DeepMind demonstrate how the private sector can lead in setting standards for responsible AI innovation.

CASE STUDY 1: ANTHROPIC

Anthropic emerged as a significant player in the AI landscape in 2017, co-founded by Dario Amodei, Tom Brown, and other OpenAI alumni. The company's mission is ambitious: to develop artificial general intelligence (AGI) that is not only technologically advanced but also deeply aligned with human values.

One of Anthropic's notable projects is the development of Claude, a generative AI model designed to rival established models like ChatGPT and Bard. Claude is distinguished by its integration of Anthropic's "constitutional AI" paradigm. This paradigm is a groundbreaking approach where AI is trained to adhere to fundamental human values such as liberty, equality, and justice. The training process is meticulously crafted to prioritize information accuracy and minimize harm, addressing critical concerns around bias and transparency in AI.

Anthropic's approach extends beyond model development to encompass rigorous testing and validation processes. For instance, Claude undergoes extensive

evaluations to ensure its responses do not perpetuate biases or misinformation. This includes testing
with diverse datasets and scenarios to assess the
model's performance across a wide range of cultural
and social contexts.

The recent investment by Amazon in Anthropic is a
testament to the company's potential in ethical AI.
This partnership provides Anthropic with access to
Amazon's vast cloud computing resources, essential for training and refining large-scale AI models.
Moreover, Amazon's diverse customer base offers
a real-world testing ground, allowing Anthropic to
gather valuable feedback and continue improving
its models.

Highlights: Anthropic's commitment to ethical AI
is exemplified by its "constitutional AI" paradigm, a
novel approach to embedding human values into AI.
This case study demonstrates the potential of AI to
be developed in a way that is not only technologically advanced but also ethically sound, addressing
key issues like bias and transparency. Anthropic's
collaboration with Amazon further underscores the
growing importance of ethical considerations in the
AI industry.

CASE STUDY 2:
DEEPMIND

DeepMind, a subsidiary of Alphabet Inc., has been at the forefront of AI research since 2010. The company has gained international acclaim for its work in reinforcement learning and its application to complex problems in healthcare and climate change.

DeepMind's ethical AI initiatives are spearheaded by its dedicated Safety and Ethics team. This team's work is grounded in a set of AI Principles that emphasize the benefit to humanity, alignment with human values, and responsible development. DeepMind's commitment to these principles is evident in its diverse range of research projects.

In the realm of healthcare, DeepMind has developed AI systems for early detection of eye diseases and cancer, working closely with medical professionals to ensure these systems are ethically designed and respect patient privacy. In climate change, DeepMind's AI algorithms have been used to improve energy efficiency in data centers, demonstrating the potential of AI to contribute to environmental sustainability.

DeepMind's research in ethical AI also includes developing techniques to mitigate bias in AI applications. This involves creating algorithms that can identify and correct biases in areas like loan approvals and hiring processes. Additionally, the company focuses on enhancing the transparency and accountability of AI systems. This includes creating algorithms that can explain AI decisions, making them more understandable to users and stakeholders.

Highlights: DeepMind's systematic approach to ethical AI, encompassing fairness, transparency, and human alignment, sets a benchmark in the industry. The company's work in applying AI to real-world challenges while adhering to ethical principles illustrates the potential of AI to be a force for good. DeepMind's initiatives in healthcare and climate change demonstrate how AI can be harnessed to address some of the most pressing issues facing humanity, guided by a strong ethical compass.

EPILOGUE:
CHARTING NEW HORIZONS

As we conclude our exploration of the ever-evolving landscape of work, it becomes abundantly clear that we are not mere bystanders but active architects shaping its future. From the primordial roles of hunter-gatherers to the emerging professions in the AI-driven world, the spectrum of work encapsulates humanity's innate capacity to adapt, innovate, and reinvent.

Throughout history, work has served as a mirror reflecting our identities, aspirations, and collective narratives. Nevertheless, the traditional boundaries defining work are now blurring, as humans and technology merge in an ever-evolving interplay, demanding resilience and lifelong learning amidst uncertainty and accelerating change.

While the initial impact of technological transformation has primarily focused on routine or repetitive forms of work, its influence is increasingly permeating knowledge-intensive professional fields, where creativity and originality are highly valued. Even occupations reliant on nuanced expertise and judgment are being reshaped by AI as its capabilities extend beyond mere automation. This co-evolution and interdependent development is transforming the very nature of work across all sectors, creating a dynamic space for creativity, progress, and transformation.

As AI evolves, its impacts grow increasingly profound. The 'technological singularity' concept, which envisions a future where machines surpass human intelligence in all domains, heralds monumental shifts in our way of life. As the traditional role of human work diminishes, societal structures and economic fundamentals will need to adapt, reshaping our pursuits and redefining the ways we forge our identities.

Linking the ongoing evolution of AI in the workplace with the theoretical 'technological singularity' suggests a natural progression from current impacts to more profound, disruptive changes, affecting not just work but all aspects of life.

The breadth and depth of this transformation are likely to exceed our current comprehension, with AI systems growing more sophisticated, autonomous, and encompassing. Although the future is uncertain, the rapid advancement of technology indicates that we are just at the beginning of a monumental transformation in human life and societal structure.

The path ahead offers immense opportunities to uplift humanity, yet it requires careful navigation. As innovations reshape the fabric of work, key priorities emerge. Organizations need to evaluate their preparedness for AI integration, focusing on infrastructure, data management, skill sets, cultural adaptation, and visionary leadership. Additionally, they must formulate adoption strategies that prioritize ethical considerations, embedding principles of ethical AI into governance frameworks to ensure data security, transparency, privacy, and fairness.

Simultaneously, we must embark on a comprehensive transformation of the three organizational pillars: workflows, workforce, and workplace. This demands a concerted effort to upskill and reskill the workforce, fostering adaptability and ensuring the seamless integration of diverse talent. Beyond that, we must envision a future where AI not only augments but potentially makes most economic labor obsolete. As we approach this pivotal milestone, our inquiries become profoundly philosophical, even existential.

Standing on the brink of a new era shaped by artificial intelligence, it's time for humanity to reassess the value we place on work in defining our identity, self-worth, and the ways we organize our lives. AI's transformative power offers us an unprecedented opportunity to redefine our understanding of work, moving beyond the age-old notion that our jobs, once decoupled from sustenance, are the epicenter of our lives' meaning and purpose.

This shift doesn't diminish the importance of work; rather, it invites us to rediscover and embrace a broader spectrum of life's riches. In a reimagined landscape, where AI assumes roles once uniquely human, we find an opportunity to pursue a deeper, more holistic form of fulfillment – reminiscent of Aristotle's concept of *eudaemonia*. Let us welcome this change, not with apprehension, but with optimism for unlocking new dimensions of human experience and community, beyond the confines of jobs and careers.

Amidst this expansive vision of AI's role in redefining work and life, we must not forget the immediate and practical implications for organizations and management. The transitional phase we currently navigate presents both significant opportunities and challenges for leaders and managers – and for economic structures and society more broadly.

This book provides guidance for navigating this transformative era, offering insights and strategies for organizations to adapt, thrive, and maintain a human-centric approach in an AI-driven world. By directing technology's trajectory towards human empowerment and dignity, we can forge a future where technology and humanity co-evolve symbiotically. With compassionate oversight and wisdom, the potential of AI can be harnessed for progress that aligns with justice, sustainability, and our collective aspirations.

Embracing AI's possibilities demands fluid thinking where we continuously challenge assumptions and established ways of analysing the world. It requires cultivating "beginner's mind" - a Zen idea of approaching things with an attitude of openness, lack of preconceptions, and eagerness to learn. This mindset allows us to envision radically new applications of AI technology unconstrained by current technological or cognitive limitations. It also necessitates cross-disciplinary collaboration, fusing concepts from fields like design, ethics, education, and anthropology to steer technology's trajectory responsibly.

REFERENCES

Arntz, M., Gregory, T., & Zierahn, U. (2016). The risk of automation for jobs in OECD countries: A comparative analysis. *OECD Social, Employment and Migration Working Papers.*

Bauman, Z. (2000). *Liquid Modernity.* Polity Press.

Bessen, J. E. (2019). AI and Jobs: The Role of Demand. *Harvard Business Review.*

Bostrom, N. (2014). *Superintelligence: Paths, Dangers, Strategies.* Oxford University Press.

Boston Consulting Group. (2017). Master complexity through simplification. *Boston Consulting Group.*

Bröckling, U. (2016). *The Entrepreneurial Self: Fabricating a New Type of Subject.* Sage.

Brynjolfsson, E., & McAfee, A. (2014). *The Second Machine Age: Work, Progress, and Prosperity in a Time of Brilliant Technologies.* W. W. Norton & Company.

Burton, R., Døjbak Håkonsson, D., Larsen, E. R., & Obel, B. (2020). New trends in organization design. *Journal of Organization Design, 9*(1).

Crawford, M. B. (2009). *Shop Class as Soulcraft: An Inquiry into the Value of Work.* Penguin Books.

Daugherty, P. R., & Wilson, H. J. (2018). *Human + Machine: Reimagining Work in the Age of AI*. Harvard Business Review Press.

Daugherty, P., & Wilson, H. J. (2018). Collaborative Intelligence: Humans and AI Are Joining Forces. *Harvard Business Review*.

de Beauvoir, S. (2011). *The second sex* (C. Borde & S. Malovany-Chevallier, Trans.). New York: Vintage Books. (Original work published 1949)

Deci, E. L., & Ryan, R. M. (2000). The "what" and "why" of goal pursuits: Human needs and the self-determination of behavior. *Psychological Inquiry, 11*(4), 227-268.

Diamond, J. (1987). The worst mistake in the history of the human race. *Discover,* 8(5), 64-66.

Domingos, P. (2015). *The Master Algorithm: How the Quest for the Ultimate Learning Machine Will Remake Our World*. Basic Books.

Drucker, P. (1985). The Future of Work: Where Are We Going and What Are the Implications for Management? *Oxford University Press*.

Elkington, J. (1998). *Cannibals with forks: The triple bottom line of 21st century business*. Capstone.

European Commission. (2019). *The European Green Deal*. Brussels: European Commission.

Fried, J., & Heinemeier Hansson, D. (2013). *Remote: Office Not Required*. Crown Business.

Friston, K. J., Lin, M., Frith, C. D., Pezzulo, G., Hobson, J. A., and Ondobaka, S. (2017). Active inference, curiosity and insight. *Neural Comput.* 29, 2633–2683. doi: 10.1162/neco_a_00999

Galbraith, J. R. (1973). *Designing complex organizations*. Addison-Wesley.

Goleman, D. (2000). Leadership that gets results. *Harvard Business Review,* *78*(2), 78-90.

Gratton, L. (2016). The New Work Order: Why Employees Are No Longer Employees and How This Is Transforming Organizations. *Harvard Business Review Press.*

Harter, J. K., Schmidt, F. L., & Hayes, T. L. (2002). Business-unit-level relationship between employee satisfaction, employee engagement, and business outcomes: a meta-analysis. *Journal of Applied Psychology,* *87*(2), 268-279.

Hawken, P., Lovins, A. B., & Lovins, L. H. (1999). *Natural capitalism: Creating the next industrial revolution.* Little, Brown & Co.

Heifetz, R. A., Grashow, A., & Linsky, M. (2009). *The practice of adaptive leadership: Tools and tactics for changing your organization and the world.* Harvard Business Press.

Herzberg, F. (1959). *The motivation to work.* New York: John Wiley & Sons.

Hobson, E. A., & DeDeo, J. (2015). The Emergence of Animal Social Complexity: Theoretical and biobehavioral evidence. *Behavioral Ecology and Sociobiology,* 69(4), 903-924.

Hofstede, G. (2001). *Culture's consequences: Comparing values, behaviors, institutions, and organizations across nations* (2nd ed.). Thousand Oaks, CA: Sage.

Iasiti, M., et al. (2020). *The AI-Powered Enterprise: How to Embed AI into Your Business and Drive Growth.* Harvard Business Review Press.

International Labour Organization. (2023). *World Employment and Social Outlook: Trends 2023.*

Jesuthasan, R., & Boudreau, J. W. (2018). *Reinventing Jobs: A 4-Step Approach for Applying Automation to Work*. Harvard Business Review Press.

Johansen, B. (2017). *The New Leadership Literacies: Thriving in a Future of Extreme Disruption and Distributed Everything*. Berrett-Koehler Publishers.

Kahn, W. A. (1990). Psychological conditions of personal engagement and disengagement at work. *Academy of Management Journal, 33*(4), 692-724.

Kapoor, R., & Lee, J. M. (2013). Coordinating and Competing in Ecosystems: How Organizational Forms Shape New Technology Investments. *Strategic Management Journal, 34*(3), 274-296.

Kearns, M., & Roth, A. (2019). *The Ethical Algorithm: The Science of Socially Aware Algorithm Design*. Oxford University Press.

Kessler, S. (2018). *Gigged: The End of the Job and the Future of Work*. St. Martin's Press.

Kiron, D., Altman, E. J., & Riedl, C. (2023). Workforce ecosystems and AI. *Brookings*.

Kremer, A., Luget, A., Mikkelsen, D., Soller, H., Strandell-Jansson, M., & Zingg, S. (2023, December 21). As gen AI advances, regulators—and risk functions—rush to keep pace. *McKinsey Quarterly*.

Lakoff, G., & Johnson, M. (1980). *Metaphors We Live By*. University of Chicago Press.

Levy, F., & Murnane, R. J. (2004). *The New Division of Labor: How Computers Are Creating the Next Job Market*. Princeton University Press.

Liker, J.K. (2004). *The Toyota Way: 14 Management Principles from the World's Greatest Manufacturer*. New York: McGraw-Hill.

Luger, G. F. (2009). *Artificial Intelligence: Structures and Strategies for Complex Problem Solving* (6th ed.). Addison-Wesley.

Malone, T. W. (2018). *Superminds: The Surprising Power of People and Computers Thinking Together*. Little, Brown and Company.

Manyika, J., Lund, S., Chui, M., Bughin, J., Woetzel, J., Batra, P., ... & Sanghvi, S. (2017). Jobs lost, jobs gained: What the future of work will mean for jobs, skills, and wages. *McKinsey & Company*.

Maslow, A. H. (1943). A Theory of Human Motivation. *Psychological Review, 50*(4), 370-396.

Matthee, S (2020). *The Gig Economy: The Rise of the New Workforce*. Routledge.

McKinsey Global Institute. (2023). The future of wealth and growth hangs in the balance (Report). *McKinsey & Company*.

Mintzberg, H. (1979). *The structuring of organizations: A synthesis of the research*. Prentice-Hall.

MIT Sloan Management Review & Deloitte. (2021). *Workforce Ecosystems: A New Strategic Approach to the Future of Work*. MIT Sloan Management Review.

Morgan, J. (2014). *The future of work: Attract new talent, build better leaders, and create a competitive organization*. Wiley.

Nadler, D. A., & Tushman, M. L. (1988). *Strategic organization design: Concepts, tools & processes*. Scott Foresman & Co.

Piketty, T. (2014). *Capital in the Twenty-First Century*. Belknap Press.

Pinker, S. (2007). *The Stuff of Thought: Language as a Window into Human Nature*. Viking.

Pirsig, R. M. (1974). *Zen and the Art of Motorcycle Maintenance: An Inquiry into Values.* William Morrow.

Porter, M. E., & Kramer, M. R. (2011). Creating shared value. *Harvard Business Review, 89*(1/2), 62-77.

Ransbotham, S., Kiron, D., Candelon, F., Khodabandeh, S., & Chu, M. (2022). Achieving Individual — and Organizational — Value With AI. *MIT Sloan Review.* November 1, 2022.

Rockström, J et al (2009). A safe operating space for humanity. *Nature, 461*(7263), 472-475.

Rossides, N. (2021). *Engaging the Workforce: The Grand Management Challenge of the 21st Century,* Matador.

Russell, S.J., & Norvig, P. (2010). *Artificial Intelligence: A Modern Approach.* Malaysia; Pearson Education Limited.

Schad, J., Lewis, M. W., Raisch, S., & Smith, W. K. (2016). Paradox Research in Management Science: Looking Back to Move Forward. *Academy of Management Annals, 10*(1), 5-64

Schaufeli, W. B., & Bakker, A. B. (2004). Job demands, job resources, and their relationship with burnout and engagement: a multi-sample study. *Journal of Organizational Behavior, 25*(3), 293-315.

Schein, E. H. (1985). *Organizational culture and leadership* (2nd ed.). San Francisco, CA: Jossey-Bass.

Searle, J. R. (Ed.). (1993). *Metaphor and Thought.* Cambridge University Press.

Senge, P. M. (1990). *The Fifth Discipline: The Art & Practice of The Learning Organization.* Currency Doubleday.

Sinek, S. (2009). *Start with why: How great leaders inspire everyone to take action.* Portfolio.

Sterman, J. D. (2000). *Business Dynamics: Systems Thinking and Modeling for a Complex World*. Irwin/McGraw-Hill.

Sullivan, T. (2011). Embracing Complexity. *Harvard Business Review*, September issue.

United Nations. (2015). *Transforming our world: The 2030 agenda for sustainable development*. New York: United Nations.

Susskind, R., & Susskind, D. (2015). *The future of the professions: How technology will transform the work of human experts*. Oxford University Press.

Terkel, S. (1974). *Working: People talk about what they do all day and how they feel about what they do*. New York: Pantheon Books.

United Nations Framework Convention on Climate Change. (2019). *The Paris Agreement*. Bonn, Germany: UNFCCC.

Van de Ven, A. H. (2007). *Engaged scholarship: A guide for organizational and social research*. Oxford University Press.

Vermeulen, F. (2017). *Breaking Bad Habits: Defy Industry Norms and Reinvigorate Your Business*. Harvard Business Review Press.

Wellman, N., Applegate, J. M., Harlow, J., & Johnston, E. W. (2020). Beyond the pyramid: Alternative formal hierarchical structures and team performance. *Academy of Management Journal*, 63(4), 997–1027

West, D. M. (2018). *The Future of Work: Robots, AI, and Automation*. Brookings Institution Press.

Wolf, M. (2018). *The age of globalization: Winners and losers*. Yale University Press.

Wolfram, S. (2019). *Adventures of Computational Thinking*. Wolfram Media.

APPENDIX A:
GLOSSARY OF TERMS

Artificial Intelligence (AI): A broad concept of machines performing tasks that typically require human intelligence.

Machine Learning (ML): A subset of AI focusing on algorithms that learn from data.

Deep Learning: A specialized form of ML using multi-layered neural networks.

Natural Language Processing (NLP): AI focusing on the interaction between computers and human language.

Large Language Models (LLMs): A branch of NLP designed to understand and generate human language.

Computer Vision: AI that derives information from visual inputs.

Generative AI: Techniques that enable AI to create new content, like images or text.

Algorithm: Set of rules or instructions given to an AI system.

Neural Networks: Computational models inspired by the human brain, used in ML and AI.

Supervised Learning: ML method where models are trained on labeled data.

Unsupervised Learning: ML method where models learn from data without labeled outcomes.

Reinforcement Learning: ML where an agent learns from actions and feedback.

Predictive Analytics: Using data and ML to predict future outcomes.

Transformer Architecture: Neural network architecture used in NLP.

Data Mining: Discovering patterns in large data sets using ML and statistics.

Synthetic Data: Artificially generated data that mimics real-world data.

Explainable AI (XAI): AI focused on making AI decision-making transparent.

Bias in AI: The tendency of AI systems to produce prejudiced results.

Ethics in AI: Moral considerations surrounding AI.

Robotics: Field dealing with the design and operation of robots.

Chatbot: A computer program simulating human conversation.

Narrow AI: AI designed for specific tasks, lacking broader cognitive abilities.

Artificial General Intelligence (AGI): Hypothetical AI with broad, flexible intelligence.

Automation: Technology performing tasks with minimal human intervention.

Internet of Things (IoT): Interconnection of devices via the internet.

Edge Computing: Processing data near its generation location.

Cloud Computing: Delivery of services like storage and processing over the internet.

Blockchain: A decentralized ledger of transactions across a network.

APPENDIX B:
AI READINESS ASSESSMENT

The AI Readiness Assessment is designed to help organizations gauge their preparedness for AI integration. This assessment covers various areas, from infrastructure and data availability to workforce skills and organizational culture. By completing this assessment, organizations can identify areas of strength and pinpoint where further development or investment might be needed.

Instructions: For each statement, rate your organization on a scale of 1 to 5, where 1 = Strongly Disagree and 5 = Strongly Agree.

Infrastructure and Technology

1. Our organization has the necessary hardware and software to support AI technologies.

2. We have a reliable and secure data storage system in place.

3. Our IT team is equipped to handle the integration and maintenance of AI solutions.

4. We have a clear strategy for cloud computing and its role in AI deployment.

Data Availability and Quality

5. Our organization has access to high-quality data that can be used for AI applications.

6. We consistently collect and update data relevant to our industry and operations.

7. Data privacy and protection are prioritized, and we comply with relevant regulations.

Workforce Skills and Training

8. Our employees have a basic understanding of AI and its potential impact on their roles.

9. We have specialists or teams dedicated to AI development and implementation.

10. There's a continuous learning culture, with opportunities for employees to upskill in AI-related areas.

Organizational Culture and Leadership

11. Our leadership is committed to AI adoption and understands its strategic importance.

12. Employees are generally open to technological changes and innovations.

13. We have a culture of experimentation, where pilot projects and iterative testing are encouraged.

Strategy and Vision

14. We have a clear vision of how AI can align with and further our organizational goals.

15. There's a roadmap or strategy in place for AI integration over the next 1-5 years.

16. We consider ethical implications when planning AI implementations.

Collaboration and Partnerships

17. We actively seek partnerships or collaborations for AI expertise and resources.

18. Our organization is open to working with startups or innovators in the AI space.

19. We participate in industry forums or groups focused on AI advancements and best practices.

Scoring:

- **17-28: Emerging** - Your organization is at the early stages of AI readiness. Consider investing in foundational elements like infrastructure, data collection, and workforce training.

- **29-40: Developing** - You have some elements in place but need to focus on strategic alignment and fostering an AI-ready culture.

- **41-57: Advanced** - Your organization is well on its way to being AI-ready. Continue refining your strategies, upskilling your workforce, and staying updated with AI advancements.

- **58-76: Leading** - You are at the forefront of AI readiness. Ensure you maintain this momentum, continuously innovate, and share best practices within your industry.

By regularly revisiting this assessment, organizations can track their progress and make informed decisions about their AI journey.

APPENDIX C:
SKILLS ANALYSIS TEMPLATE

In the evolving landscape of the modern workplace, the traditional emphasis on job descriptions has become less central to managing the workforce. The very notion of a 'job' is undergoing a transformation. Instead of rigidly defined roles, we're witnessing the disassembly of jobs into specific tasks – that can be distributed among full-time employees, contract workers, and even robots or AI systems.

This shift means that a 'job' is no longer the central organizing principle it once was. Organizations now prioritize skills and competencies that can be applied across a myriad of tasks, making the identification and bridging of skills gaps even more crucial. This template is designed with this contemporary perspective in mind, aiming to help organizations navigate this new terrain.

Nevertheless, most companies still need to follow certain policies and procedures for their own employees that still adhere to the needs of their permanent employees as they find ways to transition to more flexible work-flow arrangements.

Purpose: The Skills Gap Analysis serves as a diagnostic tool to pinpoint discrepancies between the current skill sets of employees and the skills they need to excel in their roles. By identifying these gaps, organizations can strategically invest in training and development initiatives, ensuring that their workforce remains competent, agile, and prepared for future challenges.

Steps:

1. **Role and Skill Identification:**

   o Review job descriptions meticulously to list down essential skills for each role.

   o Engage with team leaders, managers, or department heads to understand evolving skill needs.

   o Conduct a skills audit through surveys or workshops to gather a comprehensive list of desired skills.

2. **Current Skill Assessment:**

   o Conduct one-on-one interviews with employees to understand their self-perceived competencies.

   o Review recent performance appraisals to gauge demonstrated skills and areas of improvement.

   o Administer skills tests or simulations to objectively measure current proficiencies.

3. **Gap Identification:**

   o Compare the required skills against the current skills of each employee.

   o Use a matrix or a chart to visualize where the gaps are most prominent.

4. **Gap Prioritization:**

o   Not all skill gaps are of equal importance. Determine which gaps, if addressed, would yield the most significant impact on performance, productivity, or innovation.

o   Consider the urgency of certain projects or initiatives that might require immediate upskilling.

5. **Action Plan Development**:

o   Depending on the nature of the gap, decide whether training, reskilling, or upskilling is the most appropriate intervention.

o   Explore external training programs, online courses, workshops, or even hiring new talent if the skill gap is vast and immediate.

o   Consider mentorship programs or peer-to-peer training for softer skills or company-specific knowledge.

Tools and Resources:

- **Job Descriptions**: Detailed outlines of roles and responsibilities.

- **Performance Reviews**: Historical data on employee performance.

- **Skills Tests**: Objective measures of technical or role-specific skills.

- **Interview Templates**: Structured questions to gauge self-perceived competencies.

- **Training Repositories**: A collection of internal and external training resources.

- **Reskilling Platforms**: Tools or platforms that help transition employees into new roles.

- **Upskilling Platforms**: Resources that help enhance current skills to a more advanced level.

Tips for Implementation:

Stakeholder Engagement: Ensure that all relevant stakeholders, especially those in leadership roles, understand and support the analysis.

Diverse Data Collection: Use a mix of qualitative and quantitative methods to get a holistic view.

Continuous Review: Skills needs can evolve. Regularly revisit the analysis to stay updated.

Feedback Loop: After training or interventions, gather feedback to understand the effectiveness and areas of improvement.

Cultural Emphasis: Foster a culture of continuous learning where employees are motivated to self-identify areas for growth.

Output:

Upon completion, the Skills Gap Analysis will yield a detailed report. This document will highlight the discrepancies between current and required skills, offering actionable insights and recommendations to bridge these gaps. The report serves as a roadmap for HR and leadership teams to make informed decisions about talent development, ensuring the organization's continued growth and adaptability.